ORACLE

ORACLE

A Practical Guide to Card Reading, Divination, Prophecy, Omens and Seers

Published by Blue Angel Publishing®
10 Trafford Court, Wheelers Hill,
Victoria, Australia 3150
E-mail: info@blueangelonline.com
Website: www.blueangelonline.com

Edited by Cherise Asmah and Peter Loupelis

Blue Angel is a registered trademark of Blue Angel Gallery Pty Ltd.

ISBN: 978-1-922574-48-0

Printed on sustainably sourced paper, with soy-based inks.

Lucy Cavendish

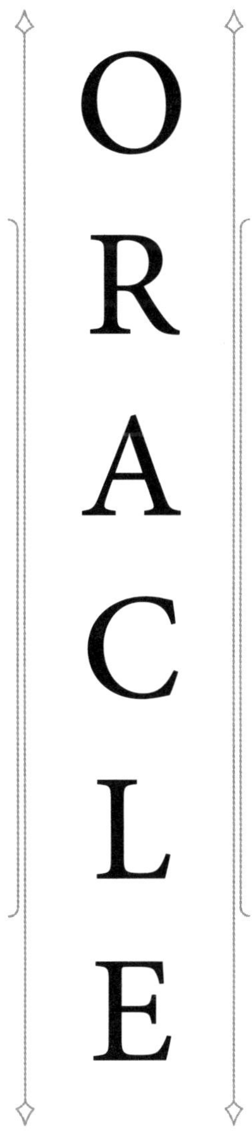

A Practical Guide to Card Reading, Divination, Prophecy, Omens and Seers

Contents

A Warm Welcome…

The first prophecies were the words of an oak.

— Socrates

Welcome to the sacred path of becoming the Oracle. Within this book, you will come to know a great deal more about your Oracle card decks and the meanings of the cards. You'll also discover methods that can work so very well with them, whether reading for yourself, for friends, or on a professional basis. You'll learn about signs and symbols, prophets and dreamers, and be given valuable tools. I will be with you every step of the way.

Please know that many of the principles taught throughout this book will hold true for any Oracle deck you may use. However, this book of teachings is specifically concerned with those decks I have created, and the principles, lessons and guidance will work very effectively with these decks.

For the very first time, I am sharing entries from my own reading journals. These have never been published before, and they are very special to me, revealing (as they do) absolutely life-changing interactions with the cards. Most are from readings I did for myself, some are from a reader I saw twice when I was living in London, and others are from my time in a teeny studio apartment in Paris. Some are from readings with friends, and some are from when I felt myself all alone, except for the cards, who saw everything — we have been so close ever since. These excerpts are raw and real, and some are emotional because I am a very emotional person, and part of my way to process emotions—especially strong, sometimes overwhelming emotions—is to turn to the cards, give control over to the Universe, and ask for the reading to help me understand what is taking place in my life.

And the cards answered, over and over again. They did not judge. And they told me truths I couldn't see without them. My sense of mystery and wonder is hopefully conveyed in these excerpts from very personal parts of my life. I've changed some names for privacy, and some grammatical errors have been tidied up, but apart from that, they appear here exactly as they were written down. Sometimes, they were smudged and blurred by teardrops. Sometimes, they brought me an intense, bright happiness. I am so, so glad I have these diaries from my younger self who lived so close to the bone. I've kept diaries of some kind most of my life, from when I was a very little girl, but these reading diaries started to explore deeply the world of magick I was exploring for the first time with real discipline.

The discipline I brought to the cards was always hard work, but the joy that work gave me was so much greater than the effort. I read until candles burned down and my eyes stung and I was tired, very tired; but I have never, in the 38 years since I first picked the cards up, felt tired of reading them. Meeting the cards was like having new friends who never let me down. The more I gave to them, the more they gave to me. Every deck, every card had a personality, and some were warm and nurturing, others daring and provocative, others light and cleansing — while others seemed to dance and sparkle like there were faeries living within them.

I'D ALWAYS LOVED SPEAKING WITH PEOPLE ABOUT OUR DEPTHS, BUT THE CARDS ALLOWED ME TO TAKE THAT A STEP FURTHER. THE JOY OF CONNECTION, OF REALLY SEEING PEOPLE, SOUL TO SOUL, IS DELICIOUS AND LIFE-AFFIRMING. AND I HOPE YOU WILL SEE FROM MY JOURNAL ENTRIES THAT I WAS A YOUNG WOMAN WITH DREAMS; AND WITH THE SUPPORT OF THE CARDS, THOSE DREAMS CAME TRUE.

Every reading was so magickal for me; they drew me in, and I loved every moment. I needed no encouragement to devote myself to this path. In this bewitching discovery was a kind of freedom to be a better version of the self I had been taught to be: more imaginative, braver to strive to become more independent, more loving, more able to listen—truly listen—as I learned this new and wondrous language of the cards. They gave me something else, something I had never found for myself before. They gave me a way to speak with people about what truly mattered in life. And they shared with me a beautiful way to connect and to be of help to people. I'd always loved speaking with people about our depths, but the cards allowed me to take that a step further. The joy of connection, of really seeing people, soul to soul, is delicious and life-affirming. And I hope you will see from my journal entries that I was a young woman with dreams; and with the support of the cards, those dreams came true.

I've also included some stories of readings I have given and experiences that changed me during my explorations in those early days. I'm sharing with you some of the most vulnerable parts of my life, times that were full of tenderness, magick, yearning, wonder and woe — and oh, how the cards lit up the path forward.

Within each chapter, you'll meet an oracular legend — people whose intuitive messages and insights resonated with the people of their time. I have always been so inspired by people who have lived extraordinary lives with courage and self-determination. People who have a generous dollop of defiance in their character, people who are willing to become conduits for spirit communication, people who sometimes have given their lives for the work they do. To be brave helps when walking the path of the Oracle. But it doesn't take much to be fearless when Spirit calls; it's as irresistible as following the White Rabbit was for Alice. These Oracles from history may just give you a glimpse into how you can make Oracle card reading a part of your life, too — no matter what people may say.

As you finish reading each chapter, you'll find a set of exercises for you to do. Please make use of them. They take me back to when I spent hours in tiny rooms in Sydney, London and Paris, in rooms dark and dingy; but my practice with the cards under the candles I burned made the room into the most beautiful place in the world. The cards made my world enchanted, no matter how much my life at the time felt like a struggle. If the world outside seemed brutal, if my heart was breaking, if I was making mistakes and hurting, the cards and their wonders took so much of that away. So these exercises are not 'homework'; they are portals into the joy of reading for yourself and others. The 'experientials' I've offered within these pages will make the cards your darling friends who are there for you whenever you reach for them.

I've put together a little list of what you may find helpful to have with you as you explore my magickal memoir. Oh — it's best to read from start to finish, in that order, because all the exercises and experientials build upon each other!

It's not a lot that you'll need, so here we go …

JOURNAL:

A journal or Book of Shadows and Light. You can call this your journal, your reading journal, your magickal reading grimoire, whatever. Make it fun and make it personal to you so that you really take ownership of your readings as you develop your reading style.

It's one of the best parts of your new reading experiences to keep a journal as you explore the cards, develop your skills, dream about the cards, or are woken at midnight by their whispers! Mine were just very basic notebooks, and I made them a little more magickal with my drawings and colouring-in pages, making my journal an expression of me. I even made drawings of many of the cards and paintings, too, in great detail, to help me really embed the symbols in my mind and memory.

ORACLE DECK:

You will definitely need one of my decks. There is an abundance of decks with many themes to choose from that I've created with amazing artists. I'm trusting that you'll know which one is calling you and make the right one your own. I do ask, please, please, please, don't give in to any temptation you may feel to purchase one of the fraudulent counterfeit decks being illegally made. The people who are making and selling them are stealing my life's work and the life's work of creative artists who spend years learning their craft. These decks do not have guidebooks, and you will absolutely need your guidebook. These fake decks are very cheap, but please, it's worth making the real deal your own.

You will feel the loving, authentic energy and the incredible quality and care poured into every deck I have made, and it will be your true friend always.

CANDLES AND ESSENTIAL OILS:

I have included some spells to work with your cards. You may wish to gather some essential oils and tea lights or tapered candles (or any that you prefer to work with).

You will, though, need a white candle — my preference is for beeswax because I adore bees, and their wax smells like honey, and the smoke from the beeswax fills the air with healthy, buzzy, sweet vibes. Soy candles are heavenly, too, so I recommend those. I am not a fan of paraffin wax as there are toxins in the burn-off smoke, and I feel we already deal with so many environmental toxins — why add more to the load? Especially when we are conducting the sacred rite of cartomancy.

CLEARING HERBS AND SALT:

You could work with ethical sage or *palo santo*. Rosemary and lavender are wonderful as well. You'll also need good-quality sea salt to help clear your deck.

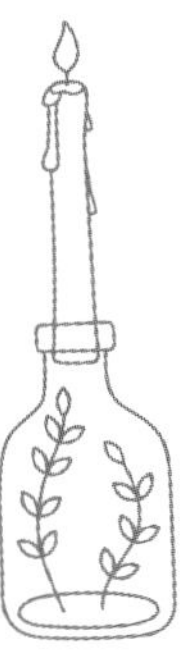

Let us begin now to consider what we are doing when we walk this path, and begin to work with these cards.

Part One

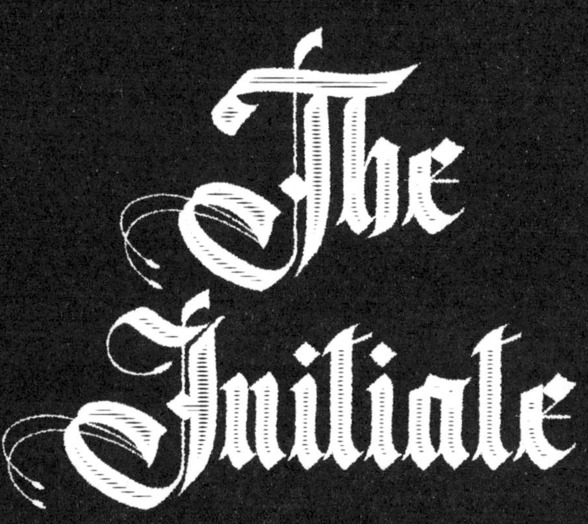

Chapter One

Light the Fire

Lycurgus, here you are. You have come to my rich temple,
Beloved of Zeus and all who dwell on Olympus.
Should I address you, in my prophecy, as a god or as a man?
I think it would be better to call you a god, Lycurgus.

— Herodotus

The Mysterious

Cartomancy, which is one of many forms of divination, is a very old art. It developed primarily in the 1400s in France and Italy and is said to have its roots in travellers' camps, becoming a substantial part of the tools of trade for those who read the fortunes of others to make a penny on the road. Cartomancy, which developed into Tarot and then Oracle cards—an evolution we will learn more about within these pages—is our own special technique of divination as Oracles. But truly, the skills, role and function of the Oracle have deep roots that stretch into the ancient past — indeed, into the times before there was any written history.

This may seem too long ago to be of any relevance, but when we begin to do this oracular work and use the Oracle cards, we are stepping into a great lineage and tradition that stretches right back to our most distant of ancestors. To understand the traditions—and why we humans required individuals who acted in the role of the Oracle—is to know what we are beginning to work with as we shuffle and turn the cards. To be an Oracle card reader is to be an Oracle — and to be an Oracle is a sacred task, one which was entrusted to those who were to become the intermediaries between the Divine and the Community. This remains our purpose to this day.

So, you can see that it's important to be aware that this is an ancient tradition we are working within. Not so that we become weighed down by the years and inheritance we are taking on, nor to have a kind of weighty self-importance, but to know that when we do this work, we step into something very old, very sacred, very diverse and very profound. Indeed, oracular skills were essential. To the Ancients, seeking out the Oracle was a matter of survival …

Even in our relatively safe and unwild lives today, when someone comes to us seeking assistance through the seemingly random turning of cards and the delivery of messages, the service we offer is often that of survival. We help those in need through dark times as they traverse a life-changing moment and navigate transitions and difficulties. When someone truly needs help, the Oracle can be of service. This is an age-old truth about Oracles. So, initially, we will look at some of the ancient roots of this tradition so that we can know our own history. In this way, we come to know ourselves.

The Nature of the Oracle

Let's think about what an Oracle is. When in human form, an Oracle is a person who stands somewhat between the worlds, one foot firmly within what most of us would agree is reality and the other in the Otherworld, where the spirits reside and deities dwell. To me, Oracles are somewhat in-between creatures. We become a kind of bridge, a way of joining two ways of being, two realms, in order to obtain and bring back messages that can be of service.

The people who come to see us are often in the same position; what I mean by this is that they are often between two worlds themselves. They are most often on the verge of making a decision or grappling with the kind of change that completely alters lives. They may be at a loss to know how to cope or handle what lies before them. In this respect, although so much has changed in our world, little of the essential function of the Oracle has changed. People who seek out the Oracle—both those of the past and seekers of the present day—are often vulnerable and uncertain. They come seeking answers, so to me, it is so very essential that we offer guidance from a compassionate, clear and conscious place.

When we look back, back, back into the history of Oracles and witness how the tradition has endured, we can see why this art of Oracle card reading is so precious and so worthwhile developing.

Why not, you may wonder, just run off pure intuition? You almost certainly have natural intuitive talents and skills, and there are valid reasons to have confidence in your gifts, so it's reasonable to wonder whether you even need to learn the art of Oracle card reading. Why not begin to practise immediately? Well, whatever our level of talent or gifts, we can all benefit from a structured and layered approach to our readings, with the knowledge that we are continuing a kind of sacred work that has endured for millennia. Even in an age when we have the most sophisticated medical treatments available, a time in which we have psychology and counselling, there is a growing demand for answers that come from the realm of the spirits, and more people than ever before seek out the Oracle. If we can combine knowledge with natural gifts and the wisdom of training with our instinct, we will strengthen the reading — it will be well-rounded. You, dear Initiate, could be about to enter this realm of sacred service, ancient lineage and compassionate guidance.

PEOPLE WHO SEEK OUT THE ORACLE—BOTH THOSE OF THE PAST AND SEEKERS OF THE PRESENT DAY—ARE OFTEN VULNERABLE AND UNCERTAIN. THEY COME SEEKING ANSWERS, SO TO ME, IT IS SO VERY ESSENTIAL THAT WE OFFER GUIDANCE FROM A COMPASSIONATE, CLEAR AND CONSCIOUS PLACE.

This can be a somewhat strange and bewildering path, even as it can be one full of rich meaning and deep communion. We live in fortunate times. Although we Oracles do face some discrimination in a science-based world, which sometimes pushes rationalism to a cult-like degree, we have vast freedoms today. We live in times when we are now at liberty to explore these paths after nearly 1000 years of discrimination, torture and oppression. It is no exaggeration to say that in many places on this planet, humanity is in the process of rediscovering innate abilities.

For many Oracles throughout time, it was necessary to journey alone in order to connect deeply with the mysteries of the world. Oracles often live in solitude and even endure great loneliness. Sometimes, Oracles lived within communities and sisterhoods, but even those had their drawbacks and restrictions. But we are no longer as isolated as we once were. Today, we can create an oracular path and life that fulfils our dreams and gives expression to our own unique gifts and circumstances. The path of the Oracle is often mysterious, and it can still be challenging, but it is perhaps even more rich in meaning than ever before. Nowadays, we can meet like-minded souls along the way to learn from, share the journey with for a time, and be of service and assistance to those who seek reconnection with the Divine.

In the Beginning

We Oracles began by simply observing Nature … by watching and interpreting the signs given to us by the elements themselves. Anomalies, unusual patterns or extremely blessed events that were out of sync with the cycle of the seasons (or different to the way things simply were) could be read. Each element had its messengers and its meanings. The elements, the environment—even the planet herself—spoke to us. Let's work our way through those elements.

EARTH: Earth and the land, the trees, its crystals and crops gave us signs and messages which we, in turn, would observe and then make meaning from. This meaning would then be passed on to the people.

FIRE: Fire and flame, with its transformational powers, was one of our greatest sources of messages. We would watch the fires, be warmed, dance to its golden light, and sometimes, be warned of what was to come as we gazed into the smoke of sacred woods, scrying for signs and portents.

WATER: The people of the coastal regions and riverlands and by the great dark lakes learned to read the waters, to predict not only the physical tides but also the ebb and flow of their own lives. They watched for messages from the whales, the dolphins and the great sea turtles; they watched the reflections upon the waters, and they looked upon the shore for signs among the shells. Sacred wells, too, provided a way to work with this element.

AIR: And we read the skies … the flight of the birds, the movement and contours of the clouds, the colour of the sunset. We read the winds and tied their power into knots, which were untied to release their powers when needed. We saw the stars and the shapes they made, and we began to understand the patterns their movements traced in the heavens.

These were all the signs through which we learned the language of the natural world and developed ways of teaching this. Generation after generation, we passed this wisdom down to others — some of whom were initiated into the oracular tradition. Those who became most adept at reading the language of the world became the Oracles of their people. They were Seers, Prophets, Wise Ones, Witches. They became known by many names, but they were all Oracles … those who knew how to interpret the signs and omens of the natural world in order to help their people.

Reclaiming the Wisdom of the Oracle

We know that these Oracles were honoured, and at times, they were so revered that those who came after them decided that their bones should be kept so our ancestors could continue to draw from their wisdom. These totemic, magickal bones held the power, the wisdom, and were a way through to the Otherworld … and thus began the work with magickal tools that could be kept, passed on and repeatedly consulted.

For many of us, our ancestors—way before agriculture and the permanence of villages and homes—were hunter-gatherers who followed the paths of the wise animals, such as reindeer, the elk and the bison. They would carry with them the sacred bones of the wisest of the departed, the Oracles. Over time, something very important began to happen. On these bones were etched messages from the departed so the wisdom they had brought through could be shared again and again. This was a revolution, and you can see how this directly links to what we do today — we read the cards. We read a message etched onto something semi-permanent so that we can return to it again and again. To be the Bonekeeper was to be the Oracle for the tribe … where to go, when to stop, where the herds would be, and when to finally rest and stay, put down roots and grow grain. When we did that, the Oracles took up residence in Holy Places.

DECEMBER 22, 1987, LONDON

•

I went to Mysteries to have my tarot cards read last week, and I asked about relationships. The woman who did the reading advised me to take back my own power, to appreciate myself, and to stop trying to be a woman of steel. She said that I am warm and sensitive and a woman, and I must use these and not run away from who I am. That I must open up and not be ashamed of crying, and if I have something to say, to say it.

She recommended to me a book, "You Can Heal Your Life" by Louise L. Hay. I've started to say in my head, "I love you, I love you, I approve of you." What this has done is show me how many negative thoughts I have and how I berate myself. Perhaps now, at 26, not 46, or 16, but now, NOW I can remake my life, improve on the best and dissolve the worst.

•

Homes of the Oracle

In time, the most sacred of the bones were housed in great tombs, with some built beneath the earth — such as the great passage tombs in Ireland now called Newgrange and Knowth. Their old names are lost today, but the echoes of the spirits dwell within these places to this day. For the first time, this meant that the ancestors would travel to a dedicated temple or shrine throughout the Wheel of the Year to seek the solace and advice of the Wise Ones, the Oracles (living or dead), and of the place — which was a direct conduit not only to their wisdom, but to the stars and the dimensions beyond the physical.

If you were to see these places in person, you would feel their power … within these Holy Places—which have their counterparts in all cultures, all over this world—you can see the symbols made by ancestors in this ancient passageway tomb in Ireland, the people of the Tuatha Dé Danann. The carvings of the symbols were the messages. Over time, the combination of the symbols, the place and the Oracle all became the way back to the ancestors, through to the Otherworld, and to the spirits who guided the tribe. The mystery of the Oracles lived on …

The Oracle as

Oracles then were people who were able to keep the sacred exactly that. They dwelled within sacred spaces, they served their community, and in today's world, they would most likely be called mad, weird or strange, or some other word that means they are 'apart' from others in important ways. Please do not think you need to be these things today. You do not need to find experiences that will make you 'different' because you have what is most needed within your own lived experience.

You have already been through circumstances in your life that have tested you and shown you your own unique way of experiencing the world. Sometimes, there is a realisation—a moment as sudden as a lightning strike, a brief second or two—that you are different, that you see things with new eyes. Life has given you initiatory circumstances in which you split from the reality of those around you and moved into a different level of perception. People like you have been called many things — over-sensitive, thin-skinned, weird, maybe even weak … you may have been teased or had your experiences when young denied and dismissed. A child runs to his mother: "Mumma, I saw lights on the wall last night." A girl whispers in wonder: "Dad, have you seen the other people who live here?" Another may confide in a grandparent: "Grandpa, I saw a beautiful lady with wings in the garden today." What is the response? So often, it is a laughing off or an angry command not to 'tell stories'. We often share these very real events with others, who, having fallen back to sleep in their own lives, will seek to protect themselves from our intuitive glimpses into a more complex, magickal world. I believe—and feel strongly—that many of the people being born today have worked as Wise Ones, Seers, Witches and Oracles in the past, and thus we have many more people working as Oracles. This is because we are now experiencing a great need in our time to reconnect with our lost intuition.

Another experience, apart from this sense of being an outsider that Oracles tend to have, is some kind of life event that has changed them. You may have undergone experiences that would be considered traumatic. For some, it can be an illness that causes a period of isolation, or even a near-death experience, which causes us to step across the threshold of one world and into the Otherworld for a time. You may have also experienced prophetic dreams, shimmering moments where you have stepped into the future for a moment in order to bring back a message for yourself or for another …

This is, in some ways, because we lack the rituals we once had within our cultures. Those who were chosen to be Oracles would have undergone a series of tests and initiations to ready them for the role and the responsibility, and the strangeness that this life can impose upon us. Today, we have eradicated these overt rituals and replaced them with commercial experiences-as-ritual. Life herself will bring us experiences that will (in essence) separate us from others and make us aware of our gift and the responsibilities it bears.

Please know that when I say this to you, I am not suggesting that we manufacture these experiences or begin to fetishise difficult experiences in our lives. It is so essential to remain grounded and keep ourselves here in healthful ways when we do this work. You are most likely already a highly sensory person, one who processes the world in a very different way from many other people. We do not need to try to create more separation from others within our lives. But what can be helpful to know is that you are part of a lineage of people who have a purpose, and that is to live somewhat between the worlds.

For me, my moment where I broke with what others would call normality came in waves … The first was a car accident when I was very young, around 10 years old. I was hit by a small truck (I know, it sounds ridiculous, but there you go) on our very quiet street in our very quiet little village, where nothing at all ever happened. I was hit in the head first, then dragged along the road, crushing my left leg, forever changing the way I could 'see' physically.

For months in the hospital, the focus was on my leg. Operation after operation, skin graft after skin graft brought it back together, and the incredible healing genes within my family worked their magick. But my head had changed … something within me had been 'cracked open'. I did not know it at the time, but I couldn't physically see properly any more, and what I did begin to notice was that I could see energy around people. My blurred vision brought its own kind of weird gift — of seeing beyond the physical—while my injuries separated me from school, from family, and put me into a place where life and death danced very closely with each other for a time. This created within me a thirst for knowledge about the afterlife — what would have happened if I had died? Where would I have gone?

This accident, which became a very early break from the former life I had lived, changed my understanding of 'reality' profoundly. It changed me. Transformed me. Recreated me. Perhaps you have experienced a moment of great loss or abrupt change, the alteration of one kind of life for another? These experiences, with all their variations and personal nature, at their essence *disillusion* us. Disillusionment is often thought to be a negative event, but if we contemplate this—and consider the context of the disillusionment and that what we are learning is a deeper, more true form of reality—it becomes clear that it is not unfortunate. It is a blessing, for it rips away the veils of illusion that make so many people live blindly, stumbling towards wisdom and true light. Some of these illusions may be:

- Life is permanent.
- That we are unchanging.
- That all is certain.
- That we have time to spare.
- That we are our roles — for example, that we are a wife or mother, rather than a Soul, first.

DISILLUSIONMENT IS OFTEN THOUGHT TO BE A NEGATIVE EVENT, BUT IF WE CONTEMPLATE THIS—AND CONSIDER THE CONTEXT OF THE DISILLUSIONMENT AND THAT WHAT WE ARE LEARNING IS A DEEPER, MORE TRUE FORM OF REALITY—IT BECOMES CLEAR THAT IT IS NOT UNFORTUNATE. IT IS A BLESSING, FOR IT RIPS AWAY THE VEILS OF ILLUSION THAT MAKE SO MANY PEOPLE LIVE BLINDLY, STUMBLING TOWARDS WISDOM AND TRUE LIGHT.

The Oracular Initiation

AFTER THE SHOCK OF A LIFE-CHANGING EVENT EASES, WE OFTEN MOVE through disillusionment. Rather than this being a negative, this disillusionment can inspire us to search for what is true, what is enduring, and what can be trusted. Thus we begin the journey back after one of these life-changing—and they are LIFE-changing—events. And it is this journey, this transformation, that reconstructs us. We get to choose how we do that, and when we return, we are often changed in very significant ways. This is what happened to me, and more importantly by far, this is what has happened again and again to Shamans and Oracles, Witches, Wise Ones and Healers of all kinds over the many thousands of years we have been here on this planet.

So, if you have experienced an event, either external—e.g., an accident, divorce, death, injury—or internal, through a mental illness or experience with a change of consciousness, (for example, you have been touched by the Otherworld)—you and the way you view the world may have been forever changed.

We can struggle against this, and we often do. I did, and perhaps this is a natural and necessary part of the process. There can be many reasons for this struggle. Sometimes, there is a surfacing of past-life fear, such as an echo of severe and life-threatening discrimination. Sometimes, it seems 'crazy' to believe we have a gift, can connect with messages and symbols, and bring back advice and guidance for others. Fears of being fraudulent or giving 'bad' advice can rain down upon us, especially if we have internalised the critical, judgemental voices of cynical people or a damning culture.

Religious backgrounds and traditions within our birth family can create a host of superstitions and worries that when we do this work, we will tap into something evil or that we will consult with energies that are malevolent. "Don't play with forces you cannot understand nor control" was one of my limiting beliefs. Yet, when we break down these beliefs, see where they come from and who they have been spoken through, and really question whether these are our own genuine thoughts and feelings, oftentimes, we find these are conditioned by society or family — they do not belong to us.

The trick, therefore, is in creating awareness around these beliefs and gently disentangling them (or powerfully cutting them away) so we can move into our own powers and freely do our work without a punitive chorus hampering our abilities. We all have these burdens to one degree or another, and for me, it is a regular practice to be self-aware, to listen to the fears and voices within, to ponder their purpose, and to free myself from their tethers and chains — again and again and again.

Please know it is by no fault or flaw within you that the removal of past life fears or current-day conditioning takes time and perseverance ... This is natural and more usual than it is not. For some of us, clearing can feel instantaneous and long-term, but most often, we have to continue the clearing work on a regular basis. This is an essential and very healthy practice to get into the habit of when we are working as an Oracle. After a while, you may feel the need to do this clearing work less and less … but still, I encourage you to make space for it on a regular basis. Life is rich and surprising, and we may often be taken unawares. This is simply the nature of being alive, becoming aware and living a fulfilled life.

A Solitary Journey to

Throughout time, Oracles have not only sought solitude—which kept them in touch with the Otherworld and untroubled by everyday living—but also developed powerful ways of entering what we would call the oracular space. Oracular space is a realm where past, present and future co-exist in a timeless moment of 'now'. Ritual space, too, becomes this place where there is no past, no present, no future. There is just 'now'.

The word 'divination' comes from the Latin *divi*, which means 'deity'. The true purpose of divination is to help us connect to this consciousness and sources of guidance beyond the personal self. To be an Oracle was—and beneath the surface, still is—to serve as a portal to assist others in expanding their knowledge and wisdom. From pre-ancient times, humanity has worked with Oracles to live more closely aligned to sacred intention and life purpose. Seeing an Oracle was an Event.

The Oracle as a Highly Sensitive Being

So, how does all of this relate to becoming an Oracle card reader? Firstly, I think considering these subtle aspects of the process begins to give us a sense of context. Our work arose from a profound need for our people to have that connection to the Otherworld, to spirits that guide us, to those who have gone before us. While we may lead very different lives — very safe, very comfortable lives in comparison to our ancestors and the Oracles who would have endured harsh and sometimes short lives, many aspects remain the same.

One of those aspects is a deep sense of Otherness. A moment that separates us from others in order to bring us home to our purpose. Another aspect could be a desire to be a source of support and assistance within the world. Still another could be that you possess talents and gifts that you are naturally drawn to explore: a sense of the Mystery that lies within us, a natural affinity for being able to read what is taking place with extra-sensory perception, a state where our senses are keen, awake, aware and very sensitive. This sensitivity can make it challenging for us to live in what is considered to be a normal or usual manner, so sometimes we seek solitude and yet simultaneously experience loneliness. We often have families and children and husbands and wives and partners and so much that seems 'normal'. But deep within, we Oracles carry a sense of being slightly apart (nearly at all times), which ebbs and flows and often breaks through, demanding attention after a shattering life event.

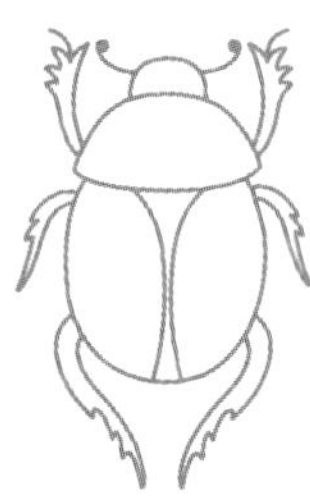

KASSANDRA — THE UNBELIEVED ORACLE OF TROY

Despite the almost universal recognition of the Oracle in ancient times, oracular visions would often visit individuals working outside of the recognised framework. For these people, being an Oracle was no easy thing. Just as many contemporary Oracles experience ridicule, so too did many Oracles in the past. We have been told (and sometimes still are) that this guidance may be evil, an illness, foolishness, superstition and most often a sign of something being very, very wrong with our minds.

This is no new phenomenon. As an Oracle, the response to our reading is, to a large degree, out of our control and, in other ways, none of our business. So, in the spirit of that truth, I wanted to share with you a little of the story of Kassandra of Troy.

Kassandra was a princess who worked outside the official 'oracular' system and was simply a very gifted, natural Oracle who was devoted to the Goddess Athena. She foretold of Socrates, whom the Oracle of Delphi called the wisest man on Earth. (Just as an aside, Socrates himself took oracular guidance from the flight of birds, communicated with animals and spoke with a being he called his 'daemon'. If ever we think our guide communicates strangely with us, think only of this wisest of all men, whose daemon communicated through sneezing ... on the left, for no; on the right, for yes. PLEASE NOTE: the word 'daemon' predates Christianity — it does not mean 'demon'. In Greek times, a daemon was a spirit. Christianity took this word and rather twisted it. Back to Socrates. He refused to explain his guidance, referring to it as his 'divine something', placing his trust in his experience of the Sacred.)

Now, Kassandra received messages that Troy would be invaded by a wooden horse. She desperately tried to warn the people of Troy when exactly such a thing was left outside the gates of the city. She begged the official Oracles not to allow the huge wooden horse to be dragged into the city, but she was not believed or even respectfully listened to. The Trojans pulled the horse in and celebrated until they slept. And then, from the horse emerged the Greek army. Troy was sacked, and Kassandra, who fled to the temple of Athena, was killed, along with most of her people. Whenever I feel I have it bad, I just remember Kassandra!

Experientials and Experimentals

- You may wish to bless and charge whichever Oracle deck you are going to be working with as we journey together. This is the very beginning of a beautiful connection for you both. (If you have already been using your card deck, please do this in any case — it will only deepen the energy between your cards and you.)
- Begin your Oracle card reader journey with your Book of Shadows and Light, reader's grimoire, or whatever name you feel most suits this sacred, magickal journal.
- Practise shuffling and handling your cards.
- Shuffle your cards, split the deck three ways with your non-dominant hand, put the deck back together, and then turn over the top card each morning when you are still fresh. First thing would be best, but anytime is better than not at all. Get into this wonderful habit, as it will help you more than you can know to get to know your deck very, very well.
- Take your cards with you as you go through your day or night. Spend time with them, and handle them as much as possible. The intention is to create a real sense of friendship, intimacy and connection between you. This is a mystical relationship in the early stages of its development, so it must be tended to with love and devotion. Have fun! Be serious. Enjoy, and also allow your heart to open to the messages and to the energies within the cards.
- Begin to contemplate your family lineage — can you remember any members of your birth family who experienced profound moments of clear intuition, psychic gifts or abilities that we are not able to explain away with 'logic'?

- Consider whether the reading of Oracle cards brings up any fears and uncertainty within you — write and wonder about these in your Book of Shadows and Light … when you can trace some of these fears to the root or a statement you can clearly articulate, write that down. If you cannot get to that place, that is okay. Just write about the feelings and sensations you may have, as these are absolutely valid, too.
- Consider whether your family or people you care about have fears and doubts around the reading of cards or the 'telling of fortunes'. If you can articulate these, please write them down, and again, this will be very valuable as you begin to clear and become more aware of why you have certain fears. Contemplating the 'why' will be of great assistance to you — the technique works, no matter our individual circumstances.

  Then, go ahead and begin your work on healing some of the patterns. Healing is a multi-layered creative experience, and I do not wish to instruct you on how. Consider meditation, journalling, exercise, setting yourself challenges and being with people who have had similar experiences.
- Journal your daily readings. Note the moon phase, the time, and how you felt. Make notes about the card. Compare these notes to the messages within the guidebook.
- Read the introduction and the instructions section of whichever Oracle card guidebook you're working with carefully. (We will move on to card spreads and card meanings later.) My guidebooks are very important and too many people skip over so much valuable material. Please begin to read this, and you may wish to make some notes of any questions you may wish to contemplate or discuss with an Oracle friend.
- Begin to see where and when you have felt the most messages or the most intuitive in your life. What factors contributed to this heightened awareness? Note these down in your Book of Shadows and Light.

You have begun your awakening,

dear Initiate,

into the oracular path.

Chapter Two

A Candle Burning Brighter

The language of excitement is at best picturesque merely. You must be calm before you can utter oracles.

— Henry David Thoreau

Dear Initiate,

Are you ready now to journey deeper along the path of the Oracle? Here, we will discover enriching information about cartomancy. We will continue our discovery of the ancient Oracles, and we are also going to explore Tarot and Oracle cards, and the differences and relationships between them. This is not a Tarot-reading book, but Oracle cards and Tarot are family. This is important to understand, for on your path as an Oracle working with Oracle cards, I feel you must know the difference between the two.

The Tarot and Oracle Cards – Siblings That Share Secrets

People regularly ask me about the difference between Tarot and Oracle cards, and it kind of saddens me that many professional readers dismiss the need to even be able to distinguish between these two great streams of cartomancy. More still are even a little discourteous regarding the Tarot. Many people who work with Oracle cards are not even aware of the Tarot or the relationship between the two forms of divination. Some people feel the Tarot is 'scary', and others are too nervous to handle it. But I think it is wonderful, and what you may be scared of has its origins in a very different culture and time.

This powerful divination tool deserves respect and understanding; when you have that, your own relationship with all of your cards will be enhanced. I wish you to know the history of Oracles and the lineage within which you are now working — and this is an important chapter of that long, long story. Knowing the tale is to know why and how we humans seek out guidance. The story of the cards (who have grown alongside us) helps us to understand how we have become who and what we are today. This knowledge—and the intuitive skill it can help nurture—can even show us who we are going to become.

A (Very) Brief Introduction to Tarot

There are so many myths and misconceptions, rumours, wild, wild stories and legends regarding the Tarot, which I consider a beautiful instrument for self-knowledge — and much of the lore does have at its heart more than a little truth. To talk of the Tarot is to talk of many things, for the Tarot is an oracular system and tool, a book of life, that has very diverse roots. Even its name is a Mystery — Tarot comes from the old Italian word, tarocchi, but it has no known etymology. It may have some of its roots in the old European word for blood, or an Arabic word that means "unknown". It is, truly, a Mystery.

You will hear and read a lot of legendary talk about Tarot — that they are the 78 lost pages of the *Book of Thoth*, an Egyptian God of Magick and Words; that the cards developed in Atlantis; that they are instruments of evil; and many other exciting, even astounding, claims and possibilities. It is up to each of us to feel what the energies are within each deck, to also respect the Tarot creators' vision, and to decide for ourselves whether a particular deck is for us and holds that special magick.

Tarot truly began to make an impact in the 15th century with the rise of a particular aristocratic fashion. The wealthy families of the Italian city-states had heard of this Tarot and of its structure, and several commissioned their own Tarot. Painted in brilliant tones by famous artists, having your own family immortalised as members of the Major Arcana was a sign of prestige.

So, even while people were the most illiterate and very bound by the dictates of the Church, here was an Oracle developing that featured imagery that drew upon alchemy, the Church, ancient systems of magick and mysticism like the Kabbalah, witchcraft and astrology. Remember, Tarot decks were very rare and costly at first, and they were often commissioned by extremely wealthy families to learn more about their fortunes. In time, and as the printing press developed, more decks came into circulation, but they were still exclusive and sometimes even dangerous to own. These early decks included the *Marseilles* deck and the *Visconti* deck, with several French and Italian variations of the 17th century containing imagery that is familiar to us today.

How Are Tarot and Oracle Cards Alike?

Both Tarot and Oracle cards are forms of cartomancy — card reading. There are many other traditional forms of card reading, and some are developments of older forms of cartomancy. Some systems use the cards as a canvas for other forms of divination — so, for example, you could work with runes in cartomancy, except instead of the runes being carved in stones, their symbols are painted and printed on cards.

Tarot Structure

Tarot is a form of cartomancy that is perhaps the oldest within the Western Mystery Tradition. Tarot decks have a very clear structure; this is where Tarot and Oracle cards are so very different. Of course, there are many Tarot decks that diverge from the traditional structure, but let's look at what that structure most commonly is, first of all.

The card numbers vary, determined by the creators and their vision, so some cards may be the same from deck to deck but may have a different number, depending on what the creators understood to be the correct numbering system.

In terms of the amount of cards, a traditional Tarot deck has 78 cards.

A Tarot deck is divided into three major parts — the Major Arcana, the Minor Arcana, and the Court Cards. Sometimes, the Major Arcana are called trump cards, and the Minor Arcana are referred to as pip cards.

Cards can be read both upright or reversed, and both of these meanings have their own nuances that can change the overall messages of the reading.

THE MAJOR ARCANA

Arcana means 'secret', and the Major Arcana contains 22 cards that depict life's adventures, joys and challenges, almost in the form of a journey. These secrets are told through archetypal imagery that has remained fairly consistent for nearly 700 years. Each card is a key that opens the door into Wisdom.

So, we have the first card of the Major Arcana, The Fool, numbered 0, through to the last card, often called The World—but sometimes called The Universe—numbered 21. The twenty-two cards of the Major Arcana walk us through a journey from innocence to experience and then to transcendence — the soul's journey, in many ways. Esteemed psychoanalyst C.G. Jung (whose works I recommend) prized the lessons within the Tarot and made it a part of his work. The Fool's journey is our own, and we can relate to the sublime moments depicted in cards like The Lovers and to the loss and upheaval depicted in cards like The Tower. There are a number of variations in the Major Arcana — for example, the *Rider–Waite* deck swapped the traditional numbers of the Strength and Justice cards. Due to its remarkable influence, many Tarot readers do not know that prior to the *Rider–Waite* deck, Justice was card number 8, and Strength card number 11. My first deck, the *Marseille Tarot*, had them in those positions. It isn't exactly going to interfere with your reading, although it can alter how you interpret the card's numbers and can also change the flow of the Fool's journey in your deck. I'm mentioning it here in case you see those variations yourself and wonder about their origins!

THE FOOL'S JOURNEY IS OUR OWN, AND WE CAN RELATE TO THE SUBLIME MOMENTS DEPICTED IN CARDS LIKE THE LOVERS AND TO THE LOSS AND UPHEAVAL DEPICTED IN CARDS LIKE THE TOWER.

The Major Arcana cards and their numbers are:

0 The Fool
I The Magician
II The High Priestess
III The Empress
IV The Emperor
V The Hierophant
VI The Lovers
VII The Chariot
VIII Strength
IX The Hermit
X Wheel of Fortune
XI Justice
XII The Hanged Man
XIII Death
XIV Temperance
XV The Devil
XVI The Tower
XVII The Star
XVIII The Moon
XIX The Sun
XX Judgement
XXI The World/Universe

THE MINOR ARCANA

The Minor Arcana deals with the more everyday events — the personal, the work day, the things of this world. They are also more about the temporary — they deal with the inevitable passing of days, the physical seasons both in nature and within human lives.

The Minor Arcana is divided into four suits, which are, in no particular order:

- **Coins, or Pentacles**
- **Wands**
- **Cups**
- **Swords**

Each of those suits has the same structure — beginning with the Ace of Wands, for example, then moving into numbered cards of that suit. Each card is a different expression and variation—or manifestation—of the energy of Wands, or Cups, or Swords, or Coins (which are sometimes called Pentacles).

Each of the suits is associated with a dominant elemental energy:

- **Coins/Pentacles: Earth**
- **Wands: Fire**
- **Cups: Water**
- **Swords: Air**

And each is associated with an aspect of Life, one of the realms of existence.

- **Coins/Pentacles: The material**
- **Wands: The creative**
- **Cups: The emotional**
- **Swords: The mental**

Please note — sometimes, you will find that the elemental attributes of swords and wands are reversed. When this takes place, forums all throughout the esoteric community light up with feverish arguments!

The suits can also share with us what healing paths can most benefit us at the time of the reading.

- **Coins/Pentacles:** We may need to become more grounded, and focus on ensuring we have enough — you know, enough food, enough shelter, enough touch, enough money, enough connection to nature … all the tangible, vital resources that enable us to care for ourselves.

- **Wands:** It's time for art and music and creativity — find ways to creatively express yourself and you'll gain perspective and wisdom about your circumstances.

- **Cups:** It's time to open up to your own emotions, to allow yourself to feel and to express those feelings.

- **Swords:** Mindfulness is the key when this suit shows up in a reading. It is the time for breathwork, clarity of thought, and mental acuity. Stay sharp!

COURT CARDS

THERE ARE MORE CARDS THAT BELONG TO EACH SUIT, WHICH ARE TRADITIONALLY called the Court Cards. These depict people relevant to the reading, their qualities and social standing. So, in many decks, you will find the Prince of Cups, the King of Swords, the Queen of Wands, the Page of Pentacles, and so on. Different decks have different beings represented by the Court Cards — some include a Princess and a Prince, and others have three male figures for every female figure. Most often, there have been more masculine than feminine court cards, which was one of my influences when I created *The Oracle Tarot* (published through Hay House) in 2002. I removed the court cards altogether, which at the time was considered a radical move.

Generally speaking, in decks like the *Rider–Waite*, we have four Court Cards for each suit:

- **The Page**
- **The Knight**
- **The Queen**
- **The King**

In other decks, like the *Visconti-Sforza* and many modern decks, there are many variations on the traditional Court Card personages.

You can see that Tarot has a structure that gives it a great deal of strength, which means it can be a very precise tool for predictions, timings and assessing what areas most concern the Querent, Seeker or Questioner. Or the person working with the cards who seeks self-knowledge, healing and wisdom. Oracle cards do not have this structure, which is unique to Tarot.

So, we can now see that Oracle cards are the siblings of Tarot cards, and today, they are made the same way, on the same mediums — but they are quite different in terms of structure and personality.

Why Are People Frightened by the Tarot?

There are images in many Tarot decks that people have found frightening and disturbing, but it is exactly that ability to look unflinchingly into life's darkness and shadows that gives the Tarot its potency. However, our world has changed in some ways that are significant, and the continual evolution of the Tarot's imagery has kept it alive as an Oracle for so many hundreds of years.

When I created my own Tarot deck in 2001–2002, known as *The Oracle Tarot* and the first Tarot deck published by Hay House, it was my absolute wish to take the cards to a true and honest place where their wisdom could shine without fear.

I had some strange experiences with certain decks when I was much, much younger. My very first deck was a version of the *Marseilles* deck, then I purchased the *Aleister Crowley Thoth Tarot*, and then the *Rider-Waite Tarot*.

I admired Crowley's deck because it was deeply sensual and esoteric, and I had been so drawn to working with it, but as I began, I found myself feeling nervous, negative and mistrusting of the cards. I was impressed by them, and they emanated magick. I gazed into the paintings by Lady Frieda Harris and I remember feeling a kinship with the Princess of Wands. She felt so alive to me, so vital and present. But despite this love, and an undeniable, strong attraction, I felt cautious. After months of varied experiences, and a recurrence of paranormal incidents that had happened so often when I was a child, I reluctantly (and a little sadly) packed them in their black silk wrap I had made myself and put them aside. I have come back to them now in my life — and perhaps I was just not ready for them at that time. I was undergoing a very deep series of psychic, magickal awakenings and personally, now, I feel I was just too open and too inexperienced to handle their energy. That does not hold for everyone, so please don't let this sharing make you feel doubtful of their beauty and power. Truly, I loved all my cards … I didn't have very much money at all; London (where I was living at the time) seemed expensive to draw breath in, and so every deck was so valuable to me: every card a wonderland full of lessons, possibilities and tantalising occult knowledge to explore.

I dreamed of my cards regularly, often lost within the world of a card like The Star, feeling myself reaching into the sky, trying to touch its shining light and transfer its promise into my body. I fell from the burning Tower in one dream, my own long scream waking me from the nightmare. The awful feeling of plunging through the air, hurtling towards the ground without any say, any control, or any way out, stayed with me for days. In others, beings from the cards began to speak with me, but I could not recall their words with any real clarity. Though somehow, I felt that they had still given me a gift and helped me understand dilemmas and paradoxes that my conscious mind could not begin to comprehend.

I sewed a little black silk altar cloth for my cards. I did this for all of my decks for a very long time; every stitch laboured with love, the deep glow of the fabric, the background against which the cards spoke to me. At the time, I lived in a house with fourteen other people in London, a wild and free post-punk bohemian household brimming with dancers, actors, artists and just an amazing collection of free-spirited young people from all over the world. We had no roof in part of the house, and pigeons actually roosted in our lounge room!

I was thrown into reading for others as soon as I came home one day with my *Marseilles* deck. With fourteen mystics in the house — Joel the dancer teaching me about chakras, Laura the artist experimenting with astral travelling and Michael telling us stories about his time with a yogi in India, my role soon became that of the … well, the card reader, an Oracle-in-training, I suppose. I would hole up in my tiny room (one of the bathrooms in the enormous, old, broken-down four-storey Georgian terrace), light my candles, chant, and read and read and read the cards. I made notes in my very funny little diaries, my first Books of Shadows and Light, and sometimes I fell asleep almost buried beneath a spread.

Soon, everyone in the house wanted readings, and as two members of the household were in bands, I soon found myself reading for their friends. It just happened naturally. At the time, I was quite the wild child, and I drank way too much, pushing the boundaries of my life in all sorts of ways. Away from everyone who had known me, I was wanting to discover who I truly was, desperate to discover what my purpose was and to know who I could become … and that remains a huge part of the appeal of both Tarot and Oracle cards, finding out who you are — a path to self-discovery.

I want you to find some of that passion — and I do wish I could spare you some of the mistakes I made! You don't have to leave your home and go completely wild—the madness and near-deaths I created for myself—to become an Oracle card reader. But you do need to read the cards for yourself and others, and I believe you need to do this a lot. Reading for others will truly help you, even if you are determined to only read for yourself. Reading for others helps with detachment and seeing the cards differently, as well as learning how to tune in and link with another being's energy without falling prey to desperately wanting to please them.

SEPTEMBER, 1988, PARIS

•

Card number four, my past: leaving journalism; getting away from my messy life in Sydney; clearing away the bad; transforming my life. Recently, somebody's help has been enabling me to change – probably an influence of my new home; Peter, Charlie, Matthew, Charlotte ... all that love and support helping me get over my insecurities and lack of real confidence, and helping me to look beyond myself and any fixed, sham, adopted, conditioned ideas. It's the best card – wonderful (tho' I love The Star the best) is The World; in the position it falls in, it means I am coming into a fulfilling time, that the hard work of the past will pay off. This is a fantastic reading so far – throwing light (Ho! Ho!) on me is card 18, The Sun. Does this mean—tying in with The Hermit—that to achieve this promise, I must continue with my self-counsel, my growth of self-knowledge? [Present-day note: Looking back on this, I can see how much I had to learn about myself – and even more to understand the possibilities of who I could become if I set forth on the magickal path that was beckoning me back then.] Perhaps I can achieve maturity, stability and confidence. And I will fine-tune my (neglected, neglected) abilities.

•

Oracle Cards — How They Differ from Tarot Cards

I feel that Oracle cards rely upon the layout or spread used by the reader to create structure for the querent. The question adds further structure. Without a clear question, and a layout that is solid and grounded, we run the risk of being very ungrounded in our Oracle card readings, lacking focus points and moments of clear guidance.

Oracle cards are more like a dialogue with the beings or energies depicted within the cards — as if you are having a discussion with a circle of advisors, energies or beings who talk to you (or to the querent, through you). They have less structure, generally speaking, but are easier to learn in some respects because of that.

Oracle Decks as Worlds of Energy

My decks have been created through a series of energies who almost … almost *asked* if they could come into the world through me, and then I began with the messages. They are speaking, but I guess I am the way they enter the world. I do feel a little like I've been chosen at times, but I would say that these beings—if I had not done the work—would have gone to another person like myself and found a way to break through into this world. They are not mine, but in some other ways, we do belong to each other. They may be like my children, but once they are set free into and upon the world, their journey is their own.

Are the beings Within the Cards Real?

I do see the beings within the cards as very substantial and never question their authenticity or validity. Yet they are very unlike us in many ways, too. Some people describe the cards as projections of our own selves, and I can see how this has validity. However, I feel they are their own beings and their own places, with their respective energies and realms, and they are not simply here to guide us — they have their own lives and purposes. But when they have felt like being of assistance, they give me messages that I can then pass on through the decks. There is a very different energy and almost a different realm and gathering of beings within each of my Oracle decks, and each has been an incredible experience of co-creating with these beings.

This holds true for many Oracle decks. One aspect of my decks that perhaps is a little different is that I work quite hard to go to the places where these beings have dwelled, or spaces within the world where there is a great deal of power and energy. The information and the beings residing in these oracular spaces are then almost imbued into the deck.

Reading within the walls of a sacred site can offer a unique atmosphere, powerful energy and heightened intuition. I vividly recall doing a reading deep within the ancient neolithic longbarrow of Wayland's Smithy, England, in 2010, with the **Wild Wisdom of the Faery Oracle**.

Liminal Spaces and Places

LIMINAL, VERY SIMPLY PUT, MEANS IN-BETWEEN. THE KINDS OF IN-BETWEENS that can hold great power, a particular kind of energy that can see us move into other realms or our minds shift into other states of consciousness. There are liminal times and spaces that we can all experience — and do each day, but we are often unconscious of these energetic gateways in time and space. Remember in the first chapter, Light the Fire, how I spoke about Oracles being the bridge between this world and the Otherworld? The being who connects the human and the Divine, or the 'Other', in order to help the

SO, PART OF BEING AN ORACLE IS BECOMING A BRIDGE BETWEEN SPACES. WE LEARN TO READ THE CARDS IN A LIMINAL WAY, TIME AND SPACE. AND WE SPEAK ... WE DISCOVER AND WORK WITH THE VOICE, AND THE SACRED VIBRATIONS OF THE VOICE MOVE THE MESSAGE INTO THE WORLD AND DIRECTLY AFFECT HOW THE MESSAGE IS NOT ONLY CONVEYED BUT RECEIVED.

querent (or themselves). The experience and energy of these liminal places are of great assistance in terms of our intuition, and they also offer the cards a certain vibration and power that comes from the blessings of these enchanted places.

Remember, too, that the Oracle is one who speaks — the root of the word Oracle is *Orare*, meaning, 'to speak'. It was also used to mean 'beseech' or even 'pray', so perhaps we could even say, "To speak the sacred." So, part of being an Oracle is becoming a bridge between spaces. We learn to read the cards in a liminal way, time and space. And we speak ... we discover and work with the voice, and the sacred vibrations of the voice move the message into the world and directly affect how the message is not only conveyed but received.

Within the Oracle Card Decks

Each of my decks has a great deal of energy woven into it, which I feel you are subtly able to pick up on. It is not the literal story that is most important here; it is the knowing that these cards are rich with their own energies and histories, which you can draw upon in subtle, poetic, oracular ways.

With the *Wild Wisdom of the Faery*, for example, there is a back-story of great personal and physical healing as a part of creating the deck, and into the images and words is woven that healing. Within the faery forest of the deck is the energy of one particular faery forest in England, which is a gateway for so many beings. The same deck also contains the energy of places like St Nectan's Glen in Cornwall and several very old beech trees at Avebury that are very significant to me, and truly powerful beings. (So powerful they connected with Tolkien, who wrote of the Ents, as he was so inspired by these trees.)

For the *Oracle of the Mermaids*, I travelled to places that held the mermaid lore, again in the old lands. There, I spent several days with marine biologists, learning what I could from those wisdom keepers about dolphins, as their energy is so prevalent in the deck. I went to the west coast of Ireland, to Japan, to tropical Queensland, and drew upon my personal mermaid experiences in Hawai'i when I was just on the cusp of becoming a teenager.

I have truly somehow made these trips and excursions happen (and there have never been any complimentary trips, nor are they sponsored or paid for). It just seemed very important to me, so some things were sacrificed so that these explorations could be made manifest. It has meant some important personal choices along the way. But this has helped create a real depth and authenticity, which I hope comes through for you with each of the decks. I feel it has been well worthwhile, and I know people can tap into the energies of those liminal places and beings through the cards, which is very beautiful and joyous. In a similar way, the energies within the deck can begin to manifest in a unique way in your own world. Trees can begin to speak. Old bodies of water rise and fall, breathe in and out and reveal their secrets. The tide recedes, and shells share their messages as you walk the shore.

Origins and Oracles

LET'S EXPLORE THE ANCIENT WORLD A LITTLE MORE, HEADING BACK IN TIME to grow our understanding of the oracular tradition and the lineage you are becoming a part of.

When we began to grow the grain and make our homes in places for longer than a season, we grew villages, and then towns, and then cities, and the Oracle would live near but still apart from us — as we discussed in Chapter One, the Oracle was the Sacred Outsider, of the community but not within the community. They were the origins of the cities and towns, which were often built around a sacred space where an Oracle dwelled.

Today, there is but a fragment left of the great town that grew around the sacred oak grove of the Oracle of Dodona in Greece. Originally dedicated to Gaia, it evolved to become the place where the voice of Zeus was heard through its priestesses. Within the centuries following the birth of Christ, the grove was destroyed, and fragments of its oaks were smuggled throughout the world, still fabled to be able to channel the voice of Zeus. Oracles endure. You have endured, too.

Ancient Greece was home to many Oracles, but none were more renowned or sought out than the priestesses of Delphi, who were the voices of the God Apollo on Earth. We know much about these priestesses: their prophecies, their age, their rituals, their symbols and their lives. The priestesses were known as the Pythia, and they were most often of mature age. They were said to be celibate, and they trained for their whole lives before becoming Oracles of Apollo.

They were elevated before the supplicant—the Querent or Seeker—on a three-legged stool, and within some of the caves in which they worked and lived, it is said that gases and fumes emerged from within the earth, sending the Pythia into an almost permanently altered state. (Earthly smudging, perhaps?) Their caves were positioned high in the mountains and were only reached after a treacherous passage. Thus, seeing an Oracle was a Journey — it was about what happened on the way, the sacrifice that was made, and then the revelations from the Pythia and whatever else took place within the cave.

When people come to see us, they are undertaking a similar Journey. The circumstances may be different, but believe me, all souls who seek have climbed that mountain to the Oracle, metaphorically.

REBEL, REBEL — ALEISTER CROWLEY

ALEISTER CROWLEY WAS THE MAGICKAL NAME OF THE GREAT magus born in 1875 as Edward Alexander Crowley. His father, a rich brewer, was a Plymouth Brother, a strange and mysterious sect not unlike the Masons. Aleister grew up to be a radical non-conformist and something of a profligate rebel. But most of all, he remains one of the oracular world's most advanced thinking figures. Though many of his philosophies are highly dubious in terms of ethics and integrity—he was not above a certain sadistic tone in some of his ceremonies—he believed the way to the light was through the shadowlands of his experiences and personalities.

He certainly explored them well. An Oracle, a Mystic and a Witch, Crowley based much of his thinking on the Egyptian model of magick. He wrote volumes of visionary poetry (his poem *Pan* is an astounding work) with some literary success, but his volumes on magick—and his notorious, theatrical public ceremonies—outraged English society. His lifelong exploration of magick and the oracular arts gave us great gifts and smaller boons as well, such as the introduction of spelling magick with a 'k' to differentiate it from magic, which had been abducted by great illusionists and stage sleight-of-hand artists.

He was almost as famed for his brilliant wit and biting cynicism as Oscar Wilde. Although this made him feared, he was also admired by many of the creative luminaries of his time — W. Somerset Maugham based his novel *The Magician* on Crowley's flamboyant life.

Crowley was a poet, a writer, a yogi, a mountaineer, master chess player, distinguished lecher, master magician, channeller of ancient Gods, and heroin addict. He revelled in being notorious, going so far as to claim he was the Beast from the bible's Book of Revelations.

Crowley developed a great advance in the oracular arts with his *Thoth Tarot*, with stunning imagery created by Lady Frieda Harris, with whom he bonded closely, and she was his friend until he left this world for the next great adventure.

This Oracle, this Tarot, is one of the most powerful tools I have ever personally worked with. It felt like a series of personalities: strong, powerful beings evoked with every shuffle. Not only highly charged, it is deeply sensual, with many references to his beloved Egypt.

Though not a joiner by nature, Crowley did briefly belong to the Hermetic Order of the Golden Dawn, and his inclusion caused seismic turmoil within the group. Such a provocateur, though some condemn him for his volcanic impact, he was perhaps the catalyst that was needed to bring magick into a more public space, bringing to an end the rigid formalism of the Victorian era that also found its way into the oracular and esoteric arts.

Experientials and Experimentals

- This would be a perfect time for you to work your way through a three-card reading using any deck of your choosing. I suggest that you practise this three-card reading several times, at least.

  The first time, I would like you to work with this three-card technique for yourself.

  The second three-card reading could be for another person. They don't need to be physically with you … but you could branch out and do this and then journal about the experience and what it illumined or brought up for you in your Book of Shadows and Light.

  This practice of reading for another person is essential, as it is important to begin to step away from time to time from the personal aspect, where we are constantly filtering the cards through our experience and pouring their potentials into our own context. It is vital to step away from the sphere of 'me' through reading for another person, which always helps us to broaden our understanding and become, overall, much stronger and more versatile readers. Even if, in future, you are reading predominantly for yourself, this will help you develop and deepen your practice and be far more accurate with your readings as it helps you to step out of habits that you may have personally developed. We create perspective, understanding and compassion when reading for others, too. It also helps us to think more quickly, more clearly, and to communicate swiftly. Even if you are simply writing the reading down in your Book of Shadows and Light, you will find this helps you develop more confidence.

  If you cannot find a person to read for face-to-face, read for them remotely. Ask them if they have a question, and then write down the reading and send it to them. You could do a video call or Facetime a reading. I personally do not like reading over the phone, although I do quite enjoy reading with a person on a video call. My preference is face-to-face, as I love to be with that person and create that sacred experience with them, see them handling the cards and feel their energy shift as the reading progresses. And I also love remote written readings, which may seem a little old-fashioned in this world of video calls, but I find I am very good at providing accurate, insightful readings with minimal information, and I find the process very deep and the energy heightened and soothing.

- Remember, keep connecting with your cards — charge them with your own energy and work with your breath with your deck. Make notes on any changes in connection that may come up for you in your Book of Shadows and Light.

- With your one-card readings, continue writing about your experience, but please begin to journal with a little more detail and structure. For example, you could include the moon phase, the time and your mood in your notes upon commencing and concluding the reading.
- Have a re-read of the introduction and the instructions to your guidebook, and begin to read about the cards and their meanings. Make notes within your journal; ponder the meanings. As you do your one-card reading each day, also include reading the meaning within the guidebook and then make notes about this yourself in your journal. It doesn't have to be too long and laborious, just spontaneous and authentic, thoughtful and truthful. Your journal is your own space — you will learn swiftly and have a broad foundation to work from when you work this way.
- Please work intentionally in a liminal space while doing readings. If you are not sure what a liminal space is, contemplate the in-betweens — what is an in-between place, or space, or time?

Have a very productive and enriching time exploring your Oracle cards, working with your three-card layout, pondering the past, and entering into the in-between, dear Oracles.

Enjoy the work! Be dedicated, for with constancy and dedication, the lessons, meanings and structures will seep deep into your subconscious.

Chapter Three

... Even the very wise cannot see all ends.

— J.R.R. Tolkien

Welcome, dear Oracle student, dear Initiate, to Chapter Three.

For the serious student of the oracular path, the reading of Oracle cards can become a way of self-knowledge. As it said over the Temple of Apollo at Delphi: "Know Thyself". When we work with Oracle cards, a reader is able to see into and within the card, using it as a doorway through which knowledge, information and insights flow. This includes knowledge about your own self and soul.

I like to think of Oracle card reading as being a fusion: we can begin with a solid knowledge of the deck, its philosophy and the card meanings. When we then team this foundation with our intuitive gifts, our readings become powerful, like trees with strong roots (the knowledge) and branches (the insights your natural gifts bring).

When you do this oracular work with this strong foundation and connection to your own innate gifts, which are being developed right here as we journey together, with every turn of a card, every intuitive glimpse into the otherworlds, you become part of this great lineage — you become the Oracle, and standing with you are the Oracles of ages past. Over time, with practice, skill and devotion, you will hone your skills again and again, weaving an unbreakable connection to the Divine. From this, you'll be able to offer strong readings and clear messages without becoming drained, overwhelmed or distressed.

As you're discovering in a very practical way every day as you do your one-card practice, Oracle cards offer us the voice of the Otherworld in one of its myriad forms … This is direct communication, and when you enter into the conversation, direct dialogue can be achieved. Oracle cards also offer us ways to embrace our true, authentic self.

We are living in a unique period of time. We are free to be the illumined, sacred beings we were born to be, and we are free to connect and speak with the Divine and with the hidden aspects of our own selves. We have become the Oracles, the Healers, the Seers. It's important to remember that we are not reconstructing an historic path. We are part of a lineage, but we are also part of an evolution humanity is experiencing at an extremely accelerated rate — almost a Spiritual Uprising, which at times feels revolutionary. So it is important to be our contemporary selves, and work within the society we find ourselves in to contribute and bring about healthy change.

I LIKE TO THINK OF ORACLE CARD READING AS BEING A FUSION: WE CAN BEGIN WITH A SOLID KNOWLEDGE OF THE DECK, ITS PHILOSOPHY AND THE CARD MEANINGS. WHEN WE THEN TEAM THIS FOUNDATION WITH OUR INTUITIVE GIFTS, OUR READINGS BECOME POWERFUL, LIKE TREES WITH STRONG ROOTS (THE KNOWLEDGE) AND BRANCHES (THE INSIGHTS YOUR NATURAL GIFTS BRING).

APRIL 23, LATE 1980S, LONDON

(From notes on a reading done for me by a reader called Franklin, who I shall never forget.)

•

What Franklin said the first time I saw him:

"You are a very, very sensitive and moody person. It takes someone very special to realise these moods and to deal with them.

You must get more control over your emotions because you drain yourself. Big problem is self-discipline and you must begin to exercise this.

You are a psychic (he described me as a perfect medium).

You are a beautiful woman, and men will always be around you. You hate to feel boxed in, you need to feel room."

He says again and again that I am very moody, very sensitive and that I pick up on other people's moods. He mentioned too that I need to take care of my left eye – although I'm unsure of what that means. [Present-day note: Years later, I had surgery on my left eye.]

He suggested that I should do some spiritual courses and urged me to not worry about money as it will come when I need it.

He said: "You are a very sensitive woman, you are psychic, a part of the New Age," which was very affirming. He also warned me to be careful of a pregnancy next June.[Present-day note: This also came to be.]

•

Why Am I So Sensitive?

There is a phenomenon taking place on the planet now. This is the phenomenon of time seeming to speed up, a kind of compression of experience, a Quickening and an increased intensity, creating a pressure many people are experiencing each day. It is as if we are passengers in a car that is accelerating at warp speed, and it can feel overwhelming and frightening.

There is a science behind this phenomenon, this breaking down of the natural rhythm of the planet in some areas. The heartbeat of the planet (in science, it is called the Schumann resonance) is speeding up in some areas where forests and natural places have been decimated and disrupted. In those spaces, that heartbeat or pulse is literally faster. This, coupled with your natural sensitivity and being an extra-sensory being, can make life seem a little harsh, and you may feel it intensely — almost as if you were born without enough layers of skin. (That's how I used to feel all the time!) Overwhelm is real, and empathic folk can struggle at times. There are, however, ways to help ease the intensity and side effects of the Quickening.

THE HEARTBEAT OF THE PLANET (IN SCIENCE, IT IS CALLED THE SCHUMANN RESONANCE) IS SPEEDING UP IN SOME AREAS WHERE FORESTS AND NATURAL PLACES HAVE BEEN DECIMATED AND DISRUPTED. IN THOSE SPACES, THAT HEARTBEAT OR PULSE IS LITERALLY FASTER. THIS, COUPLED WITH YOUR NATURAL SENSITIVITY AND BEING AN EXTRA-SENSORY BEING, CAN MAKE LIFE SEEM A LITTLE HARSH, AND YOU MAY FEEL IT INTENSELY — ALMOST AS IF YOU WERE BORN WITHOUT ENOUGH LAYERS OF SKIN.

Here are some suggestions and some simple techniques I have personally found very helpful.

SLOW YOUR BREATH DOWN

Become conscious of your breath. Many of you will notice you hold your breath when emotions become strong — emotions that may belong to you or emotions that belong to another person. Breathe out long, strong breaths for at least four counts to empty your lungs. Pause — let there be a gap between the out-breath and the in-breath. Then, slowly draw breath in, consciously expanding the lungs, filling them for at least a count of four. Again, pause, then gently let the air go. Do this nine times, and you will slow down and reconnect, coming back to yourself rather than being drawn into another person's energetic output.

STILL THE MIND

THE MIND IS FULL OF MANY THOUGHTS AND MEMORIES, SO MUCH ACTIVITY, AND so many of its processes are habitual. Certain pathways within your brain have become second nature to you. It is important to become conscious again of words you may use habitually and thoughts that have taken up residence. Internalised voices of other people, most often critical, may also be occupying your mind.

Take some time to get to know your own mind and its current inhabitants. If you notice some criticism—patterns that are harsh, words that restrict and hurt—trust me on this: you can, with dedicated, patient work, succeed at rewiring your own brain. The brain is a remarkably flexible and responsive organ and will change if you give its health your dedication.

This does not, by the way, mean to diminish in any way any scars, patterns or woundings you may have. It is simply to acknowledge that we can begin to reduce the habitual thoughts that may not serve us within our readings, but most especially within our lives. Sensitive humans need their brains to become their allies — over time, this can be achieved. There is always work to be done, but we can enjoy so many benefits.

How do we do this? First, by discovering the thoughts that are most harmful to us. Then, by acknowledging them. Judging them does not help. You do not need to deeply analyse them, revisit them or torment yourself for having these thoughts! Just see them as an observer, and then begin to understand that just as you made a space for these thoughts within your mind, you can begin to make space for adapted versions of these thoughts. Begin to choose new thoughts. And work at making them a part of your mind by writing them down or chanting them to yourself. It will take time, but they will begin to find a place within your psyche, and your levels of confidence, calm and self-love will softly, steadily grow.

MAKE TIME FOR MOVEMENT

WHEN WE MOVE, WE ALLOW THE BODY TO RELEASE WHAT IT HAS HELD WITHIN its muscles and nerves. Without movement, we stagnate, and we allow trauma from the past to find a permanent place within us. Move a little each day. Walk with the wind upon your face and feel the energising nature of movement in fresh air. Dance to music that evokes energies and atmospheres, emotions and expression. Dive beneath waves, or swim in still waters, and feel the weightlessness of your body in this delicious element. All kinds of movement—from the most disciplined of athletic expressions to the free-flow dancing of the elements—encourage a continual flow of energy. Regardless of our physical forms and our various 'limitations', we have a form, and that form can move or be moved through touch, massage and gentle movement. Yoga, our naked feet on the earth, the movement of our breath — there is a limitless amount of experiences to be enjoyed. This is one of the most accessible ways to improve the energetic and physical health we experience. I often combine meditation with movement in nature and find the recharging and cleansing vital for my wellbeing.

PLAY MUSIC

Music can clear us, uplift us, inspire us, sustain us and comfort us. Have no doubt, it is powerful vibrational magick. From ambient sounds that soothe and settle us to music that sounds like choral fireworks, explosions of pure energy with lyrics that uplift, inspire and make us laugh out loud — all music is energy. I have often been asked what music I love to work with, and it varies so much. Some of what I adore working with surprises people because there is often a fairly standard idea of what 'spiritual people' must do in order to seem connected to the Divine. But the Divine is expressed through energy, and energy takes so many forms. Art, for instance, is a form of the Divine, and music is one of the purest forms of art, which comes in so many genres, flavours and expressions. I have known people who will not listen to pop or rock music because they fear it will be 'unspiritual'. To limit what we love to listen to for fear it will disrupt us from the pursuit of the spirit is … a thin and lacklustre way to approach the world, to my mind. Seek out what you love to listen to. Experiment and consider the nature of the lyrics of songs, too, as so many messages can be absorbed through the words we sing along to. When I am teaching or reading, I choose the music with great joy and care, and I also select music that will enhance the themes of the work we will be doing in circle. And the genres are sometimes surprising!

NATURE

She's the Great Mother, the one who can help restore us. Take off your shoes, and put your feet in the dirt, or on the roots of trees, or in her saltwater sea. Nourish yourself with her gifts. If you are a person who enjoys gardening, growing some of the herbs you can use to enhance your readings, or your own visionary journeys (such as mugwort), can be a wonderful way to further intertwine your energy with those of the Great Mother. Find out which trees you particularly resonate with, and spend time with them. It may be willow for emotional healing and flexibility and easing of pain, or eucalyptus for cleansing and reinvigorating stagnant energies. Flowers all have their messages and their healing powers, and walking in flowering gardens can bring us so much connection, joy and faery-energy-inspired delight! Waterfalls—with their abundance of negative ions that create positive, optimistic energy—are special places to feel the presence of the Divine, as are caves, ocean shores, reefs and riding the waves. If any of these are difficult for you, you can connect with nature through gardening at home, watching documentaries about nature, and cuddling with a beloved animal friend (or borrowing one for a cuddle, if need be). This natural, fresh, reawakened energy will flow right through into your readings, giving them a beauty and a calm that is beneficial for you and for those who seek out your wisdom and skills.

I love reading beneath the branches of wise old trees. This shot came from one of my favourite places when I lived in Sydney, where the intricate roots of the Moreton Bay Figs formed natural, cosy shelters within which to lay out my cards. Trees seem to enjoy the cards, too.

MAKE YOUR SENSITIVITY A STRENGTH, YOUR VULNERABILITY A VIRTUE

There are many other ways to work as a sensitive being, a being who makes their sensitivity a strength, their vulnerability a virtue. Most of all, know that your vulnerabilities and your sensitivities are signs that you are alive, open and the right person to do this work. Your energy and your beautiful nature are needed within the world. Do not be harsh to yourself, but also do not think of yourself as weak or as a victim — nor as so 'special' that you cannot interact with others at all. This is not the truth. When we are in our sensitive natures in the best possible ways, we are able to work fully and openly from the heart.

I want to move on, and speak to you about the practicalities of your readings now.

The Art of the Question

As we are now learning, one way we can work with these Oracle cards is through practical structures, such as the use of layouts or spreads. These structures give our Oracle readings so much clarity and direction — they help our readings speak more wisely, and this can be of great benefit to the Seeker and, in turn, help us by giving us a strong foundation that we can depend on.

There are other aspects of a reading that are also very important, including how we communicate with the Seeker. When we read for ourselves or for others, it is a tradition in cartomancy to ask for a question. This can be more challenging than it seems. There is also a practical element to this 'art of the question' to consider, too.

If a person comes to see us for a reading and has not thought of a clear question (or asks a question in such a way that it is unlikely to create the very best reading), it is important to know we are not about to spend up to fifteen minutes instructing a person on how to ask the 'correct' kind of question. I think that would be the surest way to lose the connection and potentially intimidate the person who is seeking help. Unless we are sublime communicators, we could leave our Seeker feeling very judged.

PEOPLE ARE SOMETIMES VERY EMOTIONAL DURING READINGS. I AM NOT DISTURBED AT ALL BY EMOTIONS, MOST OF THE TIME, AND CAN HANDLE MOST OF THE INTENSITY THAT CAN TAKE PLACE. THIS IS WHERE COMPASSION ENTERS, BUT A LITTLE DETACHMENT, TOO. FEELING SORRY FOR SOMEONE DURING A READING IS NOT NECESSARILY GOING TO BE HELPFUL. FEELING BAD IF YOU DO NOT HAVE GOOD NEWS WILL NOT BE HELPFUL, EITHER. HOLDING THE SPACE WITH COMPASSION AND SAFETY WILL BE.

Instead, we can translate the query into a tighter, more compact and grounded question, which can then be relayed back to the Seeker to see if they feel it is right. Why not try doing this yourself? Start by asking a question for a reading in a very broad way, then bring it back to a more distilled and potentially positive place. The purpose of this is not to over-simplify or dumb down, nor is it to make it a 'yes or no' question. Rather, it's good to get some practice with this process of getting to the essence, rather than getting lost in the labyrinth some people (including ourselves) may bring to the question.

Knowing *how* to ask the right question is a skill, but one which we are unlikely to have time to teach those who come to us, particularly if you will work—and we all sometimes do—in crowded festival environments or in stores, where there is nearly always peripheral noise and residual energy, and not a great deal of time. At the time of writing, I favoured asking the Seeker, "What is it you'd like to know more about?" instead of, "What is your question?" When I asked the latter, all too often a Seeker would reply with an airy, "Oh, I just want a general reading." In other words, there would be no real question. And that would have to be perfectly okay under the circumstances. Some people will be quite different and have *many* questions, and begin to talk and talk and talk. It is important, if we can, to quiet those people and distil the talk into a focal point. Not to shut them down but to let them gently know they need not tell us any more, so we can allow the cards to speak.

If a Seeker speaks and speaks, we then run the risk of the reading becoming a very different kind of session, and sometimes that happens. Only a few times in thirty-eight years of reading have I had people who will not, or cannot, settle — most often because they are severely ungrounded, extremely distressed, deeply traumatised or going through a life-changing mental health crisis. In those circumstances, I allow the reading to unfold without forcing it or becoming distressed myself by events not going 'as they should'. I hold the space, offering a safe container for some kind of release. I will still go ahead with what I can with the reading, and this can be immensely healing, too. It may not be textbook ideal, but it is what was best under the conditions.

People are sometimes very emotional during readings. I am not disturbed at all by emotions, most of the time, and can handle most of the intensity that can take place. This is where compassion enters, but a little detachment, too. Feeling sorry for someone during a reading is not necessarily going to be helpful. Feeling bad if you do not have good news will not be helpful, either. Holding the space with compassion and safety will be.

People are often fragile, very hurt and often near to breaking when they come for a reading. You need to be able to handle this without becoming overwhelmed. This can take practice, and you will, in time, come to know how you can pace yourself, how many readings a day you can handle, and what you need to do to set healthy boundaries so you can sustain your work. Of course, you need to be able to handle this in terms of clearing, which we will address closely in Chapter Four.

So, back to the question. If you are reading for yourself, and a clear question is not coming to mind, the best possible approach is refusing to allow the ego to step in and agonise about this. Your default question can always be, "What do I need to know?" or, "What would you like to tell me?" This can work beautifully.

Often, too, people are unable to ask the question they truly wish to ask. They are too fragile, or hurt, or sometimes ashamed or afraid of judgement. Sometimes people wish to put you to the test and do not want to give away any information. That is okay, too. In all of these cases, we simply go ahead and read, and tell the story that emerges from the connections between the cards.

And then there are other folks who have very specific goals and will attempt to attach those to the question and the reading. "Where will I move to? When will I get married? Can I trust this person, and if not, when should I leave/sack them?" In those cases, I hear them, I understand, and I trust that the cards will express what is available for the person to know at the time.

I can help with dates — they often come to me throughout a reading, and there are positions within spreads that can help us with that information. This is the kind of work that we will learn to do in Part Three: The Adept. Mostly, I focus on what is most important for that person to know while respecting their desires within the context of the reading. Experience is a great teacher, and after thirty-eight years of cartomancy practice, I feel a reading cannot be forced. I can always help, and I am always open to being of service.

How to Deal with Unethical Questions

At times, you may have a Querent ask you about another person in their life. I have had seekers come to me wanting to know about another person and almost wanting me to peer inside that person's mind and heart. In some circumstances, that can be okay, as it is in context and within reason. At other times, it crosses an important ethical boundary.

Essentially, if we are being asked to almost spy on another person without their knowledge or consent, we need to tread carefully and make our choice wisely. Under these circumstances, I do my best to gently assert that we can work with the Seeker—not the third party—to determine what is best for them, and in that way, information can come to light about whether they can trust the other person, and so on. But if a person seems feverishly concerned with another instead of their own path, we need to be mindful and draw the reading gently back to an ethical place that we can feel 'right' about.

for Another Person — the Practical Details

When reading for another, I think it is imperative that the Seeker handles the cards. Here is how I do this. Firstly, I always shuffle the cards a little at first, as if to wake them up; it's like I am saying to them, "Hello, I'm here, I would love to speak with you!" That way, their slightly sleepy energy can be awakened, a little like shaking a potion bottle to be sure all the ingredients are evenly distributed. I keep my mind clear, soft, easy and open but also strong, relaxed and aware. If I am thinking at all in that left-brained way, I am thinking of being of service, asking that the best possible reading can happen for the person with me. I am not seeking perfection, and I simply do my best with all the circumstances both within me and outside of me at the time.

Then, I loosely line my body up with the person and ask them to uncross their legs and arms, place their hands palms up on their lap, and then ask them to take three deep breaths in and out with me. This syncs up our energy a little and often calms the person and helps them to be a little more present and open. They usually feel safer after this.

The three breaths is a technique I use when working by myself, too. It's a way for me to step into the oracular space. I drop my breath right down into my diaphragm, and the breaths are long and as steady as I can make them, with the out-breath as long as the in-breath. With each breath, I am opening a doorway into the otherworlds, the space where I can read from with most magick.

The first breath lifts the veil and opens the door between the worlds. I visualise the second as stepping through the doorway between the worlds, crossing that threshold. With the third, I am completely within the oracular space. This technique is so powerful — it shifts my energy and helps carry the person I am reading for into a different space mentally and spiritually. From that energetic space, we experience the reading at a heightened, enchanted level where we are both protected, safe and grounded.

THE FIRST BREATH LIFTS THE VEIL AND OPENS THE DOOR BETWEEN THE WORLDS. I VISUALISE THE SECOND AS STEPPING THROUGH THE DOORWAY BETWEEN THE WORLDS, CROSSING THAT THRESHOLD. WITH THE THIRD, I AM COMPLETELY WITHIN THE ORACULAR SPACE. THIS TECHNIQUE IS SO POWERFUL — IT SHIFTS MY ENERGY AND HELPS CARRY THE PERSON I AM READING FOR INTO A DIFFERENT SPACE MENTALLY AND SPIRITUALLY. FROM THAT ENERGETIC SPACE, WE EXPERIENCE THE READING AT A HEIGHTENED, ENCHANTED LEVEL WHERE WE ARE BOTH PROTECTED, SAFE AND GROUNDED.

I usually then ask the Seeker to say their name three times for me. The voice is a kind of key that can unlock the energies. Again, it can settle, ground and calm the person, and it helps me to be fully present for them. Names hold energy — names can hold memories of the present lifetime, echoes of past lives, and family patterns, even down to the way others have spoken their name. When a person speaks their own name to us three times, we are able then to link up to their own reservoir of memory and energy.

I then ask the Seeker to shuffle the deck while thinking over what they would like to know more about. I let them know that if they are not sure what to think, they can simply let themselves open up—just to feel—so the cards can connect with them while they handle them. Then, they shuffle the cards. I ask them to split the cards next. Then, I ask them to put the deck back together. Finally, I take the deck, steady myself, and begin to deal the cards out.

Sometimes, people will worry that they are not good at shuffling or chatter nervously while they do so … it's all okay. Steady them as best you can, without being harsh or dictatorial — if we do that, they may shut down energetically, making the reading hard and sticky and unpleasant. Stay open, be kind, and remember that this is ancient and sacred healing work we are doing. Remember that without getting overwhelmed by it!

I do this because when a person handles and communicates with the cards, they are better able to connect with them. When this happens, the person is usually more receptive to the cards' message. They have touched them, so psychologically, they trust and believe a connection has been made — more so, I feel, than if a reader does not permit that contact. It's harder to go into denial once we have touched the deck and had that tactile connection and become a very real part of the process. They are more open to receiving the messages without resistance. Both of us are then inside the reading, not outside, and this, I feel, is powerful for in-person readings.

If you are conducting an online reading, you could try the following technique I use. I involve the Seeker with the shuffling process by asking them to tune in to the cards and then inviting them to instruct me on when to commence shuffling and when to finish. Once I cut the cards, I ask the Seeker to tell me which pile is to return first to the deck and in what order. I also energetically tune in to the person I am reading for with that silver cord of energy I have spoken of. Finally, I find it very helpful to breathe with them for those three sacred breaths into and out of the reading — for some people, it may feel silly, but if you let go of that self-consciousness, you will find it's a lovely way to gently unite your energies with your client at the beginning of a reading, then gently disengage from each other at the finish.

THE ORACLE OF SAINT-GERMAIN — THE FABULOUS MADAME LENORMAND

Speaking of how to read for others, let's look at the example of this amazing woman, who was once the talk of Paris and who—in our time–is at the top of Amazon charts. One of the most famous cartomancers and Oracles of all time was Madame Lenormand of Saint-Germain in Paris, who achieved notoriety after reading for Joséphine Bonaparte — the ill-fated wife of Napoleon. (If you're interested, you can visit Lenormand's resting place in Père Lachaise Cemetery in Paris. She passed in 1843, and her grave has become a site of pilgrimage for many modern-day lovers of divination.) But back to her life! This is an eyewitness account of a session with this marvellous Oracle, written by Captain R.H. Gronow in his book *Celebrities of London and Paris.*

> *One of the most extraordinary persons of my younger days was the celebrated fortune-teller, Mademoiselle Lenormand. Her original residence was in the Rue de Tournon, but at the time of which I write she lived in the Rue des Saints Pères. During the Restoration, the practice of the 'black art' was strictly forbidden by the police, and it was almost like entering a besieged citadel to make one's way into her sanctum sanctorum.*
>
> *This malignant-looking Hecate had spread out before her several packs of cards, with all kinds of strange figures and ciphers depicted on them. Her first question, uttered in a deep voice, was whether you would have the grand or petit jeu, which was merely a matter of form. She then inquired your age, and what was the colour and the animal you preferred. Then came, in an authoritative voice, the word, 'Coupez', repeated at intervals, till the requisite number of cards from the various packs were selected and placed in rows side by side.*
>
> *No further questions were asked, and no attempt was made to discover who or what you were, or to watch upon your countenance the effect of the revelations. She neither prophesied smooth things to you nor tried to excite your fears, but seemed really to believe in her own power. She informed me that I was un militaire, that I should be twice married and have several children, and foretold many other events that have also come to pass, though I did not at the time believe one word of the sibyl's prediction.*

Lenormand developed her own style of Oracle cards, a kind of series of symbols with warnings and instructions that were eccentric and unique. Her reading style came to influence generations of cartomancers. There were over 30 versions of Lenormand decks available on a particular day when I investigated this on Amazon. It seems a new Lenormand deck is being released every week — an exaggeration, but not so far from the truth! I sometimes wonder what this stern woman and legendary cartomancer—this very unique Oracle—would have made of this.

Experientials and Experimentals

- Continue with your one-card readings, journalling what you intuitively receive and reading the card definitions. Stay with the conversation. Take it day by day, gently, and pace yourself. We are here for the long term, not the brief, intense burst! I would suggest you begin to structure your entries. This, again, is your choice, but here are some ideas.

  You could include the date, time of reading, moon phase, question, the card that came forth, immediate thoughts and feelings, guidebook definition and conclusions. That is just one way you could do this, but it incorporates the most significant aspects. This can be a simple, swift process or a more lengthy one — the choice is yours.

- Using the voice: Orare! To speak of the sacred. To beseech the divine with our voice. How does the vibration of your own voice convey the energy of the reading? Can you be heard? This is an interesting exercise. As a reader, you may choose to work face-to-face with people, and in time, you could work over the phone or online. Even if you choose not to read for other people and simply devote the practice to working with yourself via the cards, working with your voice can be of benefit in your everyday life. You will notice how very much your own voice changes when carrying the energy of different emotions. When working in the oracular space, if you can keep your voice warm, engaging, comforting, and calming, I feel the content of the messages you are conveying will be more willingly received.

  That is because your voice is going to carry the message. Everything about you, in fact, will convey the message. The way you move, the energy you emanate, even what you choose to wear … but for now, let's contemplate the magick of your voice. Your voice and its tone can calm or agitate, excite and inspire, heal and also harm. Work with your voice this week. Record your voice on your phone. Play the recording, and really listen to how your voice sounds. Does it convey what you would most wish it to share with people? Is it calm? Soothing? It does not have to be a stereotype — it is important that your own unique essence stay here! But listen to your voice, and slow yourself down, and allow words to flow to you.

- The Celtic Cross — Practise the first six steps of this spread. I'll share the instructions below, and you can find the visual layout in any one of my Oracle card deck guidebooks. Again, do three readings with this format. One for yourself, one for another person and one as you wish. You may want to get a little more practice this week with another person. Or, you may wish to focus on you. The choice is yours.

Working through the 10-card Celtic Cross spread can seem daunting at first. My suggestion is to learn it in two stages. Start with the first six cards and develop your confidence and skills before adding the next four cards to this insightful layout.

The Celtic Cross — The First Steps

MANY OF YOU—IF YOU'RE FAMILIAR WITH MY WORK—MAY KNOW THAT I HAVE an adapted version of the Celtic Cross that I have been using for a very long time. It's been through several incarnations; this is the one I have settled upon, and it gives me the clearest and most insightful readings. The beings and symbols within the cards open up with this structure, which gives you (the reader or seeker) a framework that makes cards that may at first seem mysterious transform into a library of guidance.

The Celtic Cross is one of the foundations of traditional and non-traditional cartomancy.

If you are just starting out with cartomancy, the Celtic Cross can seem a little bit big. Some people feel it is complex. I often teach it in two stages so that it can then be put together. Take your time if this relates to you at all, and just feel your way into it. Know that if I could learn this, so can you. It is a layout that just may take a little practice to begin to feel at ease with. When it all clicks (as it will if you take your time and support yourself), you'll love reading with this wonderful layout that can truly help guide us through the more tangled places of our lives.

The Celtic Cross addresses past, present and future, your perspective, how others see you, the right action to take, what is influencing you most, and reveals what you truly long for in relation to the question.

It can take your hand and show you a way to navigate your life in troubled times, and it does so with honesty combined with compassion.

Begin by contemplating your question. What is it you wish to know? As this forms, slowly and smoothly begin to shuffle your cards and let them guide the momentum. There is no need to rush. Simply be really thorough, so all the cards can move through your hands, picking up your energy and simultaneously connecting you with the energies within your deck. I like to think of the deck and its community of beings and energies as keenly observing you, listening to you and discussing amongst themselves who will come forward — who will speak with you and show you what is to come.

You'll feel a sort of knowing when it is the right time to stop shuffling, and when that time comes, split the deck into three piles with your left hand—your receiving energy hand—then put them back together. Now, it is time to lay out the cards from the top of the deck.

Be sure to focus on keeping the flow of your breath smooth and deep, and as you lay out the cards, begin to notice how they relate to the question you have asked of them.

There are many ways to lay out the cards. Some folks love to lay them out face down with the back of the cards showing, revealing each card one at a time. Usually (there are always exceptions), I personally prefer to lay them out with their faces up. This way, I begin to see the way the cards are speaking, not only with me but with each other. A reading is like a dance, and certain cards are in the same tempo as others — they relate. See whether you have patterns or themes emerging, for example, the same numbers over and over again. Affinities between the Goddesses speaking with you, or who you are being asked to speak with?

Layouts take practice, so if it does not feel natural immediately, keep breathing and remember to take your time. Time is always well spent with your cards!

Remember to keep the question in your mind; speak it aloud to bring you back to it and to see each of the cards in the light of that question. This will keep the coherence of the reading and its relevance flowing, and you won't get distracted as easily.

Think of the layout as telling you a story, with you as the protagonist of the sacred narrative.

CARD ONE — THE SEEKER: Who are you in this present moment? What have you become as a result of the choices you have made in your life? The cards, and the beings within them, will share this with you.

CARD TWO — THE SEEKER'S SITUATION: Card two is all about a huge influence on you at present. What circumstances do you find yourself within, divine soul?

This card will speak to you about a situation that is both current and on your mind, and has enormous potential impact on you. This could be a friendship, a love, a workplace or a legal matter … regardless, this card is here to help you focus on what must be given attention in order to move into the next stage of your life with grace and momentum.

CARD THREE — THE PAST: This card reaches into your own history and how it relates to the question you have asked of the cards. It may reveal an experience, the kind of family you had, important events or subtle moments that memory can begin to overlook. It could also represent an actual person who played a large part in your life in the past.

CARD FOUR — THE VERY RECENT PAST AND THE PRESENT MOMENT: This card offers even more about what is currently happening or what has just happened, but is still playing a major part in your life as it relates to the question. It can show you the impact of what is taking place and give you some perspective on how it is shaping your life. I sometimes like to think about how card numbers two and four relate to each other — how do they connect? Is there anything there that can help show me more about the questions I have asked of the cards? By this stage of the Celtic Cross layout, you may begin to see a story being shaped by the cards. It is your story they are telling, but from the perspective of the cards and what the beings within them want to share with you.

CARD FIVE — THE FUTURE: This card reveals what lies ahead of us, and so it offers us the opportunity to reflect on something before it has taken place — to see how we feel about it, and how we can work with it and shape it, so that it is more in accordance with what we would want for ourselves and our wellbeing.

CARD SIX — WHAT SHALL BE: This card illuminates what must be faced. It can give you some profound moments of realisation and clarity into understanding why life is unfolding as it is. Don't forget to keep connecting this card with the preceding cards — and always link it back to your question.

Now, you have walked through the first six steps of this layout. Practise this Celtic Cross part one version often enough so that you feel comfortable and can see the relationships between the cards and in the context of the question you have asked. Then, you can introduce the next four steps and begin to read with what may have once seemed a large and somewhat daunting layout! When we break challenges down into smaller steps, we will always find they are absolutely achievable!

Practising Reading

Reversed Cards

I ALWAYS ENCOURAGE YOU TO LOOK FOR THE STORY WITHIN THE CARDS AND the layout—what happened, what is happening, what may happen—and really let the cards speak with each other, as well as speak to you … But what about when a card appears turned upside down within a reading? What does its presence mean? How does it differ from an upright meaning? Is it a block? Is it that the meaning is 'reversed'? Or is it something more subtle? I want you to contemplate this. Personally, I tend to see the reversal as a kind of resistance or challenge. But I want you to feel your way into this — you can do it!

Now, to do this effectively, we must switch off some (not all!) of our logical default mindset. The people who struggle the most with an exercise like this tend to be those who are most locked into the left side of the brain — or perhaps, those who feel safest in that kind of space. Now, I am very left-brain oriented in many ways — I am right-handed, I am fairly rational (some folks would disagree), and I can cross a road and drive a car safely! But I can also see connections very easily, and I think part of that is due to the fact that I can see the 'story' within the cards … that, and letting the images speak to me truly helps. Thus, when I receive a reversal, my curiosity is ignited, and the story changes, even while the energy of the card remains.

If you are finding this a little bit of a challenge, before you read, consider this technique, even as an experiment. I want you to be sure to do the three-breaths technique mentioned previously in this chapter. Then, put on and play some beautiful music. Have a couple of items near you that really help you connect with your right-brain self. Keep your readings brief — no more than nine minutes apiece. We are learning the dance of the cards here, and we need to flow and move, and relax into the possibilities.

One last thing … I've spoken about the cards being tools—and in some ways, the Oracle cards you are working with are like scrying tools—linking us again to another form of oracular practice that, in some ways, has been overwhelmed by so many people reading cards today. When we scry, we see different things within the cards each time we gaze at them. A different story will emerge, and when we read, we must trust the story that comes through and retell it to the person who is seeking clarification and assistance, insight and guidance — perhaps most especially when the person we are reading for is ourselves. So when you work with your cards throughout this chapter, I want you to soften your gaze as you look into them — as if you were scrying. I don't want you to 'think' in a hard and linear way or look at them in a forceful and penetrating way. (There's nothing wrong with that way of working with our intellect, by the way, but why not try this way as an experiment, just to see how this might begin to work for you?)

I wish you the very best for this experiment with reversals. Enjoy—be light when you approach this—and know I'm cheering you on; I know you can do this!

Have a delightful, insightful, rewarding time with your cards, dear Oracle reader, as you move through the work — and the play.

Chapter Four

The Silence that Speaks

*Listen to an oak or a stone,
as long as it is telling the truth.*

— Plato

Ah — what joy awaits us!

In this chapter, we will explore energy exchange and learn how you can avoid energy attachments from all readings (face-to-face, online and remote). You'll also discover some holistic health how-tos and delve into card-clearing techniques, too.

You'll notice the beautiful quote from Plato above. I wanted to draw it to your attention for a couple of reasons. Firstly, I love how the very simple things are our guides, but also that the great philosopher, through whom we know of Atlantis, says quite clearly that the oak (or the tree) is a conveyer of divine messages. Remember, our cards are of the trees, too, and that paper contains that energy and spirit.

I also just loved the second part of the quote, the measure of scepticism that is present in the words. It's also a reminder to ourselves, to tell the truth within our readings. Compassionate, kind, caring, yet truthful. To pass on the message when it comes to us in the space between the worlds, which is the reading. And with that quote, Plato brings us back to the foundations, to the oak, to the stone, to the Truth.

WE, ON OUR QUEST AS ORACLES, ARE ALL A LITTLE LIKE THAT ANCIENT OAK, TOO. THE FOUNDATION OF WISDOM AND KNOWLEDGE WE ARE LEARNING, PERHAPS, ARE THE ROOTS OF THAT OAK AND THE BRANCHES THE INTUITIVE MESSAGES WE RECEIVE. THE TRUNK, WELL, THAT COULD BE OUR HUMANITY, OUR PHYSICALITY AND EXPERIENCE. THREE WORLDS IN ONE.

We, on our quest as Oracles, are all a little like that ancient oak, too. The foundation of wisdom and knowledge we are learning, perhaps, are the roots of that oak and the branches the intuitive messages we receive. The trunk, well, that could be our humanity, our physicality and experience. Three worlds in one.

Plato's quote made me think of how those sacred oaks were cared for, once, when they were listened to at the Oracle of Dodona, or when they formed the nemetons (groves) of the Druids. These places were sacred. The oaks were cherished.

I wondered, don't we need to be cared for, just as those oaks once were, in order to do this work? We don't need to be pampered or 'special', nor dramatic and demanding — we must have a strong work ethic, dedication to our craft, and practise self-responsibility and accountability. Yet, one way in which we take care of ourselves as Oracle card readers is in the area of energy exchange. An energy exchange where we are cared for in the most appropriate way for our culture and in this time is imperative.

In Chapter One, we contemplated one of the phrases carved above the temple associated with the Oracle of Delphi: "Know Thyself." We will now team this with the second phrase that was carved there, "Nothing in excess."

To begin to know ourselves and to be sure we are not excessive in our reactions (or in our approach to being an Oracle), I want you to again become conscious of your thoughts. You are sure to be a sensitive human, and I am certain you are experienced—even skilled—at noticing your own thoughts and working on them so they are truthful yet supportive of your very best self … in other words, the thoughts you have about yourself are both grounded and encouraging of your very best qualities.

Why? Because, as a reader, you will need this skill. Which, in time, will just become a habit and a way of being. You don't need talent to develop a better relationship with your own mind, although some of us are more naturally disposed to optimism than others — we ebb and flow with our emotional states.

Many of us have experienced what we spoke of in Chapter One — the Oracular Break with Reality. Sometimes, this can lead to dissonance and trauma in our lives, which can recur again and again. We often think we have to get over things and leave them behind in our quest to cease the pain.

I want to share something that I find very helpful. You see, I don't think—or feel, or believe—that we get 'over' things. I don't even know that we should. Yes, the pain and the raw edge of memory should become more easeful.

There seems nothing more sad to me than if our struggle to transform our wounds into lessons leads us to grow bitter and cold as a result of carrying the full weight of a burden. We often don't get over such things. I feel we get *through* circumstances, and we learn as a result of our experience of the difficulties. Due to these tests—because of these challenges—we become Initiates.

In traditional Celtic wisdom, there is a philosophy that is very ancient, and it is known as Geis (pronounced 'geyshe'). Geis is a kind of theme you are living with; some translators equate Geis with curse or taboo, but I think it is more subtle and interesting than that. Firstly, I feel we all have our Geis. I feel that our own personal Geis is what we are destined to work with this lifetime, what will cause us the most difficulty and the biggest challenge.

Geis certainly can be troubling and awkward to work with. And instead of trying to 'clear' it or eradicate it (a very New Age concept that, in a very real way, tells us how we feel is wrong) the presence of Geis offers us a gift, and our relationship to it works in a kind of spiral.

We spiral back to our Geis again and again, at different times in our lives, learning more each time, understanding, changing our reactions, and growing as a result. Each time we work with our own Geis, we reveal another layer—Know Thyself—and begin to alchemise the new lessons into our whole Self. We no longer hurt so much from it. We begin to develop wisdom because of this particular challenge, and because of the experiences it offers us.

We will all have themes circling back to us, again and again — and how we think and feel about the circling, the spiral path to wisdom, plays an immense part in the way we experience the echoes of the themes that recur in our lives.

Some of the very simplistic (not simple, there is an important difference) New Age philosophies have set us up to believe that we can 'clear' ourselves immediately and easily, as though we are dense, impenetrable plastic, and can be wiped down. We have been made to feel somewhat inadequate if we go through confusion, challenges, hurts and sorrows, as though we have attracted them to ourselves through a flaw in our own souls and makeup.

This, I feel, is dangerous. We are complex, amazing beings, and we must learn to make use of what has taken place within our lives—most especially the traumas—so that we can transcend the initial pain and wound, and develop a healthy scar. In time, this becomes our symbol of initiation into the wisdom of Geis.

With my own challenges in this life, I often ask myself: am I creating what I want or what I fear? Perhaps this approach could be helpful for you, too. In this way, we become contributors to our responses and move beyond reaction and towards a deeper wisdom, born of challenges.

JANUARY 22, 1988, LONDON

•

Did a reading for myself (and one for Chad) today. All points to changes in my financial and work situation. Maybe I do want much more comfort. Life is lifetimes long ... I drew the Hermit, and I am devouring books. The Hermit guides me with prudence, caution, introspection, meditation. Thoughtfulness.

And who is the man represented in the Lovers card? I feel, regardless of the Lovers card, that I need to spend time with myself. And most of all, love myself more.

•

The Exchange with the Oracle

Let's now move on to our readings, and explore energy exchange a little more. To see an Oracle in the past nearly always meant a payment of some kind was necessary. To see the Oracle of Delphi there was often an immense sacrifice made on behalf of the Seeker, such as the offering of treasured possessions or animals. And, certainly, in the 8th Century BCE, we know that a monetary fee was also paid to the Pythia.

I will need to be clear here, as this is just how rumours begin! Of course, I am not suggesting anyone sacrifice any being for a reading with you! What I am saying is that in order for a Seeker to have an effective session with any Oracle (or healer/reader/ being), you—the Oracle—must learn to accept an offering.

The form that takes is a sacrifice on behalf of the Seeker — they give up time, or money, or even their barriers and pride for a reading. Many Oracles have a great deal of trouble asking for money for their services. Many Oracles have a great deal of resistance to receiving very nearly anything, so conditioned are we to be of service and to give, and give and give. Some fear the obligation they feel comes from accepting a gift or earning money through readings.

I wish to encourage you, right from this time forth, to know that you require an energetic exchange when you read for others in order to be able to do this work in the long term. What is an energy exchange? Obviously, in some respects, it is to be paid for our readings and for the space and the energy we are sharing.

You may have begun to read for others—and I truly hope you have—however, you might notice this is the first time I have mentioned payment. Why so? Because I feel the energy exchange initially is about experience. You're gaining invaluable experience; that is worthwhile and is, as such, a kind of 'payment'.

But as time passes and you become more experienced, this will change.

If I was teaching you in person, in a classroom with other Initiates, I'd ask you to pair up, read for each other, and then pay each other, even with a small coin. That begins to break down the stigma of payment, and somehow, even when the money passed is slight, it can begin to make you feel okay about accepting payment for your sacred work.

To this day, a friend of mine feels she cannot accept money for readings because it taints the reading — even short circuits her powers. It is almost impossible to know whether this could have been part of her journey, something she was going to change her mind about once she had spent time working it through. Her commitment to this belief is so resolute. It seems to have total power over her, with no possibility of choice or changing her mind. To her, it is true. The belief in its absolute truth has made it even more true.

It is possible that she undertook some kind of vow of poverty in a past life and because she believes that to be true, she continually provides herself with evidence to support this hypothesis. Yet, she craves to be able to care for herself, and the struggles have impacted her and those who love her in ways that, I feel, could have been changed. We create so much, and this is one area in which we have perhaps more control than we will even consider at first.

I have encountered many spiritual people who feel the same way, but for some people, it is a false modesty, and a false virtue, too. To boast of being humble is not humble. To parade our poverty as evidence of goodness, and then to pressure others to care for us and admire us for our lack because it proves our virtue is no strength, nor is it evidence that we are using our gift 'properly'.

How Long Before I Can Charge for a Reading?

Personally (yes, you're about to get one of my personal stories!) it took me something like twenty years of reading before I first decided I was ready to accept payment. (You don't need to do this! I am not putting this forward as a virtue but rather as an example of how long it can take until you reach that moment. I think I waited way too long.)

I finally reached a point where I just felt that unless I began to accept that it was okay—perhaps more than okay—to make a living this way (and that it was also okay to have some conflict around this), I was never really going to step into what I truly wished to do with my life. I made a commitment to myself that somehow my spiritual work—my dedication and devotion—was going to be able to support me. And that I would be more dedicated as a result.

I also decided to accept my conflicted feelings—not to fight them, critique them or label them—just accept that was how I felt, and entertain the possibility that it would change gradually over time in that subtle and spiralling way. For years, I still felt strange and weird and a little awkward about accepting money. I felt guilt. I read for longer than I needed to. I gave people my personal books and crystals when they came for a reading. I was over-generous because I still felt that maybe I wasn't good enough or worthy of being an Oracle card reader.

Begin Amidst the Discomfort

I THINK WHAT HAPPENED, ULTIMATELY, IS THAT I JUST BEGAN TO DETACH FROM those feelings of guilt and unworthiness, and instead think, "I just need to do this." I started to trust that as I created new experiences, those feelings would gradually shift and change. I needed, as the saying goes, to get out of my own way.

It took time and work, noticing my own behaviours, and wondering about the 'why' behind my sense of obligation — why did I feel I ought to help and serve without exchange or reward? In time, the sting and the charge gradually left those feelings. They have not vanished or disappeared altogether. But there are other feelings, like satisfaction, joy, humility, compassion, understanding, kindness, reverence and acceptance that have become a part of the process.

I didn't get over it. I got through it. I integrated it … So those uncomfortable feelings are still kind of there, but they are no longer in control. I accept the paradox. I do my best. I work in a dedicated and truthful way. I learn and grow. And that is the very best I can do.

So please don't wait until you are super-comfortable with being paid for your work. Begin to learn how to accept an energy exchange, while you are uncomfortable. Let yourself be uncomfortable for a while. That is what change is! If it's true change, it won't always feel easy …

So often, we think a feeling of uncertainty means a certain action or choice does not feel right. This is something to be very discerning about. Remember, we have been taught that any discomfort means something is 'wrong'. But that is untrue.

Discomfort in the right doses, places and ways is exactly where the growth and change and magick occur. Amidst the discomfort is where the courage develops and confidence is grown. You will move through the discomfort and into a new stage of being able to accept energy, in the form of money, in return. You will evolve as a result of your courage to continue despite the discomfort.

DISCOMFORT IN THE RIGHT DOSES, PLACES AND WAYS IS EXACTLY WHERE THE GROWTH AND CHANGE AND MAGICK OCCUR. AMIDST THE DISCOMFORT IS WHERE THE COURAGE DEVELOPS AND CONFIDENCE IS GROWN. YOU WILL MOVE THROUGH THE DISCOMFORT AND INTO A NEW STAGE OF BEING ABLE TO ACCEPT ENERGY, IN THE FORM OF MONEY, IN RETURN. YOU WILL EVOLVE AS A RESULT OF YOUR COURAGE TO CONTINUE DESPITE THE DISCOMFORT.

In case this is an issue you have faced (and people who are highly intuitive often face terrible anxiety over money and whether it is okay to be paid for their services), remember that money is simply one form of materialised energy. Your time, study, dedication and development offered to another deserves energy in return. And the most recognised and validated form of energy in this world at this time is to be paid with money.

And that, in turn, helps you on so many levels in so many ways. Feeling lack is no fun. It doesn't make you more spiritual. Being paid won't make you materialistic or shallow or any of those sorts of criticisms that get levelled at people.

I want you to know that the Universe will support you once you begin to support yourself. Guilt around money is debilitating for people who are here to be of service. To help others, you need to be cared for, just like those oak groves of Dodona, just as the Oracle of Delphi was paid. Your readings are worth being paid for.

So as an exercise, I would like you to do a reading for someone and receive something in exchange. It could be a foot rub, a lovely homemade cake, anything at all — but I want you to learn how to receive, because it's going to become very important once word gets out about your skills. This is work, and as such, there must be give and take.

Please value your work as an Oracle, dear Initiate. By valuing it, you will be giving yourself positive reinforcement, which will encourage you to keep growing. Growth will see you become more and more compassionate and clear with your oracular practice.

And Now ... a Little More on

In Chapter One, I asked you to consider reading within a liminal space or time without going into great detail about what a liminal space or time was. (How very liminal of me!) Truly, I wanted to have you wonder and consider and feel it out for yourself — again, because that is where the magick is. Answers given to you without your own participation mean you are less likely to have the ah-ha! moment for yourself.

So, as you've now been pondering this, even subconsciously, here are some possibilities and suggestions for you to consider. We are learning about the liminal because reading itself is a liminal art ... Liminal times are those in-betweens, like dawn, dusk, sunrise, sunset, at tide-turn, and moon cycle points like dark moon, full moon, new moon and first quarter.

They include solstices, equinoxes, birthdays, deaths, births, transitions, ritual and magickal time! There are liminal phenomena — such as fog, mist and rainbows, sunshowers and eclipses, northern and southern lights ... We make liminal spaces all the time: An altar. A stage. A card-reading table. A stone circle. We cast a magick circle. We create these because we humans wish to have places and times when we are still slightly within the world, but not *of* the world at that moment.

Stone Circles gather and hold energy for millennia. This ancient circle can be found in Carrowmore, Ireland. Here, you can see me touching the stones with reverence, feeling out their energy and tracing the symbols made by the hands of my own Irish ancestors.

We experience this liminality in our lives; people who are sometimes not so well are in liminal space and time. People who are in trance states are in liminal space and time. People who are dreaming, awakening, falling asleep … these are all liminal moments.

Think of a doorway or a gate. Think of places that overlap or fold into each other. Think of thresholds and transitions. Liminal states are those which are ambiguous or undefined in terms of our consciousness. Times that are neither cloudy nor clear, where you are neither awake nor asleep, where it is neither night nor day.

In these states, great growth can occur because the fixed sense of self-identity, or even a fixed sense of perception, has shifted. We experience an openness. The outside world (or what mainstream society agrees is the 'real world') tends to dissolve a little, giving you the chance to have breakthroughs and insights, epiphanies and visions.

Who we are can even melt away, almost as if we become a part of the energetic field, the Quantum Universe — which we, of course, are; but we are rarely conscious of this, as our minds cannot quite cope with the deconstruction of identity, form, self and the Union that can take place in those moments that can be ecstatic. We also need to remember that although the liminal space is precious and can be extremely beautiful and helpful, we must emerge from these places and be grounded again in the natural world.

Liminality, while an important state necessary for oracular growth, can be damaging or become a site for stagnancy if we reside within it to the exclusion of interaction with the beauty of the everyday. The Pythia did not spend all her time perched upon her stool.

THINK OF A DOORWAY OR A GATE. THINK OF PLACES THAT OVERLAP OR FOLD INTO EACH OTHER. THINK OF THRESHOLDS AND TRANSITIONS. LIMINAL STATES ARE THOSE WHICH ARE AMBIGUOUS OR UNDEFINED IN TERMS OF OUR CONSCIOUSNESS. TIMES THAT ARE NEITHER CLOUDY NOR CLEAR, WHERE YOU ARE NEITHER AWAKE NOR ASLEEP, WHERE IT IS NEITHER NIGHT NOR DAY.

She was consulted only in the warmer months of the year. In ancient times, Plutarch tells us that the Oracle only prophesied once per year, being on the seventh day of the month that heralded the beginning of Spring. In later times, Plutarch says the oracle prophesied on one day each month, save for the winter months when Apollo was no longer considered to be present at Delphi. So the Oracles had their times of rest and respite when they were no longer bringing forth messages from Apollo, and perhaps we can imagine that this time restored them — made them stronger in body, and more capable of continuing the journey of the Oracle when their God returned along with the warmth of springtime.

So, too, we need to learn to work with the liminal space in healthy ways to explore, feed our work, become and quest and venture ... but we emerge again into the full light of wakefulness, and into the full darkness of rest, too. We do not stay within the circle we cast, or atop the stool, breathing in the smoke of the laurel leaves that burn as offerings to the God Apollo. We are creatures of both worlds, we Oracles.

I hope that gives you a little more to contemplate. Now, I want to speak with you about something very important. That is, your own energetic integrity and protection.

Protecting, Grounding and

When you work with other people, even when it's in a job where you do not intentionally call in your intuition or open up to others, you are always interacting with energies. When you work as an Oracle card reader, you may become both highly attuned and sensitive to energy. You are, no doubt, an intuitive and sensitive being anyway. The form that sensitivity may take will vary from individual to individual, but most of us have the ability to empathise with others. That is what makes us good Oracle card readers.

However, the shadow side of this work is that because we knowingly put ourselves in positions where we can feel and sense the energies of other people, we can inevitably become somewhat affected. Thus, we need to take very good care of ourselves. So, whether or not you are reading for others, please make it a daily practice to protect yourself.

This protection for us is going to take the form of increasing our energetic health, firstly. There is no point in building immense, protective, energetic walls about us if we are starving, energetically, within those walls. This defensive approach can lead to a siege mentality.

It is absolutely vital that you begin to connect with your own energy: feel it, understand it, raise it when the level is low, and ground it when it is too flighty and excited to serve your purpose. And when you read with others, you must take time to cleanse yourself afterwards by simply soaking in a sea salt bath, taking a dip in the ocean, a walk with the trees, feeling the fresh air — moving the body is imperative. Meditation that is mind-only will not be as effective as meditation that incorporates movement — energy shifted is energy cleared.

If you feel you are under energetic attack or a person's energy is affecting you strongly, please do not reflect or return the energy to the sender. I *never* use a mirror technique to rebound or reflect energy. It's your choice, but here is why I feel the way I do. Mirror energy bounces the energy between people — it keeps it going (you can be pretty sure they've set up a mirror, too, so you can imagine the energy ricocheting about!).

So instead, cut the energy, using one swift downward stroke of the *active* (most dominant) hand over where it feels like the energy is connecting with you. Most often, this will be near the solar plexus, as this is your power centre, and this is where people unconsciously attach. Cut the cord, then ground the energy. Let it fall to the earth, and let it be transmuted.

Most of all, relax — yes, relax. Telling yourself over and over you are under psychic attack/around bad energy will create so much anxiety. So, someone doesn't like you. Didn't like your reading. Is angry with you. Cut it. Ground it. Clear yourself with a sea salt bath and a lovely walk in the fresh air. Pat a dog. Laugh. Give yourself a hug. Have some good food and get some rest.

But what if someone really does come after you? What if it gets really serious? Here is another Lucy story. One time, the former boyfriend of a woman who attended my workshop felt I must have told her to break up with him. (I hadn't. I had never enquired about the woman's relationships.) But, he got it in his head that I had. A series of abusive messages and emails began, culminating in threats of rape, torture and murder. Then he started on other members of my family. I had one other situation where a woman—who believed that, as a witch, I ought to be murdered—began sending rather vivid threats to me. In time, they escalated into full-blown threats against my life.

With both people, I did one simple thing. I called the police. I passed on all their messages sent via email, gave my statements, and continued my work. I then discovered that the second perpetrator had been threatening other readers and healers for years, to the point of breakdown in several individual cases. They felt they must have done something to cause her hatred, and if they just sent her love and light, all would be well.

That didn't work.

She is now receiving help, as she is extremely unwell. I wish for her recovery and freedom.

Please, always do the best and most simple thing for yourself. Protect yourself, keep it simple, be strong, and know that no one ever has the right to hurt or harm or threaten you, and you deserve just the same protection and assistance as any other member of the community (even if what we do is a little strange to explain to the police).

Sometimes, if we have been reading for lots of people and our cards feel like they have taken on some of their energy, we may wish to cleanse our cards. I would suggest doing this by the waning moon, as this is the time when energy is being almost energetically vacuumed away. If they need cleansing, I do not put them out under the full moon, as the full moon is a charger and amplifier.

I may pass my cards through cleansing smoke three times. I may just leave them be in a dark place, so they can have a little rest. Or, I may put a circle of salt around them.

Now, charging our cards is a little different. Of course, you can reawaken them by breathing softly three times into them, like you are offering them your energy and essence. You can also charge them or fill them with energy by trying out some of the following suggestions.

- Taking them to sacred sites (my personal favourite!).
- Charging them by the waxing moon, and yes, the full moon.
- Taking them out into nature — they love this!
- Working with crystals or herbs you feel they would like to have about them as amplifiers and nourishers.

Re-Energising Your Reading Area

If an area you are reading in feels burnt out, or a little sticky with residual energy, you may wish to wash it down with an oil blend, or a potion — three to nine drops with pure spring water. It depends on what the energy feels like, as to what I personally use.

One cure-all I often use is to burn a tall natural candle in a circle of sea salt ran widdershins (meaning 'against the sun' — anti-clockwise for you Northern Hemisphere folk, clockwise for you Southern Hemisphere people) and let it burn down, then dispose of the remnants responsibly. (If I have the time and it feels right, I might read the wax before I dispose of it. Some I have even kept because of its unusual formation and the message it passed on to me.)

If you'd like to include wax reading, here's how to do this. At its heart, wax reading is about noticing the shape the wax has formed after a candle has burned all the way down. Sometimes, the wax will spill out into certain directions, forming shapes that resemble a moon, or a sun, a witch's face, or a tower. Shapes can take many forms, and it's more about tuning in with your intuitive gaze and allowing the image to form from the wax using your third eye. It's not likely that the wax will literally form a cat face, or a man's torso, or a wedding ring, but it will form a shape that resembles those things. I have seen birds flying west in wax, dragons, angel wings, waves, and yes, towers and brick walls. The wax becomes a way for you to add another intuitive divination skill to this simple spell. If a great deal of wax remains, it seems to me that I might need to do some more clearing work, as the abundance of leftover wax is indicative of unfinished business. If the wax burns clean away (which is rare), I feel that the work is done. If the wax spills to one side more than another, I note the direction and what may be in that part of the room, or what the direction signifies and what element may be represented. One time, I saw an arrow formed by the wax, which pointed directly to a photograph of a loved one, and I knew that somehow the clearing work I was doing was related to my relationship with them, and I needed to take steps to work on the relationship. The art of reading candle wax is called ceromancy; it is an ancient craft and one of the most available to people of the past, as candles were the primary source of light once darkness had fallen. It's a lovely tradition to revive.

If it is not the cards or the space but in fact you who feels run down, contemplate a gentle and effective detox and begin an enjoyable and effective exercise program. Your health is very important, as your vibrant, radiant well-being is the greatest life enhancer of all, and will support you emotionally, physically and spiritually, and give you the energy for your oracular work.

Optimum health for you is the aim — there are only your own goals to meet and no other person to compete with. Simply do what you can to improve your physical well-being, and as the physical self is the Spirit in material form, the articulation of the Spirit this lifetime, you will feel a shift in every aspect of your being. This will make you feel absolutely radiant!

THE PRINCESS ENHEDUANNA'S INVOCATION OF INANNA

Let us now call up an ancient voice, one of history's most mysterious Oracles.

Remember in Chapter Three when I asked you to work a little with your voice? When we use our voice within the reading, our tone, volume and cadence will convey the meaning and the message, just as the words do. This consciousness of how we use our voice in a reading harkens back to a very ancient practice when Oracles would often call on the Goddess, God or Deity — literally call to them, sing to them, chant to them. Sometimes, the call is emphasised with the beat of a drum; at others, the vibration of the voice alone hovers in the air, seeking out the divine response.

Which brings me to the *Hymn to Inanna* — one of the oldest pieces of writing in existence, written by a princess who was also an Oracle for her people. In stark contrast to Kassandra's experience, Enheduanna of Akkad was believed, and I have a sense that this prayer would have been read out as she literally says so in the lines below. Now, you don't have to, but you might want to give it a go yourself.

O wild and rampant, eldest daughter of the Moon,
Queen greater than An, who can pay you sufficient homage?
Queen of Queens, who in accordance with the spirits were greater than your mother the moment you were born.
Wise and knowing queen of all the lands, mother of men and animals, I sing your praise ...
I have entered before you in my holy garments, I the princess imperial, Enheduanna,
singing as I carried your ritual baskets,
High Priestess of the Moon.

She goes on with this song, this prayer, and it gets pretty ferocious. She was a Warrior Princess, fierce and compelling. Your voice, too, can have many qualities — soft and calm, strong and focused. Work with this part of your beautiful self a little more as you deepen your practice.

I went from a person who was shy about working with my voice publicly to developing confidence in calling in the energies with both my voice and with drum. Once I began to feel the presence of the divine responding to the vibrations, there was no holding me back.

Experientials and Experimentals

- Conduct a reading, but this time, let there be an exchange. Something must be given to you in return for this reading. It may be as simple as a cup of tea, or a small payment, or a donation to something you care about. But allow yourself to receive as well as give. Turn the cup, and fill yourself.
- Clear the decks if you feel they need this work done.
- Continue with your one-card readings.
- Please complete one three-card reading (perhaps this could be your moment to work with energy exchange).
- Complete one six-card Celtic Cross reading (found in Chapter Three).
- Complete one full Celtic Cross reading (found in any of my deck guidebooks).
- Clear your own energy field without making yourself 'wrong'. Remember, you are not a pipe or plastic, so you won't clear yourself and be 'blank'. You will still be your wonderful, amazing, unique self. But the charge of the energy that sometimes remains can be softened and moved away.
- Do something good for your energy — something loving and nurturing for yourself.
- And here is this chapter's most interesting request. I want you to dance a card. For one minute only. Find a card that you find a little hard to get, and then you know what to do — turn off the phone, turn on some music, and move like you are that being in the card or embodying the energy and the message … feel it! Flow it! Show it!
- Still have cards that just aren't opening up to you? Here's what to do. Stop being you looking at them. Imagine you are them … and then speak as them talking to you. Switch perspectives.

See how those techniques work for you. What's the worst thing that can happen? Being caught dancing to an Oracle card? Someone seeing you talk to an Oracle card? You never know. Your strange ways might just make their day — and they could even ask you for a reading!

I know walking the path of the Oracle can be a great challenge. This path is worth it, even when it feels dark and strange and lonely and unclear. You are doing very well. Keep going, Oracle.

Part Two

The Shadowzone

Chapter Five

Beyond the Border

In every crowd are certain persons who seem just like the rest, yet they bear amazing messages.

— Antoine de Saint-Exupéry

Blessings, Oracles, and welcome to the Shadowzone, the world between the worlds of Initiate and Adept, a liminal space.

The Shadowzone is the threshold, an in-between place, a little like the centre of the *vesica piscis*, where two worlds overlap to create a third.

We have finished Part One, the 'Before' stage, and so we walk through the gates and into the Shadowzone, a place of mystery and inner work. Finally, we will leave the in-between, and go into the 'After', Part Three, where you will begin to consolidate your knowledge as an Oracle.

This is a bittersweet moment for me! I love feeling like we are stretching ourselves and reaching the closing of this part of our time together; the thrill of completion is both a rush and a joy.

But I also have so many conflicting feelings at this stage. Is the path of the Initiate really over now? There is so much more to learn, one part of me says. But another part of me says, rest easy; you can always return to these parts of the book and revise, or refresh or renew again. There is so much for us to explore still together. Particular groupings of cards, blending of decks, spreads for particular questions, the nuances and detail, and the rich and varied history that we have really only touched upon ... and then there is so much more to learn about the oracular tradition. And so we will continue together, you and I, into Part Two of this book and learn together.

And that is the beauty of being a perpetual student. For you may now be on your way to truly calling yourself an Oracle, but in another very real way, you and I will always be students. We will always be learning. I know there is always more to discover, and even when we teach, perhaps most especially when we teach, we learn more about the cards and this art and craft through that experience, too.

For now, in the Shadowzone, let me introduce you to the decks and their secrets.

There are many decks to cover, and this can be a deep, shadowy journey. You are most welcome to read beyond the decks you are currently working with to understand, perhaps, more about some of your own decks' 'relatives'.

The choice is yours, but I would encourage you to explore and delve into the work here, even if you are not currently using the decks featured. You may wish to venture out and broaden your collection of oracular tools in time, including even up to three or more decks when reading. It's a little like learning about your own decks' family history, which is always fascinating and educational! Mine tend to have relationships with each other, perhaps because they have come to the world through me, in a way ... but most often because of the kinds of energies that are present within the decks, the places where they were written and that they were inspired by, and the energies present within the world that were calling for the messages of these beings. I go deeply into each deck's backstory and lore in this part of the book, and I hope it enriches and enhances your own experiences and workings.

Each Oracle deck you are working with has an energy that has been created through a combination of factors. (It is difficult to encapsulate these in bullet points, but here is my attempt!)

- The beings represented within the deck and their energies.
- The energies and intentions the author (er, me!) brought to the creation.
- The writing process — how the messages came through to me, who sent them, and what their purpose is.
- Research — I often research historical records, archeological records, eye witness accounts and much more to offer the deck depth and perspective.
- The artwork — the energies and intentions of the artist, their style, their tools and techniques.
- The physical energies — both the places and spaces where certain energies came forth to speak with me, and sometimes, the actual location of the writing itself.
- The story of the deck — how it came to be and what themes run through the lifeblood of the deck.
- Its evolution as it works in the world — as you work with the deck, it begins to be shaped by you, along with all the people working with it.

All of these factors—and more—go into the particular energy of the decks and the beings within them. So, the deck absolutely has its own lifeforce, which can be felt and worked with. This, in turn, flavours our collective use of the deck, influencing both your experience of the deck and how *others* experience it, too.

Then there is another very important ingredient. You. Your own energy and life force, story and destiny are now helping to shape and create the deck's destiny, too. Yes, you are.

Mysterious and very powerful is this work we do, Oracles.

Decks and Readings as Destiny

MARCH 9, 1988, PARIS

•

Tarot reading of the same day.

9 of swords: there is an illness and nagging worry at the moment. This card is often associated with serious misfortune, utter desolation. Misery, despair, suffering.

My question was – the right action?

At the moment, my consciousness has fallen into a realm unenlightened by reason. Hunger without restraint.

The way through is of passive resistance, resignation – or of implacable revenge. What affects me at the moment is illusion, bewilderment, hysteria – the darkest hour before the dawn; the brink of important change.

Dealing with highly charged emotions – shows everybody is muddled.

A great ordeal is happening. But the outcome is victorious.

In the future position, The Star shows me that hope, faith and optimism will be a part of what will be created, what will come for me.

There will be hope, unexpected help, realisation of possibilities, spiritual insight.

•

When I first wished to work with cards many years ago, I was a very lost, fragile and torn-up young woman. I was 25 years old and living in London after a relationship breakup and a late-term miscarriage that had brought me to breaking point.

I had survived the urges to take my own life, to self-destruct, but I was still very far away from well, and in order to find a way to live again, I left everything and everyone I knew. I took the jagged fragments of myself and left my home and my country and my family, in order to recreate myself from the soul outwards.

I didn't know that at the time. I just knew I wouldn't make it—literally, I wouldn't stay alive—if I stayed. I was in too much pain. I needed to find out who I was when I was not around all the people who previously had defined me, and I threw myself into this next step to create new memories, to somehow be reborn.

Not knowing at all what I was doing, where I was going, or how I would do a single thing, I took the little money I had and bought a one-way ticket to London. The cheapest I could find. A 36-hour flight to the possibility of a new life.

I'm telling you this story because this is how Oracle cards (and cartomancy, Tarot and my own Self) came to be.

My first reading was at a place called Mysteries. (This precious place recently closed as a retail space but is still operating online.) I will miss it, as will many people searching for answers. It was in Covent Garden, and my reading wasn't all that happened that day. I was still in a lot of pain and pretty foggy as a person. I sat down for my reading with a woman in her thirties who just felt strong, reassuring and compassionate. I don't know her name, which I regret, as I would love to thank her. But I think of her often, this kind, wise woman who showed me how powerful and life-changing an Oracle can be.

She told me many things throughout the reading. She worked skilfully, hands graceful as she turned the cards of the *Rider–Waite* deck, and her words rang with truth — hard as some aspects were to hear. Finally, she looked at me and said, "You do not truly need a reading. You need to learn how to take care of yourself." And she recommended the book *You Can Heal Your Life* by Louise L. Hay. After the reading, I gathered my change together and had just enough to buy that book right there.

I cannot tell you the whole story (too long indeed), but the second time I went to Mysteries, I bought a Marseilles deck. And I began to read. Then, in 2000, fourteen years after that first reading, I came to the attention of Hay House Australia (founded by Louise L. Hay) in some serendipitous fashion, and they asked me to create a Tarot deck. Their first Tarot deck.

So, my first reading — Louise L. Hay. Her first Tarot deck — um, me. She didn't know that. But that's how this amazing, magickal universe works. If you were to work with the Oracle Tarot, that would be a part of the energy within it. Subtle, in the background, but there. Fate. Destiny. Magick. Belief.

That's partly what I mean by backstory with the decks. Whenever I've worked with other writers' decks throughout the years, there's no doubt the personalities of those who created the cards came through in some respects. This should not overpower the work—ever—and you don't have to know the story of the creators for the cards to be effective. But in decks that do work, this energy is unmistakably entwined within each card.

The *Thoth Tarot* deck I worked with so long ago felt like Aleister Crowley, but then the more I learned about Lady Frieda Harris (the artist and an amazing woman), the more I felt her balancing presence within this deck. The *Rider–Waite Tarot* deck—with its revolutionary approach to the imagery by Pamela Colman Smith (or Pixie), who drew the stories of the cards for the first time in the Minor Arcana (rather than simply having a literal depiction of, say, five swords)—emanated her energy. Suddenly, there was an illustration that shared the meaning of the five swords, or the two cups ...

The more I worked with this deck, the more I came to appreciate Pamela Colman Smith, whose name should be sung from the tops of mountains in thanks! When I touch this deck, I feel I am touching her legacy. (If you wish to read more about the history of these decks, Tarot.com has some wonderful pieces, particularly on Pixie, which you may enjoy.)

So, let's talk about these decks. The ones within your hands, the ones you've slept with and talked to and nurtured and read from. Your own sacred tools.

My decks are almost like families with lots of brothers and sisters and cousins. I feel they all have affinities, but some 'seem' to work better together and can almost be 'learned' together.

For example, let's consider the *Oracle of the Dragonfae*, the *Wild Wisdom of the Faery*, and the *Oracle of the Mermaids*. I feel they form a kind of elemental family. These decks have works by the same artist, Selina Fenech (who created all the artwork for the *Wild Wisdom of the Faery* and *Oracle of the Mermaids*), and they can be easily read together.

They have conversations. They get along. They have differences, and they are their own selves, but they are a part of a family, and they share bloodlines. As elementals, they have a special affinity and understanding of each other and of the world, albeit from their own very powerful perspectives. They are simpatico.

It would be an injustice to each deck to try and sum them up neatly and pop them into little boxes. It would mean we are not seeing them with all of their possibilities and complexities. But each was born out of a connection and subsequent inspirational epiphanies, which then took me on a journey (and that word gets used a lot, doesn't it?). But that journey part really is important, I feel, to what you have in your hands today.

So, while trying to avoid saying the word journey over and over, let's begin to explore the decks!

IT WOULD BE AN INJUSTICE TO EACH DECK TO TRY AND SUM THEM UP NEATLY AND POP THEM INTO LITTLE BOXES. IT WOULD MEAN WE ARE NOT SEEING THEM WITH ALL OF THEIR POSSIBILITIES AND COMPLEXITIES. BUT EACH WAS BORN OUT OF A CONNECTION AND SUBSEQUENT INSPIRATIONAL EPIPHANIES, WHICH THEN TOOK ME ON A JOURNEY (AND THAT WORD GETS USED A LOT, DOESN'T IT?). BUT THAT JOURNEY PART REALLY IS IMPORTANT, I FEEL, TO WHAT YOU HAVE IN YOUR HANDS TODAY.

The Birth of the Oracle of the Dragonfae

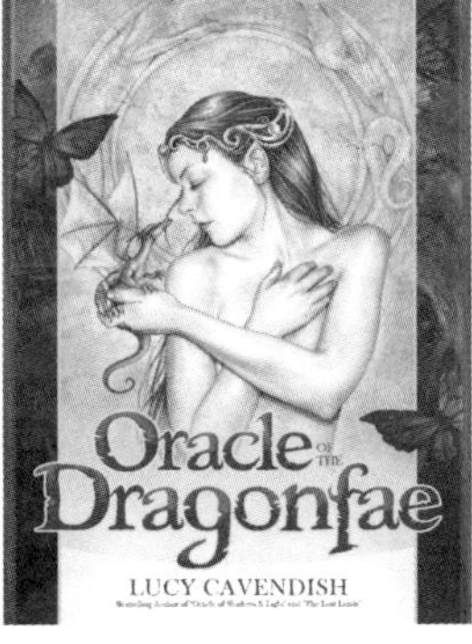

The Dragonfae began in and around 2004, and this deck was a very difficult one to get birthed into the world. It was challenging — not because of the beings, but because of people's reactions to the beings. This deck really did have a very long gestation and a long labour, too.

Because 'dragon=scary monster' was entrenched in the psyche of many spiritual folk around then, the idea was rejected.

I was very sad, and I was sure that these beings—who had absolutely appeared to me (my experience with a Dragonfae called Cecilia was most amazing and influential and is included in the guidebook)—were very disappointed in me for failing them. (They were not.)

I also felt rejected, but after having a good long moment processing those feelings, I moved on to action. I did not let those feelings determine the outcome for me or for the Dragonfae. I took those hurts and channelled them into work.

It was a very humbling and enlightening experience, being rejected. Disillusionment can be such a blessing. Fate had picked me up and offered me amazing opportunities, then just as quickly, I was left feeling lost and disconnected … and yet also I knew this dream was unstoppable. That's Dragonfae for you. They do not give in. They endure. They find a way. They reanimate.

So, I set about approaching artists. I was very open and honest with them. I introduced myself and told them I had no contract, but I wanted to work with them on an idea. And that I would split whatever royalties I got with them.

So I began. One by one, people began to join me. And then, when I had enough to work with, I approached another publisher. We were having dinner, and my book *White Magic* had just come out with Hay House and was doing very well, so he said "yes".

Even then, it took me years to complete this deck, which eventually came out in 2008. It was a complex and challenging project for the publishers, as they had so many artists to negotiate with, and I came to them with a very risky project in some regards. (Remember, dragons=scary monsters.)

All these years later, time has proven that this deck had its own lifeforce and a unique destiny. It has had two incarnations and is worked with by many people. It's in a lot of languages other than English, which is great and scary because I can't speak all the languages and check that the translations are accurate. I have to trust.

Importantly, I feel the deck empowers humans and allows these amazing beings to enter our lives and re-enter the world in a new way. There's a destiny here, and we all play a part in it.

For those of you working with this deck, know it was born out of many things: a desire to right an injustice (the depiction and treatment of Dragonbeings); to move through rejection and seeming defeat; to deal with disillusionment without becoming bitter; to rebuild and recreate; and to be patient, take time and then explode into new life. It is a story that is still unfolding and those of you working with this deck are now a part of the story — it unfolds through your use of the cards, and how you work with these beings in your lives.

The *Oracle of the Dragonfae* was published in 2008. A second edition with a changed cover and some art variations was published in 2014.

THE ORACLE OF THE DRAGONFAE: DEEPEN YOUR CONNECTION

Given this backstory of the Dragonfae, what do you think has drawn you to work with this deck? What particular energies do you sense around this deck? What more would you like to know about them?!

- Choose one card from the deck to represent you, as you are now.
- Continue with the one-card-a-day exercise. Perhaps take a peek back, see how these daily snapshots are evolving. You can focus on numbers that may be repeating or if there is a theme emerging from your readings. Or, there may be shifts in the types of cards coming forth that point to significant changes in your life. One colour may be dominant, or the cards may seem to have a feminine rather than a masculine energy. Note down any patterns you can detect, and especially see if there is a certain energy apparent on a new moon — do the same for all distinct lunar phases. This can be both meaningful and illuminating.

You may wish to build on your previous experientials while exploring this chapter. Why not complete:

- One three-card reading.
- One Celtic Cross spread.
- One reading for exchange (your choice as to the layout).
- Or you could try a new layout from your deck's guidebook.

The Wild Wisdom of the Faery Oracle Arises

I BEGAN WORKING ON MY NEXT DECK RELATIVELY QUICKLY AFTER COMPLETING *Oracle of the Dragonfae*. I found the creative process an absolute joy. It made me very happy. Besides, the faeries were calling to me.

Instead of many artists, this time, I wanted to work with one solo artist, and the artist whose work I was very drawn to at this time was Selina Fenech. I had been aware of Selina's work for a very long time. In the early 90s, I began a magazine, Witchcraft, and Selina—who at the time was very young—had sent drawings in.

I really admire people who, at a very young age, just give their dreams their all. That, to me, was Selina. Creative, gifted, talented, inspiring, brave, and with a wry sense of humour — as magickal as the beings she painted into life. I had my first chance to work with her on the *Oracle of the Dragonfae*, and her work really resonated with a part of me that was nourished by her art. One thing I adored about her work was her depiction of faeries, of course, but I also loved something else her work has that makes it very special.

Selina seems to be able to paint emotions — the artwork expresses feelings and is very evocative and eloquent. There are so many relatable feelings within her works … so much compassion, yearning, regret, optimism and joy. There is power but also a very 'fae' quality, an otherworldliness that only she can capture in quite that way. I loved that. Still do.

So, we began.

On one level, the meaning of the *Wild Wisdom of the Faery Oracle* is held within the joy, ease and magick with which it came about for me. I wanted to reclaim the fae, too, from the idea of them being weak and silly or easily dismissed or watered down — it was time for understanding and respect to be an intrinsic part of the faery experience. A return to the honouring of days of old, when faeries were royal, tall and ruled the land.

Unlike the *Oracle of the Dragonfae*, this deck was comparatively simple in many ways. One artist. Me. The publisher excited and totally supportive. And the subject matter and my affinity with it was so strong. At the time, I was in a relationship with a man who lived in what he called "Avalon", in a faery forest. He was of Irish blood, and he was

YOU CANNOT WORK WITH THIS DECK AND REMAIN THE SAME. IT CHANGES YOU, BECAUSE WHAT YOU LOOK AT CHANGES. YOU TASTE AND EXPLORE AND FEEL THE WORLD IN DIFFERENT WAYS THROUGH EVERY SINGLE ONE OF YOUR NATURAL AND SUPERNATURAL SENSES. IT'S LIKE FAERY FOOD — EAT IT, AND YOU CAN NEVER RETURN. WORK WITH THIS DECK, AND YOU WILL NEVER AGAIN BE QUITE WHO YOU ONCE WERE.

a very magickal person. I felt protected within this relationship, able to explore my connections with no fear of ridicule or being found strange.

I explored, and I travelled, and I made offerings. I picked up so much human debris from the highway that led to our forest home, and I grew and tended a very powerful herb garden. I was surrounded by belief. By faery magick.

So, on one level, magick, ease, joy, growth and protection … but there is another story within the deck. Throughout the creation of the artwork, Selina was going through something very powerful. She had been diagnosed with breast cancer and was undergoing intense treatment, which made painting painful, slow and very difficult some days.

Selina reflects on that time, "There were a lot of ups and downs actually; it was a non-stop emotional and physical rollercoaster. Probably, my lowest moment would have been at the halfway point of my chemotherapy treatments. It should have been a positive time, being half finished, but all I could think was that I had to get through as much as I'd already done all over again! It was hard, and I was feeling like a big, bald, useless blob."

Throughout her treatment, Selina continued to paint. There are paintings within the deck that capture some of this journey — cards of recovery, cards that express the hope for fertility, cards that embody the courage to go through treatment, the search for answers, and the return of hope.

So, there is undeniably this energy within the deck. Selina is a very courageous and aware soul whose inspirational approach to her diagnosis, treatment, fertility treatment and recovery are a part of this deck. This has led me to believe it is absolutely a healing deck. You work with it. It will heal you. Faeries are healers, I feel, and their healing will change you: open you up to the world in various ways, make you look at things differently, question yourself, and realise that seeing without really 'seeing' happens all the time in human-land.

You cannot work with this deck and remain the same. It changes you, because what you look at changes. You taste and explore and feel the world in different ways through every single one of your natural and supernatural senses. It's like faery food — eat it, and you can never return. Work with this deck, and you will never again be quite who you once were.

One thing that did happen when I had nearly finished—and I was working on the cover with the publishers—was I showed my partner at the time, and he said, "Another one! Isn't that a bit much." I laughed and pointed out to him that it was like telling a painter to paint one painting or a musician to play one song. But that reaction stayed with me — and, in a sense, became a part of the deck, too. Never be afraid you are 'too much'. Don't pull back.

I also love that there is a thread of connection between Selina and myself. That there was history. It adds something fated to the deck, again.

So, there are faery places within the deck. There are personal stories within the deck. There is a heroic journey within the deck. There is defiance and refusal to be constricted. There is recovery, fertility, connection and freedom. There is a grace and ease to it, and a simple honesty. It is a key — you'll see on the cover image of the box that the faery queen within it holds a key. She is quite literally offering you an invitation! The deck is a key — the key opens the door to Faerie and once opened it cannot be shut again. That is because we change through experience.

Again, there have been two editions, so this deck incarnates and evolves just as you do, too. *Wild Wisdom of the Faery Oracle* was published in a large deluxe-format edition in 2009 and in a new version in 2015.

WILD WISDOM OF THE FAERY ORACLE ASSIGNMENT

- I would recommend reading my book, *The Book of Faery Magic*, which I wrote together with Serene Conneeley.
- Knowing now what you do, how do these themes affect your understanding of your deck? What do you feel about your deck and its healing capacity?
- Choose one card from the deck to represent you, as you are now.
- Continue with the one-card-a-day exercise. Perhaps take a peek back through your magickal reading journal, and see how your one-card readings are evolving. You can focus on numbers that may be repeating or ponder whether there is a theme emerging from your readings. Or, there may be shifts in the types of cards coming forth that point to significant changes in your life. One colour may be dominant, or a feminine rather than masculine energy could be significantly more present. Note down any patterns you can detect, and especially see if there is a certain energy apparent on a new moon — do the same for all distinct lunar phases. This can be both meaningful and illuminating.

Please complete:

- One three-card reading.
- One Celtic Cross spread.
- One reading for exchange (your choice as to the layout).
- Try a new layout from the guidebook.

Dive into the Oracle of the Mermaids

Again, I wanted to work with Selina for this deck. The emotionality, compassion and depth of love her mermaids showed … their fun and delight and vigour … all attracted me to working with her. So, we grew this deck from another deck we had been working on for a time, which grew out of my book, *The Lost Lands*, published in 2009. This deck eventually became the mermaids' oracle, as we wanted this clear focus. That just flowed — the messages from the sirens of the sea swam right through my mind and onto the page.

At the time of writing, I was falling in love, and again, all the energies seemed to conspire to bring this through. This is a joyous deck, but it is also complex. It asks a lot of us in terms of self-love — it is about love and romantic relationships, but it is also about compassion and love for the self. It is imbued deeply with Atlantean and Lemurian energies, too.

In a sense, it is informed by the mythos about mermaids—the idea of the Little Mermaid—and I wanted to take that back and really get to who these beings are. I wanted to include the selkies, the red-cap merrows and all the world's most wondrous mer-beings … thus, there is a depth of research, history and travel in the deck, along with the myriad lessons around relationships and, most of all, our relationship with our own selves.

While working on this deck, I went to the ocean … I hesitate to say every day, but it was as close as I could get to every day. I took myself to the waters, and I *dived in*. For some people writing oracles, receiving the messages might be about 'channeling', but I feel I need to go where I am called, and mermaids do call. So I went to the waters, wells and waterfalls, but most often the ocean, and I dived in and immersed myself.

There's a lot of travelling in every deck, and I feel it is a necessary part of writing them. Of course, for others that may not be so; but for me, bringing some of the energies back and somehow having them energetically merge with the deck through physical experiences is very powerful. It makes the decks very strong. They 'sing' because of this.

So, from days spent on an island in Queensland with wild dolphins, surfing at dawn, to listening to the whales and watching them migrate, to nearly sitting on a stingray (I did, really), and gently examining all the little creatures of the shore and tides … they all flowed into this deck, through true physical dedication.

Learning from respected Elder Oracles has led me to faraway places. This shot was taken in 2012, on my first visit to the islands of Okinawa. I was led there by my desire to work with the matriarchal lineage Sea Priestesses. Here, I am being taught the turtle song.

I thought a lot, too, about family, motherhood and connections, and all the emotional ways in which we need each other. How we need to have people around us, and yet how we need to become who we are evolving into, and how that is an ever-changing process. I thought a great deal about what love is, how love is expressed and how relationships can be so diverse. I realised that as I was falling in love, the mermaids would help me love myself so that any challenges within this relationship could come back to me working on myself, rather than blaming the other person.

WATER IS AN INTERESTING ELEMENT. IF WE HOLD IT GENTLY, OPEN-HANDED, IT STAYS WITH US, AND WE CAN DRINK AND QUENCH OUR THIRST. FORCE OUR HANDS TOGETHER TO CAPTURE IT AND IT FLOWS AWAY, AND WE RAGE AT IT FOR BEING TOO HARD TO HOLD. SO, TOO, WITH THE MEANINGS HERE — GENTLY HOLDING OURSELVES OPEN WORKS. PUSHING AND FORCING THE MEANING WILL HAVE IT RUN AWAY.

This deck is about personal stories, our life narrative, our emotional history, the conditions we've come to expect and accept, and how to challenge those in healthful ways. How to deny burdens a home within our emotional souls, and also how the emotional body is intrinsically bound up with the physical body and the impact of each on the other.

There are cards within the deck that are quite emotive and which bring up sadness — the card *Experiments*, for example, or the card *Sacrifice*, can act as truth-tellers, helping the person reading know what is taking place, but also giving them quite the responsibility when it comes to passing on the message. It would be fair to say that my decks are like that — the reader does need at all times to act with care and compassion and deliver messages with clarity.

Water is an interesting element. If we hold it gently, open-handed, it stays with us, and we can drink and quench our thirst. Force our hands together to capture it and it flows away, and we rage at it for being too hard to hold. So, too, with the meanings here — gently holding ourselves open works. Pushing and forcing the meaning will have it run away.

This is an alluring and challenging deck to work with at times, but it can lead to so much healing in the realm of self-love, human relationships and our own past lives, too.

Oracle of the Mermaids was published in 2013.

ORACLE OF THE MERMAIDS ASSIGNMENT

- For further exploration and a deeper understanding of the mermaids, please read *The Lost Lands* by Lucy Cavendish and *Mermaid Magick* by Lucy Cavendish and Serene Conneeley.
- Knowing now what you do, how does the story of the *Oracle of the Mermaids* affect your understanding of your deck? What do you feel about your deck, and why do you think you were drawn to it?
- Choose one card from the deck to represent you, as you are now. Write about this.
- Continue with your one-card-a-day journalling and reading. Perhaps take a peek back and see how these daily snapshots are evolving. You can focus on numbers that may be repeating, or see if there is a clear theme emerging from your readings. Or, there may be shifts in the types of cards coming forth that point to significant changes in your life. One colour may be dominant, or a feminine rather than a masculine energy could be present. Note down any patterns you can detect, and especially see if there is a certain energy apparent on a new moon — do the same for all distinct lunar phases. This can be both meaningful and illuminating.

Please complete:

- One three-card reading.
- One Celtic Cross spread.
- One reading for exchange (your choice as to the layout).
- Try a new layout from the guidebook.

As always, enjoy your practice. Explore and journal and wonder and lay out those cards. They are talking to you, guiding you through the great in-between of the Shadowzone.

Shadow Work for Lightworkers:

The Oracle of Shadows and Light

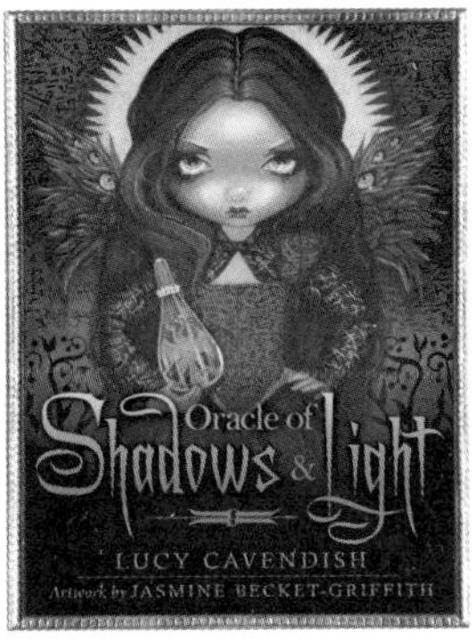

THE *ORACLE OF SHADOWS AND LIGHT* FALLS chronologically after the *Wild Wisdom of the Faery* ... but thematically and energetically, it belongs more to another branch of my oracular family — which, to date, comprises the *Oracle of Shadows and Light*, the *Oracle of the Shapeshifters*, and *Les Vampires*. There is overtly a very common binding agent here, being the collaboration between the artist Jasmine Becket-Griffith and myself. And, as always, there is a story.

Many, many years have passed since the day I entered a very sweet and small faery store in Byron Bay. Byron, at that time, was not the epicentre of counterculture that it is today. It was, of course, alternative, and busy, but it was a little less centre-stage than it is now!

I went into this store and was absolutely taken with the artwork featured on the cards. The faery was disgruntled, frowning, her stare unflinching, no smile to disguise how she truly felt. I loved her ferocity, her 'get out of my way' attitude, and that honest gaze that would stop any falsehood right in its tracks.

I purchased that card for my child, then so very young, and Thom plastered it on his bedroom door as a sign of a boundary to be kept (despite his tender age). I was so delighted by this — even though it was a 'keep out' sign, I loved how the image evoked boundaries, the designation of personal space, and the marriage of self-love with a strong, sweet, quirky faery representative.

The artist, of course, was Jasmine Becket-Griffith, and I made a wish that I could one day work with her. Jasmine, at that time, was a very young artist who worked in a style that was known as Big Eyed Art, pioneered by Margaret Keane in the 1960s and 70s, whose story also has some resonance with the deck. (For more on that energy, which is subtle, you may wish to watch the film *Big Eyes* by Tim Burton, starring Amy Adams.)

In 2009, I was approached by my publisher, Toni Carmine Salerno, who asked if I would be interested in working with an artist whose work he was captivated by. The artist was Jasmine Becket-Griffith, and so began a series of works that so far has seen three decks born into the world, changing oracular work a little along the way and giving a very fresh, unconventional and almost 'up-yours' approach to reading.

The *Oracle of Shadows and Light* is about our darknesses, and entering into them in order to alchemise what we have been told is most unacceptable about ourselves. My dream for this deck was to show that within the most abandoned aspects of ourselves lies pure gold, and I encourage us all to enter into our personal fears or rejected aspects of self and into the culturally unacceptable parts of ourselves, too, in order to find who we truly could be.

Too much of ourselves lies languishing in our own darkness and shadows, dismissed culturally or by family, but most tragically by our own selves. Until we own who we are and bring these aspects of ourselves to light, we cannot be whole, and the rejected self will grow, hidden, and sometimes become twisted and painful. Repressed, it can exert more control than ever from the deep abyss into which it was thrown. If we bring these aspects to the light of our minds and hold them with hope, the once-rejected self can become healthy and reach great heights with its fulfilled potential. We cannot do this unless we have the courage to find out who we could be if we nurture that hidden aspect of ourselves.

Many, many people love this deck. It has opened their eyes to the love of the whole self. Some do not like it, calling it negative. But it holds a special place within the world of decks, and it reads like no other. It is for the misfits, the lonely-hearted wanderers, the orphans and the abandoned, the individuals who will never fit in … and so it encourages us to be our full selves and find the freedom that lies within knowing ourselves.

The *Oracle of Shadows and Light* was published in 2010. There are two versions: the US publishers asked for changes within cards that had some nudity and perceived harshness. The US edition was published in 2012. I tend to recommend the original edition, although both are wonderful.

THE ORACLE OF SHADOWS AND LIGHT ASSIGNMENT

- Given this backstory of the *Oracle of Shadows and Light,* what do you think has drawn you to work with this deck? What particular energies do you sense around this deck? What more would you like to know about them?
- Choose one card from the deck to represent *you*, as you are now.
- Continue pulling one card a day. Perhaps take a peek back and see how these daily snapshots are evolving. You can focus on numbers that may be repeating, or if there is a theme emerging from your readings that you can relate to. Or, there may be shifts in the types of cards coming forth that point to significant changes in your life. One colour may be dominant, or a feminine rather than a masculine energy may be dominant. Note down any patterns you can detect, and especially see if there is a certain energy apparent on a new moon — do the same for all distinct lunar phases. This can be both meaningful and illuminating.

Please complete:

- One three-card reading.
- One Celtic Cross spread.
- One reading for exchange (your choice as to the layout).
- Try a new layout from the guidebook.

The Art of Change: The Oracle of the Shapeshifters

This beautiful deck was already dancing throughout my head while I was working on the *Oracle of Shadows and Light*. Its roots are very much a part of my younger years, and my own inability to change in healthy ways through some of life's most challenging transitions—initiatory moments—created the need for the deck within me.

A while back, as a child and throughout the early 90s in particular, I'd started looking into the world of animal familiars and magickal companions and became a little obsessed with animals and creatures who have the capacity to metamorphose (or radically change their form). Along with that, I became fascinated with animals who develop camouflage or change colours, and ... well, all sorts of animals, really. Though, those who change, and the role of the familiar, were particularly keen interests of mine.

I'd read a book in the 1980s about the cats who'd been placed on trial for witchcraft during what was called 'the burning times', and I'd been fascinated ever since. (If you are interested, that book is *The Great Cat Massacre* by the historian Robert Darnton). I was also really interested in the idea of shapeshifting—changing our form and our makeup at a cellular level—and how the animals show us how to find ways to live and survive and transform, again and again.

Humans seem to be forgetting their capacity to change, move and be empowered by their instincts and the wisdom of their deepest selves. We have become so domesticated

HAVE YOU EVER SEEN A BUTTERFLY COME OUT OF THEIR COCOON? IT IS VIOLENT. IT IS VERY, VERY MUCH A STRUGGLE FOR THAT BUTTERFLY TO EMERGE. IT PUSHES AND SHUDDERS AND FIGHTS ITS WAY OUT. IT BREAKS FREE. IT DOESN'T THINK OR POSITIVELY WISH ITS WAY OUT. IT BREAKS THROUGH ITS OWN PRISON — A PRISON WHICH ONCE WAS ITS SAFE HAVEN AND MOST PRECIOUS 'HOME'.

that our wild wisdom is being lost. I also had the words 'change or die' running through my head at the time. It was a little confronting, for sure, but it was also very exciting.

So Jasmine and I worked together again, and I really became passionate about how we need to change within our lives. Even if we have the same kinds of situations or themes to face, the change is in the ability to know ourselves, see what needs doing, and head straight into the most uncomfortable and confronting aspects of ourselves.

It's a complex deck in some respects because it doesn't have one clear message. Rather, it takes the behaviours and energies of the animals and asks us to think about their wisdom and how we can apply that in our lives. I loved working on this deck, and I found it was a great teacher for me, culturally as well as in terms of nature and animals, as animals are regarded in so many different ways in different cultures.

While I was writing it, I described it to someone I knew, who became very angry that I was exploring this area, who threatened me, chastised me and berated me harshly. I could see why they were concerned, but I knew this work was not at all like their work. This, too, became a part of the deck — that while others criticise you for following your heart, you can do your work in a unique way and deal with the bullying that can sometimes arise when you do so.

In workshops for many years, I'd taught about butterflies, and this is a big part of this deck, too. The butterfly, of course, undergoes an immense change of form within their life cycle. And what had always struck me most was the struggle to emerge from the cocoon and the contrast with many spiritual/New Age teachings that are all about not struggling and that difficulty must be a sign you are doing it wrong.

But I didn't agree because I had seen what happens with the butterfly. You see, a pupa in the chrysalis metamorphoses by turning into utter mush within the cocoon — a cellular soup containing exactly the same set of cells from the caterpillar being who created the cocoon. Then, it reconstructs itself, becomes something else again. Wings form, and the body is changed … but utter destruction into its most elemental, potentiated self must take place first.

Eventually, it must, of course, emerge. And here's the paradox. The very thing that kept it safe while it went into the cellular soup and recreated itself—the cocoon—then becomes its prison.

Have you ever seen a butterfly come out of their cocoon? It is violent. It is very, very much a struggle for that butterfly to emerge. It pushes and shudders and fights its way out. It BREAKS free. It doesn't think or positively wish its way out. It breaks through its own prison — a prison which once was its safe haven and most precious 'home'.

When my son, Thom, was very young, we watched a butterfly attempting to emerge. How amazing it was! Thom was so affected he wanted to run and get scissors and free them, to help them so the struggle would cease. And while I loved my child's pure and empathetic heart, I had to say no.

No. No to making things easy for the butterfly. No to avoidance. No. Why? Because if you cut a butterfly free from its cocoon, it has no strength. The green blood of the butterfly must be pumped through its wings in order to fly. The struggle pumps that blood, and the wings are fed and become able to hold the butterfly. Without that struggle, the wings cannot even unfurl.

So together, we watched as the butterfly emerged, seeming exhausted, and then dried its wings in the gentle sun. Then, strong-winged and ready, it flew away to find nectar, the sweetness of life, and drink it for the rest of its days.

This deck holds that teaching within itself … the dragons who only become strong because they go against the flow and head upstream in their form as koi. The deer whose antlers grow and fall with the seasons. The wolves who travel alone and learn to survive by adapting and changing, or the ones who have found their pack and must grow into an understanding of the relationships within their new family in order to belong. The butterfly creatures, the kitties who grow claws, the stags, and so many more, all depicted with Jasmine's big-eyed magickal beings.

Most of all, this deck is about understanding that the need to change—and the death that we undergo within the cocoon and the subsequent struggle to be reborn—make us trust ourselves. We can rearrange what we are, what we have, and make ourselves over, reborn — again and again and again.

The *Oracle of the Shapeshifters* was published in 2011. There are two versions: the US publishers again asked for changes within cards. The US edition was published in 2013. I tend to recommend the original edition, although both are powerful.

THE ORACLE OF THE SHAPESHIFTERS ASSIGNMENT

- Given this backstory of the *Oracle of the Shapeshifters*, what do you think has drawn you to work with this deck? What particular energies do you sense around this deck? What more would you like to know about them?
- Choose one card from the deck to represent you, as you are now.
- Continue to draw one card a day. Perhaps take a peek back and see how these daily snapshots are evolving. You can focus on numbers that may be repeating or if there is a theme emerging from your readings that you can relate to. Or, there may be shifts in the types of cards coming forth that point to significant changes in your life. One colour may be dominant, or a feminine rather than a masculine energy may be dominant. Note down any patterns you can detect, and especially see if there is a

certain energy apparent on a new moon — do the same for all distinct lunar phases. This can be both meaningful and illuminating.

Please complete:

- One three-card reading.
- One Celtic Cross spread.
- One reading for exchange (your choice as to the layout).
- Try a new layout from the guidebook.

You Shall Not Go into the Dark Alone: Les Vampires

All backstories are spirals and circles and weavings, and this deck's story perhaps begins with being picked on at school, or even before, with a very problematic relationship as a very young child where I was hurt and betrayed very badly. That wounding perhaps led to a series of encounters throughout my life where I just seemed to attract people who were abusive, and because I was always seeking to heal that first relationship, I was terribly vulnerable.

Now, I've long been fascinated with the concept and anthropology of Vampires — are they real, how do we work with them as metaphor, how do they manifest in reality, how do they transform over time and through cultures, and what can this tell us about ourselves and our relationship to sex, death, immortality, burial and hunger ... so many questions. I have read Bram Stoker's work, but I was also really fascinated at how, every single time people would consider the vampire fascination—even the Vampire genre—dead, it would resurrect itself.

There has to be a reason for this ... and then there is the kind of feeling I had, that if I am encountering vampiric people or situations in my life—or demonstrating these myself—how can I recognise them? What is the best action under the circumstances? And if I were to have a guide, wouldn't the best possible guide be actual vampires themselves?

One of the most prevalent parts of the Vampire mythos is that they are often on a path of redemption, yet always dangerously close to their instinctual desires, overwhelming their love or care for their human lovers, family or friends. So, although it feels risky, I wanted to explore the idea of a vampiric guide on that path of redemption working with us (the Seekers) via this Oracle.

And they did begin to speak in that magickal way. It wasn't easy — it was complex, and I knew I was very close to a kind of edge or line. I know many people who feel they are walking a spiritual path would not feel comfortable with this deck.

But those who really wanted to get through a time when they were being drained or mesmerised—when their own personal power was being sucked away or compromised by the very real vampires all around (all the narcissists and the sociopaths)—would maybe do best walking with a guide who truly knew what they were dealing with. I know that might seem overly complex, but that is truly the way I approached this and conceived the idea beneath the deck.

Vampires are metaphors for our desires, too, our yearning for long, long lives, for our wish to have great powers, our hunger for sex, and for the actual ingestion of those we adore and care for. They are also a metaphor for immense personal power at the expense of others' lifeblood. I personally relate to Vampires in that classic energetic vampire sense — one of the very first occult books I ever read was Dion Fortune's *Psychic Self-Defense*, and the concept and reality of the Vampire who devours your energy and feeds on certain emotions and personality types stayed with me.

I truly believe that many narcissists are vampiric, as are socio- and psychopaths, and that the explosion in narcissism could accurately be described as an epidemic of vampires. So, *Les Vampires* is almost like a psychic protection guide built into a deck, with beings who can share messages on how to keep our boundaries safe, how to break free of potentially dangerous people or circumstances that chain or drain us, and the inevitability of encountering these throughout our lives.

And as always, it's a story … As I mentioned, I have certain issues around boundaries and failing to protect myself. When I did this work, I revisited those events, but with new players in my own personal Geis. I encountered many people who wanted a great deal from me. Some were outright hostile towards my work.

Some were friends who no longer understood or related to what I did. Others were people who thought they knew me and projected this onto me and found me to be a great disappointment when I 'failed' to meet their expectations. Without listing a litany of what sounds like negative encounters, there was jealousy, there was envy, there were attacks.

In life, some of the most beautiful people you could ever meet are amongst the most fragile, and

ONE OF THE MOST PREVALENT PARTS OF THE VAMPIRE MYTHOS IS THAT THEY ARE OFTEN ON A PATH OF REDEMPTION, YET ALWAYS DANGEROUSLY CLOSE TO THEIR INSTINCTUAL DESIRES, OVERWHELMING THEIR LOVE OR CARE FOR THEIR HUMAN LOVERS, FAMILY OR FRIENDS. SO, ALTHOUGH IT FEELS RISKY, I WANTED TO EXPLORE THE IDEA OF A VAMPIRIC GUIDE ON THAT PATH OF REDEMPTION WORKING WITH US (THE SEEKERS) VIA THIS ORACLE.

even those people who are wonderful in many ways can have energy issues. We have all experienced the unpleasant — the person who feeds off energy, the person who almost flings their energy all over the place, the aggression and dislike flying about like arrows. There are people who dislike me without knowing me, and there will be people who may be the same in your life.

This deck is for anyone who has ever felt bullied, drained, dominated or disregarded, who has not kept their boundaries safe, and who is still haunted by the actions of others in the past, actions which are staining their present. Humans can be extremely hostile towards each other. We can energetically be difficult, and our behaviour is often less than loving.

We are under pressure in many ways, and we react out of fear more often than trust and love. When we come from love, we often come from love in a flawed way — we open up completely and let anyone's energy in. The trick is to operate from love *and* to have very strong boundaries.

So, les Vampires are a group of beings who know the very worst of us. They are able to show us where we are being messed with so we can make it through the very difficult times in our lives — particularly draining energetic interactions or hostilities, or when we have trouble letting go or find ourselves with unhealthy feelings.

It is at once among the most challenging of my decks, and yet it's also one of the most confronting for people. My feeling, though, is that if you want to do the hard work, you work with beings who know the territory. I see these beings as almost like Fallen Angels, beings who can recognise the suspect behaviours and are on their own mission to help protect, despite their own nature and reputation. This is complex and obviously not as benign or safe-feeling as decks including Archangels or Saints. Yet, these beings are so trustworthy.

When people do let this deck in, they find it is remarkably easy to read with and fosters very powerful readings and results. I also feel that some of the artwork is amongst Jasmine's best — it is just superb. Personally, working on this deck helped me hugely to detach from the energies I had failed to see clearly or had made excuses for … people and behaviours I was allowing to harm me because I was able to be manipulated.

I am still learning, as I have a very, very loving heart, and I tend to forgive easily (and sometimes I do forget!). But with their help, I am able to remain loving yet develop self-protection without feeling bitter, jaded or victimised. As always, I am a work in progress, and les Vampires have been a wonderful help to me. I thank them.

Les Vampires was published in 2014.

LES VAMPIRES ASSIGNMENT

- Given this backstory of *Les Vampires*, what do you think has drawn you to work with this deck? What particular energies do you sense around this deck? What more would you like to know about them?
- Choose one card from the deck to represent you, as you are now.
- Continue to draw one card a day. Perhaps take a peek back and see how these daily snapshots are evolving. You can focus on numbers that may be repeating or if there is a theme emerging from your readings. Or, there may be shifts in the types of cards coming forth that point to significant changes in your life. One colour may be dominant, or a feminine rather than a masculine energy. Note down any patterns you can detect, and especially see if on a new moon, there is a certain energy apparent — same for all distinct lunar phases. This can be both meaningful and illuminating.

Please complete:

- One three-card reading
- One Celtic Cross spread
- One reading for exchange (your choice as to the layout).
- Try a new layout from the guidebook

One of the great lessons of **Les Vampires** is that we must learn methods of protecting our energy – especially when we are affectionate, warm souls. For me, nothing lands quite like immersion with trees, the sea and the elements. Experiment, and find what works for you.

A LITTLE ORACULAR HISTORY ... LIMINAL LANDSCAPES AND WARRIOR ORACLES

In ancient times, entire landscapes were the Oracle. The Druid Isle of Anglesey, or Mona, was one such place where the groves and homes of the ancestors were worked with to bring back messages to the many tribes of ancient Britain. There were many such islands in the ancient western European world.

The Isle of Sena, off modern-day Brittany, was the home of nine Oracle women. The island was said to go into the mists, to the in-between, for its own protection. The Isles of Scilly, south of Cornwall, were known as the home of the ancient priestesses of Lyonesse. These islands each had their own oracular traditions and methods, remnants of which have lasted to this day.

During the Roman invasion and subsequent occupation of Britain, sacred places like the Isle of Mona were invaded, the sacred groves cut down and burned, and their Oracles slaughtered. All that remained were the homes of the ancestors. Following is an extract from *The Annals of Tacitus* (Book XIV) written in CE 110–120 by the Roman historian, Cornelius Tacitus, reporting as an eye-witness in Mona during its invasion:

On the opposite shore stood the Britons, close embodied, and prepared for action. Women were seen running through the ranks in wild disorder; their apparel funeral; their hair loose to the wind, in their hands flaming torches, and their whole appearance resembling the frantic rage of the Furies. The Druids were ranged in order, with hands uplifted, invoking the gods, and pouring forth horrible imprecations.

The novelty of the fight struck the Romans with awe and terror. They stood in stupid amazement, as if their limbs were benumbed, riveted to one spot, a mark for the enemy. The exhortations of the general diffused new vigour through the ranks, and the men, by mutual reproaches, inflamed each other to deeds of valour. They felt the disgrace of yielding to a troop of women, and a band of fanatic priests; they advanced their standards, and rushed on to the attack with impetuous fury.

When these ancient sites were desecrated, they led to a massive revolt of the people of ancient Britain. This revolt was led by Boudicca, the Warrior Queen, or chieftainess of the Iceni, in 60/61 CE. Boudicca herself was an Oracle, as well as a warrior, and she invoked the Goddess Andraste, a Goddess whose symbol was the hare.

Andraste is said to be particularly powerful during the full moon when she could most easily be spoken with for oracular guidance. In visions, Andraste advised this courageous and inspired Warrior Queen to unite the tribes of Britain against their common enemy. And so, the great rebellion led by Queen Boudicca began.

To this day, hares seen in sacred places are a sign that Magick is with you — perhaps Andraste (or even Boudicca herself) is appearing to you. It was prohibited throughout the ancient times to kill a hare. In medieval times, hares were feared, as Christians felt they were witches, shapeshifted into another form.

Today, by the Houses of Parliament in London, you can find a massive sculpture of the Warrior Queen of the Iceni and her daughters, leading the ancient tribes as one. Unfortunately, there is also a gift shop beneath her, which seems peculiar, but when I am in that part of the world, I love to visit her. I gaze up at her and remember that Oracles can be many things — part warrior, part diplomat, all mystic.

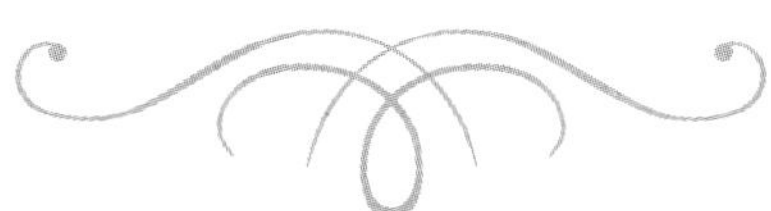

Chapter Six

Someone Foretold Your Coming

Every single human being should be the fulfilment of a prophecy: for every human being should be the realisation of some ideal, either in the mind of God or in the mind of man.

— Oscar Wilde

OCTOBER 11, 1988, PARIS

•

Last night I dreamed of the full moon – time to give in to the mystic, and arrest the intellect, the constant voice in the head. The dream was beautiful. I felt revealed.

•

WITH EVERY READING YOU UNDERTAKE, YOU WILL EVOLVE AS AN ORACLE. BE it within a noisy hall at a crowded festival or alone with one soul in your own oracular 'office' or space. Or, if it is a reading conducted for yourself, within a sacred forest, with nothing but the sound of the elements about you — we are always learning. Some of you will read within hectic environments, learning swiftly about the wild dance of energy in such places.

I know these experiences, too. They have been an important part of my oracular training and continue to be. Have trust that every reading, no matter how beautiful, flowing, puzzling or downright harsh, will be valuable for you. You will walk into the fire of initiation, stand within it, and then emerge on the other side again and again.

Please remember: there is no perfect knowing of cards or spreads. There is only our evolving understanding and the refining of technique. We are on our own spiral into knowledge, entering into the honing of our own intuitive gifts, and learning more about the right application of all these aspects of the oracular arts.

Through these layered and aware experiences, we begin to earn our place amongst the Oracles of the past, those whose path you also share, even while you are walking it in your own, very unique and personal way at this moment. You are now a kind of library of wisdom — you are moving the oracular art and craft into its future by being a light and a guide for others.

Enter into the World Between the Worlds: The Faery Forest

The origins of *The Faery Forest* are kind of hard to get clear on because I think the beings involved with this deck were around the edges for a long, long time. The threads (their presence, their energy, their messages) were quite tangled for some time, and that's one of the big themes of the deck — weaving, interweaving, teasing out our own path and making our own choices.

If I really think about it, I suspect the beings in the deck were there back in the 80s when I first started working with cards. They were in the tangled forest remnants that I explored when I moved to England during that very confused and lost time in my life. But they started getting stronger and more prominent and more recognisable when I began to explore the overlaps between (broadly speaking) Celtic traditions and Nordic/Northern traditions. This connection became obvious to me when I was in a place called Wayland's Smithy, a small and very powerful long barrow in England.

Over the years I've spent about a week there all up, and nearby there is a forest, which to me felt like this very slender vein of ancient wisdom, where everything from the past was still alive and able to be connected with. It was there, in this tiny bit of forest near Wayland's Smithy, that I really felt that there were these Elven energies mixed with ancestor energies, Druidic energies, and what we would call faery energies. I love that forest, and I've been fiercely protective of it — I am nervous that if a lot of people start going and find this kind of portal there, the farmer who owns the land could take down the trees that remain. Even if that happened, the land remains, the energy remains, of course, but these special places are very rare, and in so many ways, they are very vulnerable.

Another place that worked its way into the deck is a place about two hours away from Wayland's Smithy, an old burial mound on top of a huge hill. It's had many incarnations, such as burial chambers (long barrow) and hill fort. It's had so many kinds of belief systems work their way through this point on a hill in the land, and many people believe there is extraterrestrial (ET) activity taking place here. I have seen lights here, almost strobing lights, and I've seen columns of light erupting from the hill. But I am not convinced what I've seen is influenced by what modern people call ET.

I feel more that these are the old energies of Odin, and perhaps this hill is a point between Midgard and Asgard and Valhalla … One particular day, while there, I could just feel this braiding of energies from Viking times, from the Anglo-Saxons, from the ancient ones, the Indigenous people of the land. It was all enmeshed and very clear, and very real and almost visceral. I felt called to invoke and work with beings I had not spent a great deal of time with, and certainly, I'd never dared call them in that kind of space.

But I did, and it was really—I hate to use clichés, but I am going to—next level. Like I'd just elevated my own ability to connect and work with these beings.

I had a really profound moment, too, in the British Museum, where I felt moved to tears when I saw a Volva's magickal tools — her iron wand, the ritual objects that had been buried with her, and there they were, right in front of me. I couldn't touch them, but I felt touched by them… They spoke to me and asked to be a part of this deck.

You'll see cards like that (*Volva* and even the *Ragnarok* card), and you may notice they have a really strong, steel-clean energy. Within this group of energies, we have an interweaving of old Celtic lore and Nordic energies and elementals, just as it was interwoven within that forest, on top of that hill, deep within that long barrow. Softness, fecundity, fierceness, wildness, tenderness, watchfulness …

I HAD A REALLY PROFOUND MOMENT, TOO, IN THE BRITISH MUSEUM, WHERE I FELT MOVED TO TEARS WHEN I SAW A VOLVA'S MAGICKAL TOOLS — HER IRON WAND, THE RITUAL OBJECTS THAT HAD BEEN BURIED WITH HER, AND THERE THEY WERE, RIGHT IN FRONT OF ME. I COULDN'T TOUCH THEM, BUT I FELT TOUCHED BY THEM… THEY SPOKE TO ME AND ASKED TO BE A PART OF THIS DECK.

There is a massive presence of trees within the deck, too, which is why I included a layout based upon a tree, and the tree also references the (ash) tree upon which Odin hung, Yggdrasil, before bringing back the runes to the people. (What an iconic oracular tale!) The trees connect the Underworld, the middle world, and the higher worlds, and within the forest and curled into the sides of these ancient hills or bowed over the elven sacred sites, these trees seemed to me to be yet another living portal of energy.

Connect with those trees, and they connect with a kind of network of energies which are global, and perhaps they extend beyond the earth. For all that it is very earthy, the Faery Forest does have a slightly off-world feel to me. Not in the modern sense of ET lore, but in the sense of the deities belonging to the great below, to the earth (upon) and to all that seems to be above — the stars, and the cosmos, and the void.

These cards encourage us to have a very different perspective and to reach back through the diversity within our own lineage, to connect with the trees and the moss and the underneath. Through that, we accept ourselves, discover ourselves, and move away from clichés and conditions, which are the cages of the spirit. This could be perceived as a harsh deck in some respects, with its *Ragnarok* and *Otherworld* cards, but the lush and sensual imagery saves it from feeling too brutal, I feel.

The Faery Forest was created from 1986 through to 2016 (really). There is one incarnation of this deck, translated into many languages, and the translation of the title changes subtly at times, too. I am not sure why.

Working with Maxine Gadd was a very magickal experience. She is so talented, reclusive, and so fey herself; I feel very fortunate that both of us (introverts and hermits, to a degree) connected and met when we did to co-create this deck. It was a smooth and lovely process, and I'm forever grateful to her.

The Faery Forest was first published in 2016.

THE FAERY FOREST ASSIGNMENT

- Given this backstory of *The Faery Forest*, what do you think has drawn you to work with this deck? What particular energies do you sense around this deck? What more would you like to know about them? I've attached some stories for you to read to learn more about them.
- Choose one card from the deck to represent you, as you are now.
- Continue drawing one card a day. Perhaps take a peek back and see how these daily snapshots are evolving. You can focus on numbers that may be repeating or if there is a theme emerging from your readings. Or, there may be shifts in the types of cards coming forth that point to significant changes in your life. One colour may be dominant, or a feminine rather than a masculine energy may be more prevalent. Note down any patterns you can detect, and especially see if there is a certain energy apparent on a new moon — do the same for all distinct lunar phases. This can be both meaningful and illuminating.

Please complete:

- One three-card reading.
- One Celtic Cross spread.
- One reading for exchange (your choice as to the layout).
- Try a new layout from the guidebook.

CARL JUNG

This renowned Swiss psychologist, professor, scientist and mystic developed the concept of archetypes. He likened this to a Tarot deck, calling archetypes the internal Tarot of the subconscious and representative of the journey of a person towards individuation (the fullness of their soul's expression). He compared the Tarot and the I Ching, two divination systems he explored and worked with, and studied the ways in which humans can form impressions of what is to come that are valid.

He believed that the selection of a card (or a symbol) was a conscious connection between the past and the present and could reveal how the future may come to be formed. In a 1933 lecture, Jung spoke extensively about the Tarot, its history, its association with alchemy and its usefulness in psychology.

He felt the I Ching and the Tarot both present a "rhythm of negative and positive, loss and gain, dark and light."

Jung spoke openly and wrote beautifully about his paranormal experiences and participating in seances.

His mother was a medium who channelled another being, as did Carl Jung, referring to the being as his anima, or internal female principle, or even "Number Two". Jung records that between his eighth and eleventh year, "the nocturnal atmosphere" at home "had begun to thicken." In his book *Memories, Dreams, Reflections*, Jung recalls:

At night Mother was strange and mysterious. One night I saw coming from her door a faintly luminous, indefinite figure whose head detached itself from the neck and floated along in front of it, in the air, like a little moon. Immediately another head was produced and again detached itself. This process was repeated six or seven times.

In late 1913, during a trance, he experienced an initiation into the ancient Roman mystery cult of Mithras.

The language of Jung is now almost everyday for so many modern Western people. He coined the term "collective unconscious" — he sometimes referred to this as "the spirit world" or "the land of the dead". We speak of our inner child, and we feel we have many potentialities, all Jungian concepts, which we are all now so utterly familiar with that the ideas seem innate.

To this scientist and psychologist, gods did indeed connect and communicate with humans. He explored reincarnation, possession and the spirit world. He sensed that what others called madness could be instead a kind of initiation into the inner mysteries of being-ness. An essential Jungian work is *Memories, Dreams, Reflections*, which is full of his musing, mystical experiences and personal revelations.

Within the Space Where Healing Happens: Faery Blessing Cards

Art inspires me so much — I love artists, and I am always honoured to work with them. I explore art galleries and can ponder images for hours. I've travelled far away in search of images that stir the soul, and I feel something spiritual comes through the hands of the artist, through the mind and the soul and through the veins and into the blood. I feel that when the energies are finding their way through into this world, they will often come through in art, television, film and children's drawings, or in random markers and mysteries in nature. I'm saying all this because so much of my soul feels faerie, and through beauty and wonder and imagination, I can feel and see faeries even more. One artist whose work made me feel the delicate otherworldliness of the fae is Amy Brown. Amy has been one of the most devoted of faerie and mermaid artists and such an inspiration to so many others. I love the sense that the watercolours convey, that they are beings made of elements and colour and light. I was drawn to her faeries … one is in my room, and she found her way into the *Faery Blessing Cards*.

Blessings are an area I have long been compelled to explore, that sense that beings of either the material or elemental or angelic worlds are there for us in energetic and active ways. Blessings to me are an ultimate sign of support — real, true, active support, one where a being can intervene for us when we are in need. And it is in the everyday—as well as in those landmark moments—that we both crave and need those blessings. When I contemplate some of my turning points, and what I've seen as a friend, mother, partner and colleague, I see that most everyone—strangers, friends, family—often are in a kind of despair. Hope may be there, but the sense of aloneness so many of us feel is overwhelming. Thus, I created my blessing decks. I have, silently and often, blessed people. It's not so much saying, "I bless you," instead it's more offering supportive energy, giving the gift of time, and definitely demonstrating that support through real action.

I know that I have craved this in my own life. What have I most yearned for in this life? It's to be held, reassured, comforted. To be heard and to be understood. The faeries have been extraordinarily generous, gifting me exactly those blessings. I have received so much from the faery beings, and I hope I have given in return. They are so generous and beautiful, even with many hundreds of years of propaganda being bandied about by church, authorities, and people mistrustful of almost any form of magickal energy. To me, faeries are astonishingly life-changing, and they can offer us surprising blessings in so many ways. One of which is that deeper connection with nature (which we humans are a part of), and they can also reawaken the magick of our own enchanted blood. Their words did not always come when I was inside; I had to carry notebooks everywhere I wandered so I could note down the messages as they came. This, in turn, deepened my connection with the faeries, and my own relationship with nature grew more wild and intimate. I would go to a small creek deep in a forest filled with eucalypts, monkey gums, apple gums and mountain ash. The ground was rich with varieties of moss and lichen, and ancient rocks with glittering secrets that shone suddenly as filtered sunlight fell on their subtle hues. Rock orchids the colour of cream and lemon clung to the shaded walls, and every spring, vivid wildflowers would rise and fall as the light would lengthen … Tiny constellations of wonder, within which were healing energies, love, lessons and blessings. Within this space, hearing the language of the creek intermingling with rocks and air and roots of plants, their blessings would come through. I was in need, too. I was in a new world, uprooting myself from one life and being transplanted into another. My family was changing; death's hands were reaching for my father, but so slowly. Experiencing these huge life changes, the feeling of separation from everything I'd been familiar with, and not knowing anyone in my new home apart from my partner (who was busy) meant that I needed to rely on the otherworldly beings. So, I focused on my connection with the faeries. I asked for their help and blessings in my new life, hung art featuring them on the walls of a strange new home, and journeyed in meditation to visit with them in a

WHAT HAVE I MOST YEARNED FOR IN THIS LIFE? IT'S TO BE HELD, REASSURED, COMFORTED. TO BE HEARD AND TO BE UNDERSTOOD. THE FAERIES HAVE BEEN EXTRAORDINARILY GENEROUS, GIFTING ME EXACTLY THOSE BLESSINGS. I HAVE RECEIVED SO MUCH FROM THE FAERY BEINGS, AND I HOPE I HAVE GIVEN IN RETURN.

different space. All of these wanderings between the worlds led to a better understanding of how to access the times and spaces of the fae, and my work allowed me to encounter so many different nature spirits.

And so, through they came … one after another, and another again. Then they began to come through at all times — I didn't need to be right in that natural space. I could be in a room, cleaning a cupboard. I could be hanging with the dogs and the wombats. I could be walking the beach alone, wondering what I was doing, where I was, and why I was there. I knew I needed to grow new roots like the fae. I could be a wanderer, and now I was trying to grow into a home, like the faeries who were devoted to a single place and space. Could I be both? Could I continue to be the evolving being I wanted to be, living a life where there was space for growth? Would I fade here? And each time, the messages and the blessings came. Strange beings, sensitive and weird. With their help, and thanks to my own commitment to following their guidance, I began to accept their messages and understand that they contained a kind of truth that came from somewhere beyond the usual places people search for answers. With their help, I began to sink into the new earth, my roots burrowing deeper and deeper into the Underworld realms of Faerie, which held so much to teach me if I had the courage to go and to grow there.

Within this deck are blessings that are particular to the faery realms: there are the blessings of the Seelie — the 'court' of the wise and the good, of those who have alliances with humanity and who have shared their blood, ways and healing skills with us over and again throughout the ages. It also shares the blessings of the Unseelie, the other faerie court, who are often characterised as wicked and troublesome, contrary and difficult. However, as members of the Unseelie court came through, they seemed to be no such thing, at least not as I experienced them. The Unseelie are the faeries who are easy to label, as they are disruptors, have a different point of view and do not agree with dominant patterns. They are rebellious and wish to break apart that which harms us all and keeps us imprisoned. Rebels and protestors, their blessings help us to resist what is unjust and create what is better for all. They are fighters and will help you in every battle you face.

There is Queen Mab; there are the Trouping Fae, the walkers and wanderers of the pathways, songlines and leylines (the energetic pathways of the planet's lands). They have their resting places and their trails, which hum with their energies and the health they bring back to the land. Sight, Glamour, the White Hart (the sacred white deer of the forest) are all within this deck, and all I have encountered. Some at a distance. Sometimes close. Sometimes in places where it seemed impossible for them to be. But they came through, and they shared, and their blessings are here for you within this deck, as you deserve this connection. All they ask is that you offer some time, energy and blessings in return. We and they are bound together, and the cords cannot be cut without us destroying each other and this blessed earth.

THE FAERY BLESSING CARDS ASSIGNMENT

- Be open to being blessed by the elemental beings — as you are. Search for the ways in which you are blessed each day, and, especially, the beauty and healing powers of nature.
- Arise early one morning. Watch the sunrise and speak with the light as it dances over the dark land. See what you can see in the liminal, in-between time.

  Or, watch the sunset — both have their wonders.
- Bless yourself with dew from flowers, grass or leaves first thing in the morning. Clover is especially wonderful for this.
- Take your cards somewhere special where you feel connected with the faery.

  Draw a faery star (seven-pointed) energetically about them with your finger, asking the faeries to visit you in your days and your dreams. Ask them for their blessings.

  Then, draw a card. They will help you with that area of your life.

  Allow your energy to be reinvigorated with their presence.

ORACLE OF THE

THERE ARE SO MANY PLACES AND SPACES THAT ARE in between all the ones we primarily notice. Most people on the planet currently are wedded to very limited versions of what they—we—call reality. Reality is shaped and created generally by the dominant beings within a culture or group. What one experiences, another may be ignorant of. What one feels, another may never sense. When people challenge the dominant paradigms of reality, there is often discrimination and even punishment. There may be denial, demonisation, invalidation. There may be mocking, pain and hurt associated with being open about a form of reality that is not held by those in power. This is just one of the thoughts between the words and forms of the *Oracle of the Hidden Worlds*. At the time, I was contemplating who shapes reality, how it is shaped, why we have certain biases and tendencies, and how this impacts upon our experience of our own personal spiritual experiences and revelations.

Back then, my father had been experiencing his own version of the hidden worlds. Since around 2010, my father had been slowly changing, almost vanishing into a hidden realm of his own, created and shaped by a physical reality with which he was dealing. He eventually was diagnosed with Parkinson's, which was soon amended to Lewy Body Dementia. I watched him move in between the worlds, almost disappearing from us into the otherworlds and then reappearing, but as he had been at different ages and stages of his remembered life. He was dwelling in a Hidden Realm and would ultimately go to be in the lands beyond this life.

While he was changing, I called it, at first, 'sparkle time'. Dad could gaze into a space and see beyond in the same way that I could after my injury. However, for him, it was the changes within his brain that led to this journey inward and outward. I saw the energy about him transform as his consciousness changed — sparkle time referring to the lightness, the free-flowingness of his associated state. His visions were plentiful, his memories beautiful and strange, his perception of the world—both inside of him and the one he had shaped and played a part in creating—was vastly altered.

So within this deck are explorations of consciousness and the journey of the soul before birth and during this lifetime — our perceptions as we change and grow older and ultimately pass from this form and return to the air, the wind, the fire, the water, the earth. In the visions I had with the *Oracle of the Hidden Worlds*—many of which were inspired by journeying literally into the images created by Gilbert Williams, the esteemed and wonderful artist for this deck—I stepped beyond the border and title of the painting. I let myself take those three breaths and move beyond the realm. From the 'outside' to the inside of the image … in those realms, I asked questions, wandered, and heard languages formed of elements. I saw libraries growing in light on trees everlasting in the afterlife; perhaps I was connecting with Akashic records. Certainly touching and experiencing deep fundamentals of our humanity — our dreams, their purpose, the astral plane, the world beyond this lifetime, the ways in which we continue once this form returns to the Universe as energy, and our possibilities as human beings if we begin to step away from the constructed 'reality' and move within the multi-faceted potentials of time and space. The mysteries of perception, our ancestries throughout

I SAW LIBRARIES GROWING IN LIGHT ON TREES EVERLASTING IN THE AFTERLIFE; PERHAPS I WAS CONNECTING WITH AKASHIC RECORDS. CERTAINLY TOUCHING AND EXPERIENCING DEEP FUNDAMENTALS OF OUR HUMANITY — OUR DREAMS, THEIR PURPOSE, THE ASTRAL PLANE, THE WORLD BEYOND THIS LIFETIME, THE WAYS IN WHICH WE CONTINUE ONCE THIS FORM RETURNS TO THE UNIVERSE AS ENERGY, AND OUR POSSIBILITIES AS HUMAN BEINGS IF WE BEGIN TO STEP AWAY FROM THE CONSTRUCTED 'REALITY' AND MOVE WITHIN THE MULTI-FACETED POTENTIALS OF TIME AND SPACE.

lifetimes, mythic truths that are beyond definition yet influence every moment of our ever-unfolding journeys. All of this, and profound changes within my family's own landscape, came into this deck. I had vivid dreams and intense journeys in unknown worlds. As I researched, I checked in again and again with Spirit, asking to be guided to share what could be valuable for the seekers who knew of more than one version of the world, who were wishing to connect with the myriad possibilities their life could take and be the forms they could inhabit. I felt I was bringing through a work for wandering, wonderstruck souls like me, grounded yet free, our spirits unchained from living only one version of this miracle called life.

My publisher, Toni Carmine Salerno, is a great admirer of Gilbert, and I felt an immense responsibility to do his work justice — to meet the beauty and truth of the paintings with an authentic exploration of the worlds that we can all discover. I loved working on this deck, as it was a source of great comfort and healing for me.

Grief, exhilaration, transcendence, the realms betwixt and between, and shadowy vales of myth and legend all became clearer. The libraries of the soul opened, and for a time, I truly walked more within those hidden realms where I could meet the untrammelled form of my father. I dwelled there, and not within what the consensus reality continually reinforced around me — the construct that can leach our lives of so much imagination, spirit, and deep understanding and experience more fully lived.

PLAYTIME WITH THE ORACLE OF THE HIDDEN WORLDS

Journeying into the cards is something you can do with all my decks, but I especially encourage you to do so with this deck. Find a way in, beyond the borders, and explore.

- Consider the path of the soul — not just the 'you' who you are at present, but the lifetimes-long adventure that your soul is undergoing.

  Consider how you can bring your own reality into the reality others feel you must live. Question authorities who are insistent on pathways that may not feel right for you. Contemplate what art and beauty you wish to explore, and which sensations and sensual experiences matter to you. Wonder where you go when you dream.
- Keep a record of your most vivid dreams — within them, see if their symbols link to the cards. To stimulate dream lessons about the theme of a card, sleep with it by your bed or under your pillow.
- Experiment with altering your consciousness in safe and healthy ways, for example, with meditation, yoga or witchwalking. Witchwalking is a ritual practice that is very simple and full of gifts. I have relied on it throughout my entire life (well, since I could walk!). A love of long walks by the ocean, down ancient paths in a forest or through the oldest parts of a city fills me with wonder, and the movement helps me to 'walk out' troubled feelings or unresolved issues. There is a Latin phrase, *solvitur*

ambulando, which translates to, "It is solved by walking." It's so true for me, and I feel it could be true for you, too. I also like to make each step a kind of spell-step, infusing intention into every footfall. Other times, I consider a part of my walk a time to receive messages, and collect the leaves, notice the symbols or bird cries. Those moments of my witchwalk are offered up to destiny, and destiny speaks with me.

I love to go witchwalking by the ocean's edge, along cliff faces, or through ancient pathways of a faery forest. It eases any worries I may have and becomes a kind of moving meditation, often in which I receive clear messages from Spirit. I feel movement enhances intuition!

- I find moving meditation or active magick suits me very well. I am not always very good at being indoors (or staying still), and after days of readings and writing, a long witchwalk soothes me, relieves my body, and helps me let go of any exhaustion and accumulated energy and mental tension. Movement takes me to the inner parts of myself in a most natural and healthful way — some of my writing, messages from beings, insights and aha moments have come to me in my witchwalks. Sometimes, I carry a small notebook; other times, I practise using the sacred gift of memory.
- Dance, too, is a wonderful way to connect and communicate with your deep magickal self. So, too, is mindfully experiencing natural light in all of its variations. I sometimes gaze out at the ocean, watching the light glancing off the water in the shapes of stars, and I feel energised and inspired by moonlight and starlight, sunrises and sunsets. Do not live too much under artificial light, for in every moonrise, in every sunset, there is a universe of wonder and knowledge being shared.

Blessed Be: Mystical Celtic Blessings to Enrich and Empower

ONCE, I WAS VISITING MY ETERNAL FRIEND RAVYNNE Phelan's home, and I became spellbound by an entrancing image on the wall. In it was a woman, and crows. Trees. Greens and blue-blacks. I particularly remember the crows ... The way in which the colours gleamed out from the paper they were painted upon, hues filled with a divine luminosity. I cannot remember if I made a note in my mind of the artist that day, but I was awed by the talent for colour and form, the jewel-like intensity of the tones adding to the richness of the experience of gazing upon this work. I know I would have asked about them, but all I knew was that I thought them a person whose paintbrush showed an exquisite beauty, an aching rendering of the mystic — with birds, flowers and intricate knotwork as their hallmarks.

In time, I was offered the chance to work with this artist — this keeps happening, and it is a kind of magick. I suppose it is the culmination of what I experienced so long ago that if you focus on what you say you wish for in real, practical terms and devote your imagination and skill to shaping the dreams, they have a kind of inevitability to them. Life is a spell, lived through the marriage of your dreams with your intent and your actions.

Jane Starr Weils is the artist of the *Blessed Be: Mystical Celtic Blessings to Enrich and Empower*. Now, let me explain to you what I mean by blessings. It is somewhat removed from the idea of only a 'holy person', like a priest or guru, offering some kind of blessing from God to we ordinary humans! It is more that we can all bless each other, be a blessing to each other, and articulate those blessings by truly valuing the well-being and dignity of all who we encounter — and saying so! When I was far more active on social media (for these days, it seems to draw from me energy I wish to plant into works that will outlive my lifetime in my current form), I had a habit. I would often arise, and, after my own practice, I would post 'blessings of the day' on my page for my community. The day would kind of speak to me with what it felt might be rather helpful (or freeing) to bring into our collective consciousness as we went about our often very different days. A thought to keep, which ultimately served to remind each of us of our value. I would often end the day with a blessing of the night — for that, too, has its own wisdom and its own challenges. I had long ago happened upon old blessings, Celtic blessings, that were written in beautiful, poetic language that bypassed the prosaic and spoke to the richer, deeper, more rarely expressed part of ourselves. I wondered how it would be to find my way into the place where blessings could be offered directly for circumstances, so that the blessing within those situations—its teaching, its kindness, its honey—could be discovered and savoured. In this way, blessings could alleviate the tendency towards cynicism and bitterness that can turn the freshest water stale, the sweetest nectar sour … cause us to pluck at raw nerves until all we can feel is pain. If we can see the blessing in all, even the beauty of the pain we experience, the suffering, too, has its reward and its beauty. Not in the old-Christian-Church way of suffering being a punishment, but rather as a most human response to a circumstance in which we discover what it means to let go of those we love, to grow old, to confront the diminishment of strength, or to find misunderstandings between friends. Of course, the deck also embraces the ecstasy of life — a blessing can be found in all if we wholeheartedly delight in the gift of life, in all of its sorrows and sublimities.

IN THIS WAY, BLESSINGS COULD ALLEVIATE THE TENDENCY TOWARDS CYNICISM AND BITTERNESS THAT CAN TURN THE FRESHEST WATER STALE, THE SWEETEST NECTAR SOUR … CAUSE US TO PLUCK AT RAW NERVES UNTIL ALL WE CAN FEEL IS PAIN. IF WE CAN SEE THE BLESSING IN ALL, EVEN THE BEAUTY OF THE PAIN WE EXPERIENCE, THE SUFFERING, TOO, HAS ITS REWARD AND ITS BEAUTY.

I found this deck comforting as I navigated (again!) great changes, some even within my own form of faith. It was evolving, and I was changing, and some of this was because of suffering. Some of it was because of the endless discovery of beauty in the everyday. So within this deck, everyday troubles become the place where the blessing can shine — a benediction, a rapture, and a sense that your existence on this plane in this form and at this time is more than a random accident of biological probabilities. You are a divine being, in a finite form, but with infinite energy of the soul. The Celts knew this, and we once blessed each other's days. We searched within and without for the shining truth, for the luminous path, and we truly wished each other all that is good in the world. And when we bless each other, it becomes undeniable that others care for our happiness, our well-being and our ability to be connected with a divine source of inspiration. A blessing can convey meaning and clarify our circumstances, offering us a moment to contemplate the bigger picture of what we are experiencing. Blessings can ignite the fire of courage within us, and make us brave. And when we live from a blessed place—with courage—our lives are lived in more meaningful ways, every day, in every moment.

PLAYTIME WITH YOUR BLESSED BE: MYSTICAL CELTIC BLESSINGS TO ENRICH AND EMPOWER DECK

- Bless yourself, to begin with. Morning and night, take a moment to place a hand on your heart, throat, belly, and back of the neck, and say to yourself, "With love, Blessed be."

  Think more often of yourself as a divine being.
- Wish yourself well. Practise thanking yourself, being grateful and acknowledging what you do. Make doing your best the way.
- Wish those around you well, even when you cannot be in each other's company for a time. We are still energetically connected to those we think about, yet are estranged or distanced from.
- Consider what it feels like when you know other people care about your life, your well-being, your living soul incarnate in the form made manifest this lifetime.
- A final note: Do not bless people as a strategy for bending their lives to your will. You can certainly offer your thoughts, but please refrain from using spiritual well-wishing to change another person's path. Remember that consent is all-important.

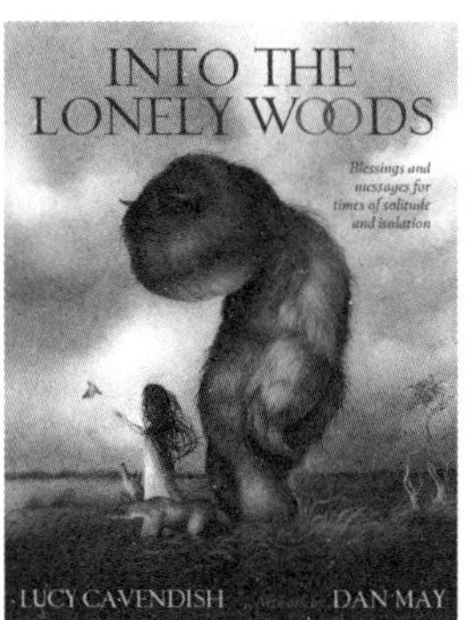

Then came the unthinkable, even what I thought unimaginable. At first, the stirrings of change didn't capture my attention as much as what we were immediately working with — an out-of-control season of fire known as Australia's Black Summer. Where we live is remote, within a forest, in a national park. There is a lot of land, home to many animals. When the fires of 2019 exploded—making their way down the south coast of NSW during the hottest months of summer—years of drought, scorching west winds and devastating heat meant Australia was, in all actuality, an inferno. We had wombats, dogs, ourselves, and a house whose frame was up while we lived in the shed. The fire licked and twisted around us month after month, leaving us traumatised, grateful, blessed, and numbed by the evacuations: time spent huddled on beaches under blankets, digging water bottles into sand and watching towns incinerate. Somehow, we made it through. So, when the murmurs of a virus solidified into people becoming sick, and then suddenly, lockdowns, restrictions, and distancing from friends and family (when we had already been separated by the fires) were all enforced, we entered that with a sense we could get through.

The world changed around us, and people changed too. Cults arose, accusations flew, people who had never experienced a kind of mass event were angry and frightened and thought it all a plot. Whatever it all was—and I've had COVID-19 and I was very, very sick—what we undoubtedly were was isolated. The world, once roamable, became very far away. Some of us were locked down within homes for years. We had a five-kilometre radius we could travel within, and I longed for my family, for friends, for touch. During this time, I wondered about the hermits of old. I had never been a person who could not be alone. I've always loved reading, music, writing and meditating, and really being deep inside myself where I feel somehow less distracted and more connected to the natural world. But I adore company, too. I love laughter, camaraderie, warmth, circles, sharing, companionship. And I am very much a person who touches. I felt lonely at times and angered at others, but ultimately, I worked at using the time. I began podcasting and loved it, and it worked … the quiet gave me the space to do that. I connected with people in new ways. I found out far more about people, and who they would abandon and who they would love in order to feel special and important, the keepers of secret knowledge — which was just another form of the propaganda they were so against. They were not entirely wrong, but they were nowhere near the truth, I felt — and still feel.

In times of great trauma, people can be influenced in terrible ways. This is what I saw.

So, during this time—of ties and boundaries, restrictions and penalties, knowing people who died from the disease and people who died from the cure—I began to wonder about how we would work our way through whilst still being compassionate and kind, increasing our love for each other and cherishing the moments we all once assumed would be ours forever.

I felt that isolation, perhaps akin to the yearning for silence and space the great wanderers and hermits of the past had felt. I'd touched it briefly before, on the silent retreats I had been on as a child with the catholic nuns, where I didn't feel any closer to the God they told me about. I'd felt it within nature, in meditation, in the great cathedrals of the stones. This time, I felt closer to a divinity that was within me and all around me. After silence and contemplation, the world was more keenly seen, and more could be shared. Every gesture and all of our expressions of love took on great significance.

And so, the words that would form the basis of *Into the Lonely Woods* were born. Because I saw this time (and any time when we are isolated from others) as a way through to something beautiful, when we commune with our most unknown self. When we lose the voices and instructions, the comfort and the colour and glamour—all of which I love—who can we become in the silence if we listen? If we learn how to hear. Within the deck, I explored ways to tend to the deep self. When we are made an island, what is it we can do or feel, to somehow bring to this experience its best potential?

Writing *Into the Lonely Woods*—bringing through the messages that felt like they came from souls finding their way—was a great solace to me. The words were whispered, and they often made me cry with their love. We were so loved, we beings, and never alone. Not truly.

The transformation of painful loneliness into healing solitude and connection of a different kind became the purpose of the deck, and I believe that although it was created in this time of strangeness, its purpose outlasts that three-year period when the world stilled and we changed. It is for every moment of loneliness, rejection and restriction, when we feel somehow apart from the world and those within it because our experience—or who we are—makes us live within a different place for a time. Its purpose is to comfort and to console, to help us create and conjure into being a deeper, wiser, more loving self. I have felt its magick.

It is the tenderness of Dan May's sublime artworks—with his wild creatures, so gentle and alone, finding their way through stark landscapes, sleeping alone in caves, clutching to the craggy shores of tiny islands—that spoke to my soul. These beautiful, tentative, awkward creatures were like me — looking out into the wilderness, searching for someone or something to be with. They were searching the world for connection, either with themselves or with a kindred soul. There they were, diving deep within the waters to find again their own thoughts, each painting articulating the compassionate journey we can all take when the hermitude of life or feeling or personality or circumstance awakens our soul. His work has a poignancy and bittersweet quality that makes my heart ache a little and my eyes tear up, because to be so gentle in a world that can be so lonely is very beautiful to me. I love this deck very much. It moves me. It comforts me. It is what came through, I feel, from our better angels, when so many of us were feeling the world was a punishment, that fear was rampant, and that unkindness was everywhere. It brings us back to the best of who we can be, and who we must choose again and again to be, in order for us to continue.

WALKING WISELY WITHIN THE LONELY WOODS

- Spend some time in solitude. I do not mean to shut yourself off from the world by scrolling, or wearing earphones, or going deep within and freezing inside.

  I mean to go to a place or an experience you would love to do and go alone. Of course, be mindful of your safety, but spend some time alone in the world or within nature, and you will begin to see again with fresh eyes.
- Contemplate a time when you have felt alone and lonely — for they are not always the same. Contemplate, too, a time when you have felt alone but in perfect companionship within the world. What do you think the difference was?
- Read for your own self. So often, we read for others, but read for yourself too, and often.
- Consider the animals or other kinds of beings you have formed strong heart bonds with, apart from those with humans. Are the trees your friends? What of the seasons, the sky, the sunshine? Is the rain soothing to your heart? Learn more about the bonds between you and the elemental world.
- Begin to speak with your self — and, perhaps in time, the aspects of that self. You see, we are many beings, people, within one. There are 'parts' to the being we call the self. I

feel I have not only an inner child, but I have within me a rebellious child, a feral child, and a wounded child. They are different ages, with quite distinctive characteristics that I recognise as part of my larger, complete self. All are aspects of myself. Likewise, I have an inner wise woman, an interior nurturing mother, a young defiant teenage part of myself, an inner patient teacher, an inner ferocious warrior, a manager part to myself, and a boss aspect to my personality. I definitely have a leader inside me. I sometimes see all these parts of myself sitting in circle, deliberating upon a problem I may be having. This technique helps me to come from a place of higher consciousness rather than letting my wounded child lead in certain situations. It has assisted me in being responsive rather than reactionary. It has taken me from flight, fight, fawn and freeze to more confident, clear, compassionate and courageous communication.

- Practise connecting with two strong core aspects of yourself. One I would like to suggest is connecting with the Maiden within you — your younger self, perhaps about 17. Ask for her thoughts and invite her to share with you what she may think and feel about a problem you may be experiencing.

  I often visit my older self, my inner Crone, and she comforts me, shares her wisdom, and sometimes the contents of a cauldron she always seems to have hanging over a fireplace. She always reassures me that I have the strength to make it through my challenges; she makes me feel that I can find a way, no matter what the circumstances.
- Go on a retreat with your cards — it can be in the city or the country, the suburbs, anywhere, but within that space, practise being with yourself. Consider who you truly are.

  By doing so, you may discover aspects of yourself. When you do, be very welcoming to them. The unmet parts of yourself may only have the opportunity to become a part of the whole of you when you give yourself time, solitude and experiences without the benefit of others' presence to tell you how to experience them. Be very mindful that you are the keeper of your own perceptions of the reality you dwell within. Value your own perception, and nourish it with solitude and gifts of time that aren't lonely but nourishing to the soul.

  You are a treasure. Your purpose is self-discovery, over and over, for you are infinite.

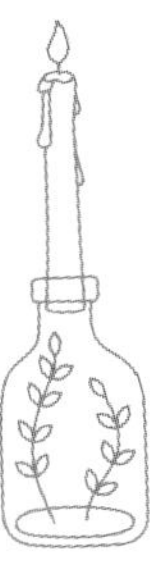

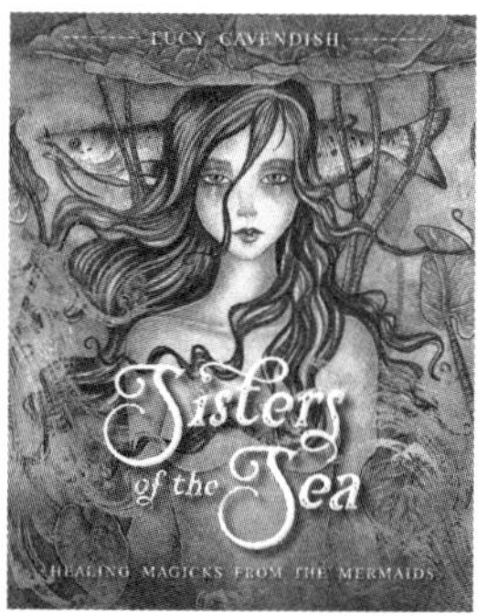

THIS MORNING, I SURFED. THE WATER WAS SILKY BLUE and green, the sand coarse and filled with shells and wash-off from the river mouth. Five women were out, and the waves were small but beautifully shaped, and it was cold. That beautiful cold that has not yet grown teeth, that feels like a form of aliveness, like biting into a crisp apple. It was a divine winter's morning. What made it even more heightened was the sense of all of us having each other's back. I didn't know two of the women who were out, but very soon, they told me their names. I shared mine with them, and we encouraged each other, shared waves and laughed. A kind of sisterhood and camaraderie that is almost instantaneous when people extend care and delight towards each other, just because. The day, as it will, changed. The sea never stays the same. The westerly wind rose up, herding dark clouds like black sheep towards us; the waters deepened into an inky, mysterious deeper blue, and soon, most of the women went in. One of the women I had just met looked over at me and asked, "Are you okay being out by yourself?" I said I was, and she said she'd go in after a couple more waves; she was just letting me know. She wanted me to be safe and comfortable, and she, a stranger, had checked in. Because that is what sisters of the sea do. I felt that the awareness each of us had for the other was so beautiful, the kind of caring that ought to always be present but too often isn't. That is the sisterhood of the sea.

This deck was born in the time after COVID-19, yet before the world had found its way back to most of its old ways again. It was created in the beauty of the friendships that formed when women, waves and winter come together … when caring co-mingles with laughter, a keen sense of the ridiculous where playfulness and courage meet and happily share space.

After a time when I had felt I did not truly connect with anyone in the new land I found myself within, I made a friend (unexpectedly) at the sea's edge. Something about the woman, who I had seen before, drew me in. Her eyes sparkled, and a gentle warmth flowed from her. I sensed a generosity of experience, kindness and love of laughter. I approached her, suggesting that if she ever wanted to surf with someone, I would love to … and over time, we formed a bond that saw us dance into the joy of discovering the love between friends.

The sea gave me this friendship. The mermaids brought to me the precious treasures of new connections.

Despite their absolute necessity in our lives, friendships are often discarded or demoted, and often distance can play havoc with our soul friends. Some connections are sparked by a rare series of events and gather and grow deep roots. But these too can flow into a different stage where the intensity is lessened — not through lack of love, but demands of time and family, or partners or injury or … that inevitable truth, that change will come. We can nourish and nurture, yet keep an awareness that we cannot grasp these bright gifts of friendship. For who knows where they come from, these people who become so vital. They may not be there in the same way forever. But the forever is in the love and the difference we can make in each other's lives when we are gifted that presence.

That brew of qualities helped me not only within the water, but it seemed to me that these women had within them the qualities of the mermaids I had so often heard, sensed and felt about me. During this time, more and more people referred to me as a mermaid. This made me happy, as I had so wanted to be a mermaid as a young person. It helped me to grow older, too. My spirit felt beyond age, and perhaps in the water, I could be as Maiden, Mother and Crone. In friendship, too, we could connect with parts of ourselves that were old and had lived through epochs and with our eternal spirit free and unbounded by the dictates of earthly time.

I also feel very, very mer — I feel so at home within the waters, yet I have full respect for the power of Mother Ocean. Often before entering her waters, I speak with her telepathically, or sometimes I bow my head and open my arms and ask for her to allow me into her depths. To her, I offer my respect. In this way, this utterly simple, innocent way, I have been blessed with being amongst all manner of sea creatures. The thrill of a dolphin driving wildly beneath me, their lustrous, sleek bodies—hard with muscle—blasting through the face of a wave, propelled by the momentum of mother ocean. The juvenile sharks, their grace often lost in the fear we have been taught to have of them — and they do demand respect, mistake me not. But they do not 'infest'. They are their own creature, a wild predator, all with their unique natures. Only days ago, a friend (one of these women) found a very young Port Jackson shark, its deep blue and charcoal-grey banded body dragged from the sea by a fisherman who pulled it up to the beach to die, to drown in the world of air. She found the young shark and helped them return to the water. To me, this is a

THE SEA NEVER STAYS THE SAME. THE WESTERLY WIND ROSE UP, HERDING DARK CLOUDS LIKE BLACK SHEEP TOWARDS US; THE WATERS DEEPENED INTO AN INKY, MYSTERIOUS DEEPER BLUE, AND SOON, MOST OF THE WOMEN WENT IN. ONE OF THE WOMEN I HAD JUST MET LOOKED OVER AT ME AND ASKED, "ARE YOU OKAY BEING OUT BY YOURSELF?" I SAID I WAS, AND SHE SAID SHE'D GO IN AFTER A COUPLE MORE WAVES; SHE WAS JUST LETTING ME KNOW. SHE WANTED ME TO BE SAFE AND COMFORTABLE, AND SHE, A STRANGER, HAD CHECKED IN. BECAUSE THAT IS WHAT SISTERS OF THE SEA DO. I FELT THAT THE AWARENESS EACH OF US HAD FOR THE OTHER WAS SO BEAUTIFUL, THE KIND OF CARING THAT OUGHT TO ALWAYS BE PRESENT BUT TOO OFTEN ISN'T. THAT IS THE SISTERHOOD OF THE SEA.

mermaid's blessing, an act of one who loves all creatures, one who is a sister of the sea. The sting rays, the fish, the kelps and the corals all have their magick, and within the waters, they spoke with me of the connections and the beauty of being within a form, yet having a soul that may indeed be beyond time's measure.

In the artworks created by the talented Amy Brown (who I was so, so pleased to work with for the second time), there are selkies, mermaids, sirens, sisters and sea witches. There are merbeings who are at the very height of their power and strength and others who are delicate and learning to navigate the depths. Some are fragile, others exhausted, and there are those whose vitality is fresh and endlessly renewed. Some are creating loving friendships with sea beings, while some are alone upon the waves, waiting for the call that will bring them to their kin once again. They have voices, and they murmur in sing-song to us of their lives, telling us stories that are laden with lessons and wisdom. The deck has interwoven into it the growth of friendships, blossoming in what seemed like hopelessly lonely places. It is about strength and understanding — the awareness of the waters and their ways, their wisdom and the beauty and the very great power within the element so often considered to be weak. It is a reclaiming of emotions as strength, of caring as courage, of friendship as being—at the very least—as important as the myths of romantic love our cultures have glorified. It urges us to find solace and companionship, true love, with those friends of the heart.

The sisters of the sea are the merbeings of so many kinds, the flowing, the rippling, the gliding … the many ways in which the sea manifests herself are the mermaids, and those themes and characteristics also are manifest in our friendships and connections. It teaches us, too, that we cannot tighten a fist around a friendship, for like water, it cannot be held in such a way. We must open our hands, join them together, receive, and learn the joy of allowing others to give to us. It is also about what can happen when we give to our loving friendships more time, regard, respect and attention. What can form is what the mermaids have — a true sisterhood of the sea, flowing, changing, never the same from day to day, but as constant as the tides, as awe-inspiring as the whales, as playful as the dolphins, and as sleek and wild as seals. I love this deck, and I hope it brings to so many of you deep, true, loving friendships and connections. Oh, and may its very natural, graceful sensuality, that innocent receptivity of pleasure and the divine through the physical form, be made even more manifest with the connection to this deck.

PLAYTIME WITH THE SISTERS OF THE SEA

- Be a friend to yourself first. Consider how you must have your own back — be there for you first, each day, and know you deserve to be treasured and loved.
- Gaze into a mirror (a tool of the sea sisters) and share the beauty of your own self with the being looking back at you. Tell yourself you are loved, and honour the being that is you, looking into your own eyes with endless love.
- Go into the water. If it cannot be the sea, or a pool, waterfall or (safe!) river, let it be the bath, shower, or even the washing of hands or feet in water. Let this bathing in the

waters uplift you, fill you with new movements, and allow you to fly within the world of water and its special relationship to gravity, breath and movement that is free.

- Drink pure clean water, each day.
- Work with salt — its cleansing properties are unsurpassed.
- If you cannot swim, consider just wading or bathing. Always be mindful of your safety, and learn of the body of water where you will spend time.

Before I go into the sea, I gaze at her for a while. I observe and notice the pattern she is making, the language she is speaking that day. I wonder, "What is Mother Ocean telling me today?" What does that mean? I notice where the rips are, what the tide is doing, where the swell is coming from, the way the waves are forming, and the lightness or strength and direction of the wind. Apply this to your life.

- Make time for friendships within your life. Become a friendship-former, an enthusiast for bonds of the soul between those who share their lives in freedom, inspiration, care and compassion.
- Let go of friendships where you may no longer be valued … seek out and cultivate a sea of friendship that you can swim within.
- Take your cards with you to the beach. Or, have seashells about when you read from them. Know wherever you are, even if it is far from Mother Ocean, she is always with you. Feel her within the sacral chakra, within your belly. Dance and feel her. See light upon water, and be transformed by her healing.
- Are you a mermaid? How would it feel to be described as one? What would that mean?
- Ponder this: What does freedom mean to you?

I love sharing fresh air, sunshine and waves with my cards — the Mermaid Oracles I've created are cleansed and refreshed by a trip to the ocean. Once I return to a reading room, my cards long remain bright and sparkling with energy, their messages clear and strong.

The Great Goddess

AT THE TIME OF WRITING, THIS CO-CREATION BETWEEN me and the artist of this deck, Jake Baddeley, has yet to be born into the world. I have seen all the art—amazing—have written all the words, have puzzled over aspects with the editor, and now am awaiting the designs.

Jake Baddeley is an astonishing artist — old school. I'm not sure if you've seen Jake's work … he's a bit mind-blowing. Paints with feathers, quills and filed wood as the Goddess commands him. This deck is an act of devotion for us both, to Her, for you.

That super-talented, non-stop creative force, Jake, and I teamed up to bring to life this dream of an Oracle deck exploring the triplicate form of the Great Goddess — the many trifold ways in which the Great Goddess shows herself to we human beings, as she has done throughout time, across every one of the world's cultures. Working with Jake was intensive and demanding: I sent him page after page of notes on the deities we had discussed and considered including. These notes consisted of what I had unearthed from poring over the most ancient sources I could find on each of these forms of the female divine. I'd highlighted all aspects that described them, which some do in surprising detail, to the colour of hair, the texture of skin and the power of their touch.

Because we were going to be showing the Goddesses—and some of them would not have been depicted in humanoid form, as we Westerners since Rome tend to represent our Goddesses—I felt it was essential to find the most authentic references to their form possible. So the plants and the flora, the herbs and the season, the animals and the emotions that appeared in sources as old as I could find were the ones we worked with to come up with their imagery and their expression through language, also. The deck took on a shape that was unusual for me, distinct from most of my work by the very strong structural element, the representations of these female divinities coming in maiden, mother and crone forms. The alignments of the deities to the earth, to the Underworld and to the skies are included in this structural reference, and each deity has two depictions. In one, she is the Goddess appearing magickally to you, the reader, speaking for you a message, a prophecy, a gift, a warning — a transmission of energy spoken in her own voice. The second depiction is for the call to the Goddess, a prayer and invocation from you to Her for when you have need of assistance, support, the lending of power and the bringing of justice.

It was a powerful and heady process, one in which I felt a great responsibility to honour the task by respecting the Goddesses with time and energy. I had more of a relationship with some of the Goddesses in the deck than others. So, I needed to really go deep, to be humble, to open up to them, and wait.

I am not much of a speedy person when it comes to relationships of all kinds. I tend to move quite slowly, even if my feelings are strong and intense. I feel I must be welcomed in, that I must know I am not impinging on the space of others or inhibiting the sacred expression of their free will. So, too, it is with me in creating bonds with other beings. I check in, observe, wait and listen. And stay still … until the invitation in the form of the voice coming to me presents. It does not mean I do not give — I make offerings and devote myself to the understanding of who and what I will be working with, and also, I focus on that most important aspect, the why.

Throughout the creation of this deck, the deities spoke, and as it so often happens when doing this work, it is not always when you set aside that time. I did do that — offering apples, or incense, or grain, or lying upon the ground to feel the warmth of Persephone's return, or going within a darkened cave to begin to connect with the Underworld journey of Inanna. Sometimes, after these adventures, I would wait, and often, not very much at all would take place immediately. Patience is required. I may feel the brush of cold wings, or a momentary whisper may become audible to my extra-sensory hearing, but it may not happen when I have made the space, placed the offering upon the altar, or made my devotions to Her. Her silence is still articulate. And I know I am not in charge; she is. I am in the strange position of waiting — and not being in control, and doing all I can to open up this channel between us, but knowing that I don't get to choose when (or even where) that conversation may happen. I feel strongly that the offerings and the work create trust between us, and that when they choose, through they come. And they did.

Hel was one of the most beautiful deities I have yet to experience. I was familiar with her but not intimate. That changed throughout this deck's creation, and I am not sure her energy has left me. One night, the cold woke me up, though it was not a winter's night. It was as if a cool wind had come in the unopened window, and frost was about. The air seemed thick, and cool, and illuminated, although it was dark. And I went and sat in the shadows and waited. When she came, it was in a series of whispers from a silver face that rose like a half moon, and half her mouth working in the face I could see, the other half still. It was not that she was fearsome, though I felt filled with respect and gratitude for her presence. She did not speak, but I felt within me a great peace, and her words seemed to come from a cold place that was fresh and alive. Though she is often depicted as half dead, half rotting, in my visions, one side of her beautiful face was sometimes blue, sometimes very old, sometimes corpse-like. The 'alive' half of her visage did not change — by which I mean, did not change in terms of her appearance, and her expression was moderate, too, grave and still. Her eyes were grey and flinty, and I cannot recall them closing. Her mouth was pale and full, her skin fresh and young and very beautiful. The two great feelings I received during that time with her were peace—a kind of loving acceptance—and courage. She moved from being a face to a maiden made of cold flesh and streaked silver ice, and she moved in and out of a great waterfall that may have cascaded with water, but the water seemed to form the shape of icy swords, faces crying out, horses, and swords, again and again.

She eventually merged with the waterfall of swords and ice, her voice faded, and I gazed down at the notepad I had and found the words she had spoken to me, the words she'd given me to seek her out. I cannot remember hearing it, although there was a voice, serious and soft. For a while, it was as though the voice was still echoing within me, like she entered me for a time and showed me her form. I may have seen her with my eyes. I may have seen her with my third eye. But I heard that voice before I awoke, in my dreams and before I stepped from the world of wakefulness into the realm of sleep. I don't know why we had this connection, but it was strange and cold and beautiful. I noticed after the connection that night that my body was shivering, and I'd wrapped myself up in shawls and made a hot water bottle, and went back to bed. Strangely, none of the dogs had awakened. Our blackish wolfhound, Magick, is the dog most sensitive to spirits and most often aware of presences I can discern, but she had lain quiet throughout the entire encounter. The memory of this apparition of Hel still haunts me, but in a strangely pleasant, shivery, sweet way.

The other beings in the deck I met when gazing at their images — it seemed they would come forward. Isis came in vision after vision, filled with aching emotion. I could feel her desperation as she searched for the scattered parts of her beloved, her commitment as she brought him back together and restored him to life. My world filled with dreams of Nephthys and her hair made of mummy's bandages, of corn stalks on fire, of flowers changing to feathers, of a woman's soothing voice becoming the soft call of an owl. Over and over, the voices, images and stories collided with all the ways the magic can come through to us.

Creating this deck was very disciplined, very intuitive, and very creative. Jake and I thought, wondered, questioned and had a few disagreements about things, too. It was a vigorous, passionate experience, and one which left me brighter, braver, and filled with reverence for Her and all that She is.

I hope that when she comes to rest within your hands and home, She will guide you with all that you need to live a life that burns brightly and burns long.

TO CONNECT MORE DEEPLY WITH THE GREAT GODDESS

- Create an altar to a Goddess you wish to connect more deeply with or shuffle the deck to see who may wish to come forward to you. Place her image upon the altar and set aside time each day or night to speak with her. If you wish, simply repeating her name in a kind of slow, hypnotic chant will begin to form a strong bond between you both.
- Consider her symbols: when you are about your daily life, stay open to seeing her in the everyday — for she will come to you. It may be the appearance of pomegranates in the supermarket, a conversation about the afterlife, the contemplation of justice.

You may even see her image unexpectedly, within the faces of the women in your life, or in those you pass on the street. Stay sensitive to such manifestations of her.

- Plan a pilgrimage to one of her sacred sites if you are blessed to manifest such an adventure. If not, create your own by surrounding yourself with her symbols, imagery and music. Films from the part of the world where she arose can also bring you closer. Energy is often held within language and the spoken word.
- Delve into her origin stories — understanding why they are as they have come to be relies upon knowing what took place, why they were formed, who formed them, and what their purpose was. Some Goddesses do not stay true to a purpose they were 'created' for — they change.
- Consider which Goddess energies may be within you.
- Work with the aspects of Maiden, Mother and Crone. Consider that you may not only move through these stages throughout your lifetime, you may move through them every day. Please know you need not be a woman, either, to crave this connection to the Goddess. Nor must you be a biological Mother to move through that aspect of the caring, nurturing, creative Goddess fecund with possibilities, fertile with ideas.
- Notice who you are working with, and consider why she may have come through to you at that time. Take note of your visions and dreams when working with the deities within this very, very powerful deck.
- Make time to visit exhibitions where Her imagery throughout the ages is shared with us all.

Magickal Spellcards — Reworking and Reweaving

My very first published work, aside from articles with *Witchcraft* magazine, was a deck. It was firmly within the realm of witchcraft, and came out long, long ago, under very different circumstances to those in which I work now. The deck was a grouping, a gathering of my own spells, and the deck was called (of course!) *Magickal Spellcards*. This was back in 2002.

Several people, lovely folk who had small spiritual stores (the backbones of so many communities of magickal people) began to contact me around 2017, saying they were unable to purchase copies of the *Magickal Spellcards* deck. I looked into it and discovered it was out of print. And had been for some time.

Bad news, right? Um, no. I danced about in absolute delight—literally!—when I was given the news in writing that the rights had been returned to me. After some months of work in which I combed over the spells, simplified some, made amendments to others, and included a little chant with each, the reweaving was ready. It felt very approachable, inclusive, and demanding enough, but accessible too — and all very magickal and very personal. The concept was still so unique and beautiful. And now, it was back in my hands. The spells could re-enter the world, even more truly themselves!

I wanted an olde-worlde feel to the deck, so I carefully combed through archives of imagery, choosing what would work beautifully to bring a vintage feel to the deck, as the spells themselves have often grown out of traditions that are very, very old. I loved doing this, and currently, I am working on a companion deck to *Magickal Spellcards*, not of spells, but of … well, I won't say too much. But it's very exciting, and once again, those archival vintage images will be a part of the look of the deck. It's called the *Oracle of the Wise Ones* (at least it is right now), and it's going through the various processes creations go through before they emerge into the world.

The themes of this deck seem to me to be about naïvete, growth, realisation and reclaiming your power. *Magickal Spellcards* is a phoenix deck! It's not only about the potent strength and courage that can come from wholeheartedly committing to the working of positive, nurturing magick but also really trusting yourself and asking for what it is you want, what it is you most definitely deserve — and that includes asking the Universe right out loud! By working with this deck, I know you can enter into a more trusting and sound relationship with the energies that are both outside of you and within you. We begin to fully enter into a relationship with the Universe that is not fearful, but based on understanding the rhythmic cycles we are all a part of, and bringing these out and into our lives in order to create what is best for us.

THE THEMES OF THIS DECK SEEM TO ME TO BE ABOUT NAÏVETE, GROWTH, REALISATION AND RECLAIMING YOUR POWER. MAGICKAL SPELLCARDS IS A PHOENIX DECK! IT'S NOT ONLY ABOUT THE POTENT STRENGTH AND COURAGE THAT CAN COME FROM WHOLEHEARTEDLY COMMITTING TO THE WORKING OF POSITIVE, NURTURING MAGICK BUT ALSO REALLY TRUSTING YOURSELF AND ASKING FOR WHAT IT IS YOU WANT, WHAT IT IS YOU MOST DEFINITELY DESERVE — AND THAT INCLUDES ASKING THE UNIVERSE RIGHT OUT LOUD!

So many of the spells were worked over years for me. Some come from my young self; some are much more recent. Others are ones that were given to me by deities who offered insights into connecting to realms of energy and beings that would (and could) be there for me if I took the time and acted upon what I desired. Spellworking required me to understand myself and what I thought I wanted. This deck also allows you to leave it up to the Universe to suggest a magickal working that would be in the best interests of your life and soul. There are spells for our human situations—work, success, travel, love and romance—and there are also spells for justice and courage, clearing your home, establishing boundaries, and drawing to you enriching friendships. I love that spells I worked myself to purchase a home when I thought I didn't have much of a chance of doing so (indeed, I didn't) are here. That the mistakes I made in love magick (so many!) meant I could offer truly worthwhile spells to draw love to you in healthful, enchanted ways, respectful of the energies of all involved. I love that the challenges I had with people I worked with who were bullies and cowards gave me the strength and creativity to learn how to face these difficulties and work magickally to peacefully bring about change. It's all within the deck, all the ways I learned to help myself. All the ways I learned to help those I love.

It is one of my favourite projects ever — partially because I was able to reclaim Her. Through this deck, you, too, can be empowered and come to know the ways in which asking for what it is you want is no sin. It is what is utterly required of you in order to live the life you are born to live.

HOW TO ENHANCE WORKING WITH THE MAGICKAL SPELLCARDS DECK

- Spend a little time questioning your attitudes towards magick and spellcasting. Many people feel fear about such natural practices — as we have been taught to fear relating with Spirit and natural energetic cycles. We've been told it is unsafe and best left to those in authority.
- Do you have any natural gifts as far as sorcery is concerned? Are you able to naturally draw to you what it is you want? Have you felt a kind of power flowing through you, especially during certain cycles of the moon? Are you a person who has an affinity with herbs, essential oils, and crystals? You can, if you wish to combine these, work spells.
- What are spells? What do you think that means? To me, it is a way of praying through our actions, making a commitment to aligning energies towards a goal or desire that will bring benefit to those you love, including your own self.
- Do you feel spells and magick are 'special', or are they part of the everyday, as natural as breathing in the air from the trees?
- Offer yourself the gift of permission to be powerful. Destigmatise that word for you. Understand that power is natural, especially when vital life force, cyclic energies and the understanding of the rhythms of the Universe line up with respect.
- Think of spells as a form of self-sufficiency and self-respect. No matter how unsure you are, the Universe is on your side and has your back, most especially when you activate the energies that are yours to work with, simply by virtue of being alive and in this form this lifetime.

  Remember, thou art blessed. And so is the crafting and casting of spells.

  Have a try at crafting some spells yourself, and see how these could work with your Oracle card reading!

True story. A year ago, not long after my book *The Lost Lands* had just come out, an artist in Canada found herself resonating with the work, the memories of Avalon, Lemuria and Atlantis, and perhaps mainly, the way these were expressed. She was a painter, and she thought to herself, if ever I work with someone, I want to work with Lucy because there is something about her that touches my heart. She felt this so keenly that she shared this wish with her husband. And she kept painting her charming, poetic paintings, which were born out of her life amidst the trees, her communing with the owls, and her love for her little one.

Another true story.

When I was about six, perhaps younger, in my home in a beachside suburb of Sydney, I had a little artwork that I had pasted to my white wooden bedhead. It was of a girl holding flowers, her face in profile, her dress old-fashioned to my eyes, and with lovely patchwork pockets. Her sweet profile was alluring — I never saw her whole face, of course, and so I probably saw a part of myself in that little girl. I scrambled over barbed-wire fences to pluck flowers from the fields that were still there in those days and drank the sweetness from honeysuckles, especially sweet at dawn with dew or after a shower of rain. I picked blackberries and mulberries and went on walks to the horses in the fields, the horses I longed for so much and wished were my own. That little girl on my bed, and those times alone singing in tree branches, playing with the willow tree, and coming in with a mulberry-stained mouth and clothes were all melded into a beautiful, almost faerytale time for me.

I wasn't the kind of child who didn't have friends, but I was the kind of child who didn't mind being alone. Some other children daunted me, and I was sometimes teased, sometimes pushed around. I was a brave and fearless, curious child in the main, but what did cause me to keep a little distance between myself and others were the experiences I had when alone in nature, or under a tree, laying on rocks by a stream, seeing if I could feed myself with only the water and the nectar and the berries. I think my own path to being a solitary witch came in those moments as a child when the inexplicable would take place. When the air would change, when I could feel the closeness of the natural world so much so that it leaked into my body, and I finally merged with it and saw through different eyes, into a different world. Light, water, leaves, creatures … all were my fascinations, and the gentle wonder and profound tranquillity I found in those experiences shaped who I am still becoming.

When I first saw Lady Viktoria's art, I witnessed, simultaneously in my mind's eye, a kind of rapid montage of myself as a young person, as a child, a Maiden, but also a Mother, and a Crone. I felt the sense of wonder moving off the screen and into my heart. Her images had that sense of nostalgia, charm and sweetness that the little girl on my bedhead had. I was utterly captivated by the works' femininity and sense of a world that had escaped being touched by machines, or war, or unkindness. These were works in which solace lived alongside quiet, simple beauty.

There was another factor here that drew me in. I adore tea. I drink so much tea I am often teased for it. And in these paintings were tea-drinking witches. Their garb was slightly old-fashioned, their hair long and wavy, and sometimes within that hair were owls, or flowers, or ribbons filled with dreams. In the paintings, beings like me slept under trees, held cats in their arms while gazing at the full moon, shared tea with witch sisters, prepared herbs by the hearth, and stirred cauldrons filled with potions. They were Viktoria in some ways, but all of us in others. There were old, old women who had the twinkle of mischief and adventure in their wrinkle-webbed eyes, their long grey locks braided with spells.

THE RAPTURE OF LIVING IN COMMUNION WITH WORLDS OTHER THAN HUMAN IS RESONATING WITH SO MANY OTHER WITCHES WHO ARE SOLITARY BY CHOICE, CIRCUMSTANCE, OR EVEN NECESSITY. I AM NOT ALWAYS ENTIRELY SOLITARY — AND YOU NEED NOT BE EITHER TO FIND THE GENTLE WONDER OF THIS DECK STEAL ITS WAY INTO YOUR LIFE AND REVIVE SOME OF YOUR OWN FORGOTTEN MAGICKS.

These works inspired me and helped me remember something I hadn't forgotten, but made the memory so available in the present that it seemed a work of magick.

I contacted Lady Viktoria, and all the way away in another land, in a colder place with pine trees and bears and her baby, we spoke about working together. I presented her works to Toni, my lovely publisher, and we began the work together. It was a joy from start to finish, working with someone as gentle, kind, emotionally pure and lovely as Viktoria. She is a piece of something rare and beautiful, perhaps from another time, and definitely able to bring through realms that many of us encounter rarely, if at all. I revisited the times when I'd been most solitary in my craft — which is to say, most of my practice as a witch. I drew on my experiences, old and new, as a child, a young woman, and a woman growing into her crone years. I also wove in the eight seasonal festivals in the Wheel of the Year, the Maiden and Mother and Crones, the gatherings I've loved, the people I've shared magick with, and conjured up potent brews with.

After our deck had been published—and we were both a little overwhelmed in the very best kind of way by the reception—both of these solitary witches shared their stories with each other. Viktoria told me in a very moving message about her wish, all those years ago. I shared with her my gratitude and why I felt her work was so special.

In a world where so much art is now being created by algorithms (regardless of what you feel or think about AI art), paintings like Viktoria's are, to me, like food grown in a garden in love that feeds our soul and spirit. I have adored the experience of working with her, and what I have found is that working with this deck is doing the same for others — they are entranced and charmed. The rapture of living in communion with worlds other than human is resonating with so many other witches who are solitary by choice, circumstance, or even necessity. I am not always entirely solitary — and you need not be either to find the gentle wonder of this deck steal its way into your life and revive some of your own forgotten magicks.

WORKING WITH THE SOLITARY WITCH ORACLE

- Brew some tea! You could hand-make some herbal or floral tea or purchase a wonderfully magickal brew from Kohli Tea (an Australian tea I love with many potent variations and blends). As you sip your tea, really tease out the tastes of the ingredients. To make this even more potent, you could do this in the dark to heighten the sense of taste.
- Practise working with your own senses in this way. Take away sight and work on touch, seeing how keenly you can feel when you can no longer see, how your body feels in space. Please do this safely. When you do this, you may wish to practise shuffling gently in darkness, or blindfolded, and see what imagery comes to your third eye. It nearly always increases your clairsentience and your clairvoyant capacities.
- Charge a witch's tool. Choose either a wand (this could be as simple as fallen wood from a beloved tree), or a chalice (again, this could be a favourite tea cup, or go op-shopping and find a charming old porcelain cup or even a chalice of copper may be amongst the forgotten treasures you can discover). Perhaps find a cauldron, sword or athame, a staff, or a witch's hat! To charge, first clear the witch's tool by moving it through smoke, incense, or the smoke of an herbal fire three times, then place it within a circle of salt overnight. Do this at the darkening moon, and it will be cleared of all incidental or intentionally engrained energies.

  To charge, take beneath the waxing or full moon, and hold it up to her light. Ask for her energies to be put into your tool. See in your mind's eye the silver light of the moon flow like liquid into your cup or chalice, flow down your sword or athame, pour into your wand or staff! As you visualise this, give to your sacred witch's tool a purpose or intention. Really focus on this and put it in so it exists with the moon's most growth-filled, expansive, celebratory energy. You can clear and recharge as needed and as you wish.
- Learn how to cast a magickal circle and bring protective magick into your own oracular reading space.
- Include tea and tools with your oracular readings.

  It need not really be said, but conducting readings with friends by the fire is beautiful indeed with *The Solitary Witch Oracle* deck.
- Spend time outside at night and watch the moon rise up with a companion who is not human. Share the magick with your familiar!

- If it is safe for you to do so, go camping with your cards or sleep outside with a tent under the trees. Take away the forms of media that so often are forming too much of our consciousness. Slow everything down to a natural pace, and listen for the messages that come through on the wind, the light, the earth, the waters, and the sounds of the natural world.

I think all Oracle cards have a special relationship with trees. After all, they're part-tree themselves and resonate with their own kind. I've taken my cards to particular trees time and again, and every time, it feels like they've received a blessing from these wise, kind beings.

- Consider following, for a year and a day, the path of the witch. A year and a day takes in each of the eight great festivals on the witches' Wheel of the Year, as well as the lunar cycle, with an emphasis on full moons. My path includes each phase of the moon, but if that seems too intensive to begin with, you could simply observe full and dark moons or full and new moons, for example. This need not be rigorous so much as immersive and delightful. It is about connection, and a sense of belonging to the natural world and being in deep relationship with her through the intertwining of your own life with her sacred cycles. If you would like to explore this path more deeply, you could explore my books *White Magic, Witchy Magic* (written with Serene Conneeley), *Witches and Wizards* or *Spellbound.*
- Practise sometimes speaking predominantly with your energy rather than just your words. Hold feelings within you and emanate them out, and see if you can be understood. You may notice a deeper kinship with animals, plants and trees after this work.
- Pour love into the food you prepare to eat. Eat consciously and with love. Nourish yourself, and this way, you will be a most healthful, wise and beautiful solitary witch.

Alice: The Wonderland Oracle

I WAS WALKING THE BEACH THIS MORNING, UNDER A stormy sky and mirrored sea, and with every step, I pondered this deck, looking at it from this way and that, wondering how to express what it means to me and how it came into being. It seemed as varied and mysterious as the sea and sky: changing, mutable, wondrous, and a source of joy and courage.

The stories of Alice and her initiatory trials through her dream/vision/actual journey to Wonderland and her voyage through the looking glass are mystical texts that can be enjoyed on so many levels. If you have this deck, you'll notice that at the beginning of each of the messages, there are one or two lines from Lewis Carroll's books. While some seem to be 'nonsense' to me, they are ways of approaching, viewing and understanding the world. There are profound dollops of delightfully put wisdom within the pages of this enchanting book that highlight a young girl's journey through the world of adults, who all seem to be ridiculous — painting roses red to appease a Queen quick to fury, mad tea parties (tea! No wonder I love this world!), sage advice from Cheshire cats and a caterpillar puffing on a hookah, smoking who-knows-what! I love the way the world of Alice is an immersive journey. This young girl—with her practical mind, her views on what is and isn't nonsense, and her sudden growth—shows us all how to travel through the world. So many of the lines became card messages but viewed through an overtly spiritual lens. The artwork is lush, and it too travels through timescapes, as the prolific and uncanny artist, Jasmine Becket-Griffith, had painted Alice not only within her world but in the style of famous and iconoclastic artists. To me, this speaks of Alice's ability to not only travel through maddeningly upside-down realms (and come back to the 'real' world with knowledge and experience), but also that she is relevant in all sorts of times and places.

In the guidebook, I've told the story of how I felt a little like I was going into a Wonderland when I first was invited to tour and teach in Japan. My values, beliefs, customs and traditions were put aside for a time so I could experience this very enchanting culture with open eyes, heart and mind. Within the days that became over eight journeys back and forth to that land, I continued to carry Alice with me. I would open the book like an Oracle, and I would take the three breaths and open my eyes to the lines that came into view first. Then, I would intentionally allow their wisdom, questions, humour or challenges to be my guide for that day. It was a truly delightful way to work as an Oracle and walk into a new land with a sense of being a stranger who was there to be taught, rather than to teach.

The cards themselves have beautiful, thought-provoking messages: They invite us to consider what it means to be ourselves, to refuse to be defined by others' dreams and realities. Instead, we must live within our own dreams, as Alice asserts. We must also attempt impossible things like having jam before breakfast and forgetting who we are in order to become ourselves. We must not drink poison (especially when we know it to be poison!), and we can challenge authority by questioning the difference between law or justice and nonsense, even if spoken by those with power. There is a reason that this story isn't for children and is so often underestimated. It is for all of us. It can be a guide into our own power and sovereignty, showing us eternal, practical wisdom that will help us move between the realms of dreams and responsibility, discipline and distraction — overthrowing oppression and liberating our minds from the thought-prisons of those who prefer to live without daring or imagination. These cards can help us to be brave in the face of anger and injustice — and to understand we are not everyone's cup of tea!

Indeed, when these cards first came out, I was the recipient of some unsolicited criticism. In Melbourne for workshops, I was told by one of the hosts that this deck wouldn't sell nearly as well as my others, while other people asked if the deck was only for children (a little like how people often consider faerytales for children, when I feel mostly they remind adults who they were before the world burrowed its way into their bones and tied them up with rules and regulations). So, a huge part of this deck is looking at where you may be underestimated by others and where you underestimate yourself! It will encourage you to believe in your own dreams, to make your own precious mistakes, to help others who will listen, and to know when you are being swindled. Most of all, it will awaken you to where we can swindle ourselves and change that propensity forever! Once we have entered Wonderland, the world of change and questions and talking cats and flowers, the world will not seem as solid, and your dreams will be empowered.

Oh — and it is a kind of confirmation for me that despite the doubt she received, Alice has been one of the most beloved decks I have ever created. She is translated into so many languages, and she has touched so many hearts. I absolutely know that while she may not be for everyone, Alice can find her way to those who are willing to look at their lives in new and adventurous ways, and to make every day a dream of daring and wonder.

And remember, everything can be an Oracle when you are willing to live in that way, approaching everything like it is a conversation between you and the otherworlds — or the wonderlands!

DOWN THE RABBIT HOLE WITH ALICE

- Try something new each week.
- Approach a stagnant situation in a fresh way. Try not to change what must be done, but change the ways in which it can be done. Make of it a most peculiar adventure!
- Remain curious, and always do something mad every day!
- Challenge prescribed authority that does not seem just.

- Understand that if you do not create your own life—or undertake to make real and live within your own dream—you will become a part of someone else's dream. Endeavour to give your own dreams the space and time to be freed from the realms of maybe, to the realms of absolute probability!
- Do you have thoughts or habits that you know may be toxic for you or for others? If so, consider the advice to not drink the potion!
- Challenge your own thinking when it is not offering you support and encouragement. Say, "Nonsense" to negative thoughts, and embrace your version of the story!
- Find a way to make every moment count. This does not mean to fill every moment with productivity or work. Rather, make it count as in the moment must mean something to you. Put your own dreams (perhaps of being an Oracle card reader) to the forefront. Daydream about what that could be like. Imagine who you might read for. Dare to imagine being offered energy in the form of money for your oracular insights! Dare to dream, and be sure to serve your own life's dream.
- When instability comes, as it does for Alice, and you no longer know who you are or are thrust into a situation that you don't know how to work with, embrace the opportunity to recreate yourself through knowing who you are within this challenge. Of course, you will have moments of doubt—this is natural—but you will rise if you offer yourself the faith you so often put in others who are not living your wild and precious life!
- Spend some time revisiting hobbies, pastimes, special places, and iconic people who were there with you at a time when you felt open and full of curiosity, questions and delight. Go horse-riding, splash in a puddle, write a letter of appreciation to a person who made all the difference in your life in this way. Play games! Reconnect with the childlike adventurer who dares to make life a dream of discovery!

Foxfire: The Kitsune Oracle

I LIVE IN A COUNTRY WHERE FOXES ARE NOT LOVED OR respected — sadly, through no fault of their own. They were brought to Australia by English folk longing for the hunt, for the cruelty and terror of fox hunting. So, these wild and beautiful creatures were brought here to be killed. Like so many introduced creatures, some slipped their bonds and made their way into the bush and ultimately thrived, to the detriment of many of the native creatures who have no defence against the claws and teeth and wild hunger of the fox. It hurts my heart to know they are still hunted here and that humans once again punish animals for problems of their own making.

I love the way foxes move, their red sheen and bright eyes, their strange calls and purrs, and their almost feline, delicate, wide-awake energy. But I understand the dilemma we have here in Australia.

So, to travel to a place where foxes are considered to be semi-deities with magickal powers—and are revered for their luck-bringing, manifestation skills and a very special fire they can conjure—was a revelation to me.

When first travelling in Japan, I was taken with the many small temples along streets, outside of homes or places of work. Some had raccoons, and many had foxes. The foxes were clever-looking, with a glint in their eye and a knowing grin on their face. They were not at all humanoid, but their intelligence and cunning and wit were transparent. I was told their stories by many people in Japan, and it became clearer to me that the fox in this culture is a being who is very, very special.

"At fifty years of age, the fox can turn into a human; at a hundred, it can know something a thousand miles away; at a thousand, it can communicate with heaven." So said Guo Pu, in around 276 CE. Guo Pu was a Chinese folklorist, poet and writer, a Taoist mystic, geomancer, and wise one who collected mythologies and legends of the East. In Japan, according to the yokai folklore, all foxes have extrasensory abilities, and the older they become, the more formidable their powers.

Over many years, I travelled to Japan until I began to feel that the beings there were truly beginning to speak with me. In these temples, I would stop and pay my respects — again, ignorant of traditions in many ways, opening myself up and willing to be a student of the energies that may come to speak with me if I had patience and was silent and respectful in their presence. The teachers came, some in human form, others in the spirit-whispers of the foxes who work with the deity Inari.

Maybe they were both because Kitsune can shift into human form, and the older they are, the longer they can stay in that form. They can speak many languages, but to me, they spoke in a language that was of the spirit. I finally began to hear them clearly in a temple of Inari, with its red gates and offerings, where they began to share messages with me. I took these in, and in time, began to write them down.

I struggled with this a fair bit. It's inevitable as a writer who works in this in-between realm that I may encounter beings who are not within my own culture this lifetime. So when the Kitsune prompted me to write of them and share their messages, I wondered if this was the right and ethical thing to do. In the end, I decided to do as they asked, but I am deeply aware that I am not Japanese in this lifetime. One aspect that may have significance is that I have a strong past-life memory of being in hot-spring stone open-air baths—the onsens—in or around the 17th century with a man who was not from my world. At that time, it seemed to me that I was a Japanese person, and there was a man who was an outsider. I was teaching him how to be a civilised human, as he was a sailor and unsure of how even to bathe, to dress, to speak with courtesy. He was my charge to educate and to teach the civilised language so my lord could communicate with him and learn of his wishes. He wore a cross, and so he was under guard. There was a deep mistrust of their Christianity, for there had been missionaries who had taken children and harmed those who would not convert. But we were a powerful clan, and the power was ours. If I could not reach this man—if he could not come to us with respect, truly felt in his deep self—he would die.

This lifetime seemed to play again and again. I felt in my present lifetime, I must be respectful of the ways of Japan (naturally) and let them instruct me, as I had been the teacher in the past. Everything had such grace and honour, so much respect imbued in ordinary moments. I was very taken with the polite, kind people I encountered and their intriguing spiritual lives, which were very old, very close to nature, very clean and pure to me.

The gates of Inari can be found throughout Japan in temples devoted to this mysterious deity. Walking through her gates becomes an experience imbued with blessings and a kind of prophetic energy. I emerge from Her changed, and set again on the right path for my soul.

The beautiful energies of Inari and the sacred fires of her Kitsune made their way into my **Foxfire: The Kitsune Oracle**. I have walked her gates throughout all my travels in the enchanting land of Japan, and her revelations are included in that special Oracle deck.

The foxes of the deity Inari were the most vocal, along with the raccoons and deer. Inari is a deity who is sometimes feminine, sometimes masculine, gender fluid and beyond definition. The foxes of Inari bring to them/her/him the grain that will feed the people. (See, pronouns were a thing long before the present day!) The rice symbolises, of course, much more than grain — it is wealth, prosperity, the ability to feed ourselves, nourish our minds and learn and teach, to be intelligent and clever, to be humble in the presence of that which is unfamiliar and mysterious to us, as Inari was to me. Kitsune have various numbers of tales, each number with its significance, and in my mind, a deck was forming. Yet, I wondered how I would find an artist who knew of the folklore and had captured their forms. I did not know any Japanese artists, and despite searching for one, nothing seemed to align with ease, as it does when it's all meant to be. The Kitsune told me that Inari would manifest this artist for the deck, so I needed to stop trying and attempting to control events and instead let it happen. I would sometimes see them speaking and caught a glimpse of a fiery tail out of the corner of my eye. Sometimes, they warned me of natural events like a typhoon or an earthquake. They were especially good at matters of trust, such as whom to trust. When I look back now, I can see their warnings so clearly. They must have wondered what they must do to make me understand!

THE KITSUNE TOLD ME THAT INARI WOULD MANIFEST THIS ARTIST FOR THE DECK, SO I NEEDED TO STOP TRYING AND ATTEMPTING TO CONTROL EVENTS AND INSTEAD LET IT HAPPEN. I WOULD SOMETIMES SEE THEM SPEAKING AND CAUGHT A GLIMPSE OF A FIERY TAIL OUT OF THE CORNER OF MY EYE. SOMETIMES, THEY WARNED ME OF NATURAL EVENTS LIKE A TYPHOON OR AN EARTHQUAKE. THEY WERE ESPECIALLY GOOD AT MATTERS OF TRUST, SUCH AS WHOM TO TRUST. WHEN I LOOK BACK NOW, I CAN SEE THEIR WARNINGS SO CLEARLY. THEY MUST HAVE WONDERED WHAT THEY MUST DO TO MAKE ME UNDERSTAND!

So, I did my best to allow this to be brought through by Inari and her Kitsune, and to just trust that if they were determined for me to do this, they could make it come to pass. One day, while thinking on this and preparing workshops for an upcoming journey to Japan, I had a phone call from Toni. He's so wonderful at this! He said he was going to send me some artists' work to look at. I looked at some, and while it was so skilled and quirky, it wasn't quite my vibe, and even though Toni was super enthused, it didn't feel right for me. I looked at the next artist's work, and my breath may have just stopped for a little while. A few heartbeats passed, and my heart felt like it burst into the flame of the Kitsune — their very special foxfire, their *Kitsune-bi*, their flame that lights our way when we are lost or warms us when we are close to becoming lost in our own beauty and feelings. My heart felt afire, and my mind, too, was aflame. Here was the artist — Meredith Dillman. And here were the Kitsune, some surrounded by the fire that had led them to me, and me to them, that would mean we would create together.

So, what is the heart of the *Foxfire: The Kitsune Oracle*? Perhaps it is to trust. To be open. To know that you may not always know who you are going to be taught by. To know that there are cultures, ways of being, thinking and approaching the world that are spiritually advanced. To know that we can be humble in the face of and be bathed in a wisdom that stretches our boundaries and allows us to experience the world in a different way. We can connect with the lives and journeys our soul has already taken and be reunited with that life's knowledge and lessons, which can make this life even more exquisite to experience.

The fire of the Kitsune has stayed with me. During the fires here, I asked for protection, for the fires to teach me, to be awe-inspired by the power of nature, to be guided by the flames unlit by the human hand, or lightning strike, or even heat. To have the holy fire in my life, to be lit from within whenever my inner flame dwindles and threatens to give out. For the passion for life to burn bright, but to endure.

It helps me, too, to contemplate the constellations above, celestial fires that we are connected to, and to which we may return as our soul will journey through the stars (as well as this earth).

I hope that you, too, will allow the Kitsune to enchant you, guide you, cleanse you, inspire you and show you whom to trust.

CONNECTING WITH FOXFIRE: THE KITSUNE ORACLE AND THE HOLY FIRE

- Explore your own past lives. You may find you have a connection to cultures and people that are way outside of your experience — even your comfort zone.
- Trust. Practise trusting, and allow the Kitsune to guide you in this. You do this primarily by feel, and it will come through to you via your own skills, perhaps your various 'Clair' senses. It can also be of great help when becoming an Oracle, to trust what you get, to trust what you are told.
- Work with the element of fire: Fire is often feared, but it is more beneficial to face that fear—if you have it—and to learn to work respectfully with the element of fire. This principle applies, of course, to all the elements — and to spirit as an element, too! Work with visualisation first. See a small flame offered to you by the Kitsune and follow the flame in a visualisation. Let the fire surround you, cleanse you, move through you, or if it spears outside of you, see where or what it guides you to.
- Respect your own growing older and ageing process. Defy the conditioning around age. After all, the oldest trees can bear the brightest blossoms. So challenge the negativity around ageing, and consider how becoming an elder will give you deeper insight and more opportunities to learn and explore, to nurture, to laugh and find joy.
- The Kitsune often are playful, so be playful in your quest on the path of the Oracle. Be the one who can find delight, who is always kind, but who is able to smile through tears. The Kitsune will always bring to you the grain of rice.

- Make offerings to the Kitsune and to Inari to help you begin to create a nourishing business that will feed your physical body, nourish your mind, fill your heart, and stretch the soul so it can reach its potential.
- Explore your past lives or dimensional lives, as time is not a simple line. Find a reputable regressor and explore this within a safe and trustworthy environment where you are not 'fed' expectations and prompts. Some of my most amazing and vivid (as well as helpful) past-life experiences have been in temples, shrines and sacred sites within nature.

Experientials and Experimentals

Find an Oracle in history you would love to know more about and learn about them. Ponder who they were, what they did, and why you wish to explore them more. What do you think might be drawing you to their story?

Part Three

Chapter Seven

Walking the Mystery Road

And I shall destroy everything I created. Earth will again appear as primordial ocean, as endlessness as in the beginning. I then am everything that remains — after I have turned myself back into a snake that no man knows.

— Hermann Kees

Dear Adept,

Welcome to the third part of this book, in which we will be working together to build on the strong foundation you developed throughout Part One: The Initiate and Part Two: The Shadowzone. We explored not only the cards you were working with, but we simultaneously walked the path of the Oracle, wondering, discovering and being open to the possibilities presenting themselves. Now, we enter the gateway and ready ourselves to begin to walk the path of The Adept.

As an Initiate, there can be a sense of wanting to find ways to solve the mysteries before us, as though they are problems or puzzles to unravel and make sense of. While within the Shadowzone, you explored the deeper meanings and mysteries of the decks, developing a strong bond and close understanding. As an Adept, it is my hope that you will begin to enter into the Mystery so deeply that you feel as though you are living the ways of an Oracle naturally — without effort, burden or pretension. As an Initiate, we explored the wonderful ways in which we can begin to bring our intuitive, mystic side into our everyday lives. In the Shadowzone, we practised pouring our soul into the cards, exchanging energy with them, and learning the importance of story. As Adepts, these ways will be woven into your days, and it is my hope that you will no longer feel the effort.

Instead of fretting and worrying you are not doing enough or doing it 'right', you may find that you are simply dedicating yourself to more development and learning, challenging yourself with various rites of passage which will help you burn through your own unique obstacles. Some challenges you encounter may be self-created, while others may be external. Regardless, Adepts do … so action, work, and offering yourself and your work in the service of others will be a part of the breakthrough moments you will experience as part of the Adept's path.

While working on this chapter, I was reminded of the card from the *Oracle of the Shapeshifter*'s deck, *Little Owlyn, Wisdom as Light as a Feather*… And I would like you to consider this idea of wisdom being 'light'. Knowledge can be a burden, but wisdom is light.

When walking this path of the Adept, it is essential to be dedicated, to put ourselves to the task, and to truly work and place effort into our learning. Without the beautiful work, we would remain neophytes, engaging with the work but not moving through it experientially.

KNOWLEDGE CAN BE A BURDEN, BUT WISDOM IS LIGHT.

As an Adept, what you will discover is that what is as important as the tasks themselves is the energy with which we complete them. When we bring a heavy, negative or needy energy to a task, it is usual that the path begins to feel too hard. We find ways to talk ourselves out of doing further work. We are all different souls, and we know each of our lives include unique challenges. But when we do this work, we must do our best not to make a burden of it.

That is hard, at times, as there are many models of spirituality that have glamorised their painful path to mysticism. They have made their sufferings seem grand and noble, and there is a dramatic quality to the path of the spirit being one of self-denial, even self-harm. We have no need to manufacture suffering in our lives, for we will all experience the many faces of emotional and physical pain that are a natural part of being here in physical form. We can learn extraordinary lessons and develop wisdom and compassion from suffering, but I feel we must not become like the monks of old, flagellating themselves in order to grow closer to Christ. If you live, pain will come. For many people, it will be extraordinary. For others, it is simply a part of everyday life.

PERHAPS ENLIGHTENMENT IS NOT ABOUT THE LIGHT OR BEING HIGHER-THAN, BUT ABOUT BEING LIGHTER IN HOW WE CARRY OURSELVES THROUGH OUR LIVES AND OUR CHALLENGES. A CERTAIN COURAGE, A LITTLE HUMOUR, AND THE WILLINGNESS TO DO THE WORK ON OURSELVES AND AVOID DRAMATISING THE DIFFICULTIES WE WILL ALL EXPERIENCE ARE HALLMARKS OF THE ADEPT.

Others claim that to experience challenges is due to some kind of inability to understand the 'Law of Attraction'. I would ask that regardless of the deck (or decks!) we are working with, we turn to the energy within this *Little Owlyn* card and think of the energy of the Egyptian Goddess Ma'at, just for a moment. Contemplate the qualities of grace and gratitude, of grit and generosity. This Egyptian Goddess is a being of truth, balance and ethics — most of all, of Justice. She will weigh your heart and its intent against the weight of a feather—most often depicted as an ostrich feather—and your heart must be lighter than that feather. Without this lightness of a truthful, guilt-free heart, we cannot successfully move into a new stage in our lives, nor can we progress into the afterlife. She is stable, and strong, and absolutely impartial in her justice.

I do love Ma'at. She is the spirit—the very being—of truth and justice. When we contemplate her in regard to our oracular work, she can help us be balanced and light in our approach. So, ask yourself, if you were to weigh your own soul at this time, would it be light as a feather on Ma'at's scales? What can you begin to do that will help you let go of purposeless negativity?

Thus, when we continue on this path, we begin to see how very essential it is to also do the work on ourselves. To be courageous, to be aware of our own self-talk, to consider how that self-talk impacts upon our readings, and to make adjustments when we are creating difficulty (even drama) so that we move back to a more centred, true and en-LIGHT-ened approach.

Perhaps enlightenment is not about the light or being higher-than, but about being lighter in how we carry ourselves through our lives and our challenges. A certain courage, a little humour, and the willingness to do the work on ourselves and avoid dramatising the difficulties we will all experience are hallmarks of the Adept. You have knowledge now. But the Adept must demonstrate wisdom, which is the best possible application of knowledge. Consider Ma'at, consider this, and do not make this path a burden. This is simply a suggestion, an observation and a truth I have lived. Let's walk in joy, together.

One Deck or Two?

At this stage of your work, I would ask you to consider having two decks. One with which only you work (for more enquiry, philosophising and deep mystical journeying), and another for your readings with others. That way, you would have a deck devoted to the service of others and one deck devoted to your own evolution as a spiritual, sacred, very human being.

Essential Meanings of the Cards — Do You Know Them?

At this stage, I would also encourage you have within your memory the general meaning for each card — a sense of really knowing your deck.

That is, generally speaking, about 45 meanings per deck, and you would do well to have these within you now, a part of you. More on this in the Experientials section at the end of this chapter.

What Is an Adept?

Let's talk more about what an Adept is. An Adept, I feel, is able to work with others whenever it is needed to provide the readings that are requested. An Adept rarely will require elaborate preparation or experience hesitation before readings, as the work has been done regarding the meanings and the practice is regular and natural — it has become a part of who you are. We have acquired the knowledge and integrated the information, and our light, strong approach creates Wisdom.

I would also like you to contemplate that an Adept is not a person who no longer engages in the world, who lives in separation and exclusion, or who feels they are above others or more special. This is a phenomenon I see over and over within spirituality; the sense of being more enlightened and thus better is a kind of spiritual snobbery that does not serve any of us well. We are all works in progress, and we must measure ourselves only against our own achievements and our own soul's development, not in comparison to others. Yes, we may be different — but perhaps we are people who are being readied for a role of service to humans and the energetic world. We are a part of our communities, and in some ways, we are assisting everyone to reconnect with the Divine, as we spoke of in the Initiate section of this book.

Please do not fall into the egoic trap of feeling superior. An Adept wears their wisdom lightly, shares their knowledge without pomposity, and does not interfere with the free will of others. We have power, and we are responsible for the working of that power.

Your Trial by Fire

All of us have the same amount of time with every cycle of the sun. We all have choices as to what to do with this precious gift of time we have been given. Yes, each of us has varying responsibilities and demands, and some of us may feel ours are more demanding than those of other people. More important. More oppressive. More, more, more. But the truth is, we all have the same time. We also have many choices as to how we decide to move forward. I would like you to consider that you are strong enough, ready, more than able to move through this challenge.

One of the truest things about card reading is that if we truly want to do this, we will find ways. And what I would like to offer is a challenge that will test all of us, without exception.

For many of us, we often think, "I don't have enough people to read for," or, "I am so sensitive, perhaps I will wait until I feel stronger/healthier/more grounded/happier/more settled before reading for another person." Some people even share with me that they only wish to read under 'perfect' conditions, as that will result in 'superior' readings. Others say that their commitments and the demands upon them make this task impossible. All of this powerful self-talk creates an atmosphere in which we fall away from our true potential.

There is a world of difference between acknowledging the conditions and situations that challenge us—which we all have, without exception—and allowing these challenging conditions that arise again and again in our lives to prevent us from reading and doing the work as an Oracle. Please know that I am not speaking of exceptional circumstances—a death, a breakup, an injury—but even throughout these, we can work with the energy at hand to help us be perceptive and compassionate and continue with our work.

Because, as you will recall, when we read, we step into an in-between space, and thus, it is not all about us and what our anxious and worried self tells us is taking place at that time. I would gently offer you this: We need to read. If you intend to do so as a professional, there will be challenges. You will have a less-than-ideal situation confronting you at times. Therefore, you must find a way through these — by doing the work and focusing on the cards, the task before you, and not being self-absorbed. Developing resilience and rising to the challenge is a wonderful way to develop.

READING WITH FRANKLIN,
DECEMBER 1987, LONDON

•

Franklin reiterated – I'm very psychic, have an affinity for the spiritual. I hate to feel boxed in. I need a job where I don't feel that. And a relationship needs to be the same. I want a relationship (marriage) but I have not given myself, have not relaxed. He said my cards say that I live off my nerves and must take steps to learn how to relax. Affinity for languages and music. A confusing time incoming but I must concentrate on myself and on my path – there will be a man around me who will want to influence me, but I must concentrate on my goal.

He said I must learn to finish what I start and surround myself with more spiritual people.

•

One powerful way of developing quickly is to have a kind of 'Trial by Fire'.

Firstly, you will need to be doing your regular daily readings for yourself — just simple, grounded readings, so that you keep getting to know your cards. They are immensely layered beings, and doing this will keep revealing more and more to you. Be sure to bring in the question each day and see how the question shapes the interpretation of the card. Really be sure to work with this.

I would also think that many of you are growing comfortable with reading more regularly for yourself and for friends. If not, please keep this up or recommence.

But what I want you to do now may really stretch you. (And for some of you, you may say, "YES! I am so ready for this!")

I want you to read for a lengthy period of time — perhaps a day, half a day, or an evening, with very few breaks (or at least minimal breaks), and you could do this for a cause you believe in as well as a payment. You can volunteer for a charity, organisation or a group of people you love who need assistance … really, any worthy cause you feel passionately about. Your most valuable energy exchange or payment is going to be honest feedback from the Querent.

This truly is a ritual, a trial by fire, and after you have completed this, you will know your strengths and be amazed at what you can do when you get out of your head and into the readings. It is supposed to be a test and help you break through any self-imposed limitations.

I would like to offer this challenge to you all. I will never know if you do or do not complete this task I offer, but make no mistake: it is perhaps the very best way for us to move through from the stage of the Initiate to that of the Adept. This is a personal challenge, and I am cheering you on. I do believe in you, and I know you can do this.

GUIDELINES FOR THE TRIAL BY FIRE

- Keep the price you read for reasonable — this way, you will most likely draw lots of folks to read for.
- The very best way to do this is face-to-face — if this is utterly not possible for reasons of geography, ability or other, then yes, do read online. However, I urge you to make every effort to read face-to-face. This can be done at local markets, wellness expos, mind-body-spirit festivals, psychic fairs and music and arts festivals. Or at events like renaissance fairs and historic-themed local happenings, for example, Ironfest festival in Lithgow in NSW or Winter Magic in Katoomba, also in NSW (Australia). Medieval fairs are also wonderful places to undertake this rite of initiation. If you find out about these gatherings well ahead of time, you can prepare a table, a cloth, and some ways of setting up your space that make you feel magickal and ready to read.
- Know that with this task, you are entering into a liminal space with your own journey as a reader. It's a transition.
- You will be reading continually, except for sensible small breaks for some food or water and going to the bathroom. We want this to be person after person after person.
- You need to read so much that you stop your mind from being predominantly occupied with the concerns many Initiates have mentioned to me through the years: "I feel blocked. I worry I will not be accurate. What if I give incorrect information? What if a person reacts negatively?" This all falls away as you focus on the cards, the person, and what flows between you all.

THE MAGIC OF THIS CHALLENGE

WHEN WE DO THIS—READ, ONE AFTER ANOTHER AFTER ANOTHER—SOMETHING wonderful can happen. Our inner critic is too occupied with doing the important and sacred work at hand, and we simply begin to fall into the readings. There is no time to fret, worry or second-guess. Instead, we focus, we read and deliver, we thank and farewell, and then we read again, over and over.

When we read for strangers, we do not have that sense of familiarity, and thus, we are not colouring many of our words based upon what we know of their experience, nor do we have to worry about relationships we already have with the Seeker. The dynamics are very clean. When we read in this way, too, we begin to trust the process and stop feeling like we are at the centre of the reading due to a (completely understandable) self-consciousness. We simply read, move through, deliver, and move on. Our minds do not have the opportunity to step in and sabotage us.

When we read for many people, we will learn how to pay attention to the people we read for. We can incorporate a beautiful spiritual practice of the Indigenous people of Australia, sometimes called Dadirri, which is a deep, healing listening, a kind of respectful space we can create for the person we read for and with. When they speak and ask the question, we listen and give respect. Of course, we do not remain silent during the reading — we speak and offer insights.

We can take this moment of Dadirri into our practice, and contemplate further that being an Oracle has much to do with being unafraid of listening to the vast, open, fierce truth of the natural world. We can wait for messages even while we speak the messages we have already received, without burdening the Querent with our waiting. We flow, and move, and listen to the cards, listening with our eyes and with all of our senses, allowing the messages to come through to us. All the while, being observant, calm, respectful, patient and still within.

CHALLENGES CAN LEAD TO BREAKTHROUGHS

- You learn to stop pushing for results and do not get attached to being 'right'.
- You deliver the information with compassion and care but do it without guilt and fretting.
- If challenging messages come through, you deliver them without feeling like you are the cause of those challenges. You are not. You are the messenger, not the creator of another person's fate (although you are engaging with the person's fate when you read for them). Listen to them, respect them and observe on their behalf.
- You will get very clear and professional about the process you have — the way you explain what you do, ask the Querent to shuffle and cut, then lay out the cards.
- You will learn how to move through the cards in the time given.

- You will get much, much better at the overall reading, developing a smooth beginning, middle and end point, which also helps you to not go over time.
- You will begin to see which questions suit which layouts.
- You will be able to introduce some spontaneity and in-the-moment decision-making rather than worrying or fretting.
- You will learn how to bring a reading to a close, especially if the Querent is emotional, troubled, or if their energy is negative or clingy.
- You will have a much better idea of how you personally travel and where your strengths and weaknesses are.
- You will have more confidence and buoyancy and will build resilience, which we all need in conjunction with our sensitivity.
- If you feel you experience blocks, or wonder how to move forward, this Trial by Fire will absolutely help you break through this. Believe me, telling yourself over and over that you're blocked will only serve to strengthen the block you say you do not want to experience. Instead, choose to break through!

Experientials and Experimentals

- Think of a clean, clear way to describe what you do for people in one sentence. Practise saying this to yourself now as a mantra or affirmation or spell — a prayer that will see you finding your way into the reading in no time at all.
- Write up a three-line description of your practice — almost a brief description that you could place on a business card or website or that you could say in person. It needs to be true to you and clear, yet somehow convey the sacred nature of what it is that you do.
- Take steps to organise this Trial by Fire (the day of reading). Think of the details, how you will present yourself and the stand, how people will pay, what you will charge, and who you will offer the money to.
- Your memory of the meanings. It is an absolute given at this time that you have memorised the essence of the 43–47 cards within your chosen deck. I do not mean word-for-word from the guidebook, but that you've gained enough experience with the cards to read smoothly and freely without needing to consult with the guidebook. You have a reliable inner library of the meanings to draw upon.

  If not, please make a commitment to work on this. This is the foundation of our work. Make notes, write out the meanings, and really commit these to memory. Test yourself, challenge yourself, and read over your card notes from the first part of this book. Without this foundation, you can come unstuck during readings — especially when we work in stressful environments, with challenging people, or within our own personal obstacles. With these meanings committed to memory, we have stability and energy to flow forth from.

Difficult Cards — An Experiential and an Experiment

Find a card within one of your decks that you find puzzling or a little challenging — do some practice timed readings with it. Don't stare at the card or force the energy of it. Experiment and play, and go back to some of what we spoke of in Part One of this book. Imagine that the being in the message of the card was talking to you directly and giving you information. Dance with the card. Sleep with the card. And commit the meaning to your memory!

Let's have a look together at some of the cards that have provided some puzzlement — they'll begin to appear here and in following chapters. For some people, these cards can seem abstract. For others, they are too precise. For all of us, different cards will feel obtuse, make us feel uneasy, or feel like they are a code that we just cannot break. This is no failure at all on your behalf — it is a very natural part of the process and will be a familiar part of most Oracle card readers' experience. We resonate more with some forms of imagery, symbolism and the power of the word than with others.

In order to fruitfully explore these cards, we need to be light in our approach and find this enquiry interesting rather than intimidating.

One of the cards that many people have mentioned to me as challenging is the card from the *Oracle of the Mermaids* titled *Conchomancy.*

A lot of folk may find this card a struggle because they are not familiar with the term 'conchomancy'. Let's begin there. Conchomancy is divination through working with the seashells and their profound, oceanic magick. Just as crystals hold energies and messages for us, so too do these beautiful living homes and structures of the sea creatures. Each creature resonates with a particular energy, and by connecting with their shell—holding it, feeling its qualities and understanding its connections—we can begin to heal a part of ourselves. And these messages and healings from the natural world are beautiful, healthful and freely available to us all!

Low tide is the most wonderful—and practical—time to search for shells, but a low tide on a new moon will take the waterline even further out, leaving even more of her treasures available for viewing, respectful collecting and admiration.

So, let's see how we can work with this beautiful 'problem child'. (By the way, even if you are not working with the *Oracle of the Mermaids*, reading through this section will be helpful for you, so do not skip this bit!)

So, this is a card about the pure magicks of the sea. Yes, it is about a system of divination and magick that is sea-based … but if we think of it further, as we discussed in the forum, it is about the pure energies of the smallest of creatures. It is about that oceanic energy being of benefit to us, listening to it, and supporting its health.

Because we are primarily oceanic—our blood is akin to salt water, and our wombs hold salty liquid in which we all grow—conchomancy is also about being able to feel the messages of the oceans in small and sensitive ways from within. Guidance can be small, subtle, delicate as shells, but it is there for us if we simply make the space to listen, observe, feel and be fluid …

Consider, too, that the question itself will give us a lot of context in which to interpret the card. When I see this card, the question of the Querent gives me a lot of ambience and environment in which I can offer suggestions. So, for example, if it was in the distant-past position in a Celtic Cross spread, and a person said they wanted to know about career direction, for example, I could glean from this card that they had always wanted to be involved with the sea, and study of the sea and its creatures. That they were attracted to the hidden, too — as shells are often revealed at low tide, so they had an ability to detect what was often hidden and unnoticed. That is just ONE possibility in terms of interpretation. Just one. If a person was asking about their love life, and it appeared in the present position, depending on the other cards and the energy of the Querent, I would suggest that they might find the energy of the sea and its creatures to be very supportive of their love — so, perhaps long walks at low tide, observation of the small, forgotten and fragile moments within their relationships, and plenty of salt-water swims/and or baths.

Of course, use this principle regardless of the card you find challenging — research, wonder, learn, discover and integrate! None of this is ever wasted.

Symbology of a Card Deconstructed—Artemis of the Forest

Let's talk about the symbology within a card and the varying ways in which it can be read. The best way in which to do this is to deconstruct or take apart, piece by piece, the card's imagery. Below you'll find an example of how you might wish to go about this. It can be a fascinating exercise, one full of revelations and discoveries. You'll see it's a series of prompts rather than "facts" — so, by doing the same for yourself, you'll happen upon previously unseen, or even misunderstood, aspects of the card and its message. I'd love you to work with these examples and fill in more detail — jot down any impressions you receive in your Book of Shadows and Light. This simple exercise will light your sixth sense up, help you develop a greater repertoire to draw upon, and help you to trust your own instincts and intuitions.

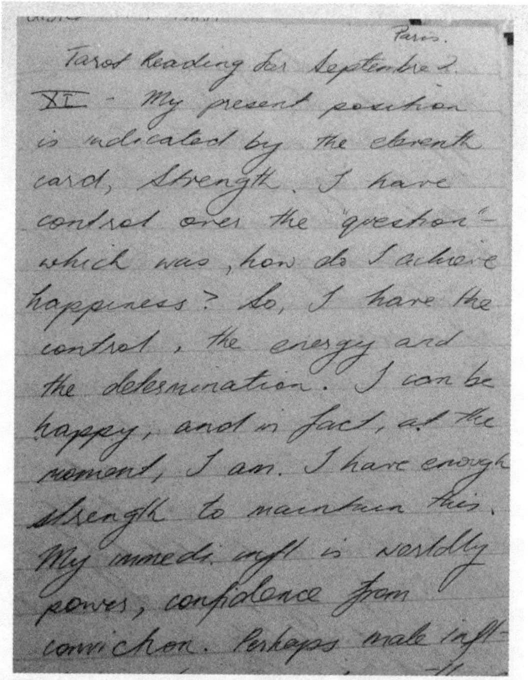

Paris.

Tarot Reading for September 2.

XI - My present position is indicated by the eleventh card, Strength. I have control over the "question" - which was, how do I achieve happiness? So, I have the control, the energy and the determination. I can be happy, and in fact, at the moment, I am. I have enough strength to maintain this. My immedi. infl is worldly powers, confidence from conviction. Perhaps male infl-

These yellowed old pages from my Book of Shadows and Light are filled with my writings from my 25-year-old self, and I treasure every page. With them, I revisit the passion and wonder of my first readings, and to this day, I am awe-struck at their accuracy and innocence.

Card: *Artemis of the Forest*

Now you are independent and free
Oracle of the Shapeshifters

ARTEMIS: Who is she? What is her energy? Is she a Goddess you feel familiar with? If not, explore her story and wonder how this may relate to a question.

CRESCENT MOON HEADDRESS: How would you read this? What does this crescent moon represent? What difference does it make, being a headdress, rather than a necklace or pendant or bracelet or earrings? Does this perhaps connect to a chakra, such as the third eye?

THE STAG: What could the stag represent? Is it mature? It has fine antlers, a strong gaze, a noble presence — all these aspects, including colour and appearance in the background or foreground, add to the meaning. What are the visual messages in the card conveying? Why is the stag here in this image? What does its presence add? How would the image be different, or what meaning would be lost without the stag being present?

THE FEMALE DEER: What is her part in this card — what does she symbolise to you? Is she gentle or proud? Is she strong or weakened? Is she to the left or right or behind the figure of Artemis? What is her relationship to Artemis? What is her relationship to the stag? Really notice the detail, as these small symbolisms will all enrich your readings.

ARTEMIS UNCLOTHED: What does her nakedness represent? How does she seem to feel, being naked? What is revealed, and what is hidden? What does nakedness mean to you or to the person you are reading for? Does being naked represent something other than being unclothed? Could it represent innocence, or being vulnerable, or being unafraid, or beyond conditioning and shame? Could it be symbolic of a kind of authenticity and truthfulness? No answer is right or wrong; all you need to do is really play with the ideas represented in visual form.

FINGERS OF THE RIGHT HAND: The figure of Artemis — take a look at her right hand. The pointer and the thumb are looped and closed … what could this convey? Is it a kind of sign language? Is it a mudra entering into the image? To me, it looks like the yoga mudra—hand gesture and position—that increases focus, awareness and psychic knowledge. Again, none of these prompts are necessarily the ones that will come to mind in the reading, but exploring their possibilities will provide you with a rich treasure chest of meaning at the ready to come to you during a session with yourself or with a client. (Once, this gesture sprang out at me in a reading, demanding I notice it, telling me it was of significance in the reading. I said to the Seeker that, for some reason, using the hands and the body to speak was significant. As it turned out, the person I was reading for was learning Auslan, the sign language used for and by the majority of the deaf community in Australia, and they were wondering whether to continue. My point is, don't pigeonhole the meanings — just think of them as possibilities to draw from.)

LIGHT: Notice the quality of the light in the card. What is the source of the light? What time of day could it be? Does the light seem bright and hopeful, or does it seem ominous or dark? Remember that how this expresses itself can shift from reading to reading, as the cards are in some way alive, and how they seem one day may change the next, due to the energy of the reading and the situation they are relating to.

BLUE ROBE: What could be the significance of the colour blue? What is the difference between this kind of blue, and a turquoise, sky blue, or duck-egg blue? What does the tone convey? Why would this colour have significance? Is there a chakra, energy centre, deity or angel that is associated with this colour? Why would it be appearing here with Artemis? Blue is sometimes associated with optimism, openness, royalty, cheerfulness, and an open-hearted nobility. It is also connected with strong communication skills. All of this does NOT have to be conveyed when you are reading for another — the card will 'show' you what is meant to be read during the session, and the layout and the surrounding cards will all assist in creating meaning.

THE CARD NUMBER: What could this signify? What are the various ways of interpreting this number? How could this number relate to timing, if it was in the past or in the future position of a three-card spread?

Now, find a card within the deck you are working with that you'd like to deconstruct in this way. Make a list of the symbols that appear within the artwork and go further into these. Be curious and ask lots of questions.

Timing and the Cards

You've just looked into the card above, *Artemis of the Forest*, and investigated its number.

Now, let's imagine we are doing a three-card reading, and this card is in the past position. How long ago do you think we could say the event took place, given the number of the card and the visual evidence of the card?

Have a practice with this, using a question and a one-card reading, or a three-card reading, and begin to see how you can put timing together. This is an experiment, so see how you go and what you get, and we will explore this further!

THE YUIN ELDER AND THE GREAT WAVE PROPHECY

Oracles, and their portents of the future and how it may unfold, come from every culture across this blue and green planet. Here is a recent prophecy, made from Guboo Ted Thomas, Initiated Elder of the Yuin People, NSW, Australia. It helped to inspire the film, *The Last Wave*, made by Peter Weir and released in 1977 ...

I was in Dreamtime.
I see this great wave going.
I tell people about this wave.
It wasn't a tidal wave.
This was a spiritual wave.
So, to me, I believe that the Dreamtime is going to be that.
I believe the revival is going to start in Australia when we're Dreaming.
It's the humming bee that I'm talking about.
And love.
We've got to learn to love one another.
You see, that's really what's going to happen to the earth.
We're going to have tidal waves.
We're going to have earthquakes.
That's coming because we don't consider this land as our Mother.

We've taken away the balance, and we're not putting back.
I look at the bush, and those trees are alive.
They're not dead, they're alive.
And they want you to cuddle them.

Well, this has been quite a long chapter, so I will leave you to digest all of this for now. Remember, you have so much wisdom within you. Let's all make a pact with ourselves to allow ourselves to be light as a feather and shine out.

In that way, we begin to walk the path of the Adept.

Yours, in the spirit of oracular love and magick.

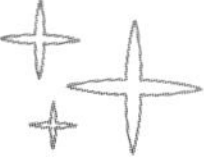

Photo © Leonie Dawson

I'd always loved speaking with people about our depths, but the cards allowed me to take that a step further. They gave me the joy of connection, of really seeing people, soul-to-soul, delicious and life-affirming.

Chapter Eight

A Secret Language

We have this language of the omens, the language of the signs. It is an alphabet that is directed to us. If we do not fear to commit mistakes, and if we take the language as a help to cross that particular day, then we start to get deeper and deeper into the soul of the world …

— Paulo Coelho

Dear Adept,

Powerful, magickal and infinite, sacred symbols and signs empower all our work as Oracles. From the Celtic to the Nordic, to the Wiccan and the Hermetic, they are imbued into our cards and worn by the people who seek the guidance of the cards, and they come to us intuitively amidst the reading. They may visit you in meditation, trance, even dreams ... at other times, they will reach you in the most ordinary of ways: A billboard with a triquetra, a truck with a Pegasus, a giant carousel wheel in a major city in the shape of a seven-pointed star.

These sacred symbols and 'secret' signs reveal how spirit is speaking to us ... which deities we may be communicating with, which past lives we may be linking with, and which magickal principles have the most to teach us. Within a reading, understanding what symbol we are seeing with a Querent, or which numbers occur again and again within their cards, or why their reading predominantly features certain colours will help us all give deeper, more nuanced and layered readings. They can assist us with timing and the influences about that person at that time.

THESE SACRED SYMBOLS AND 'SECRET' SIGNS REVEAL HOW SPIRIT IS SPEAKING TO US ... WHICH DEITIES WE MAY BE COMMUNICATING WITH, WHICH PAST LIVES WE MAY BE LINKING WITH, AND WHICH MAGICKAL PRINCIPLES HAVE THE MOST TO TEACH US. WITHIN A READING, UNDERSTANDING WHAT SYMBOL WE ARE SEEING WITH A QUERENT, OR WHICH NUMBERS OCCUR AGAIN AND AGAIN WITHIN THEIR CARDS, OR WHY THEIR READING PREDOMINANTLY FEATURES CERTAIN COLOURS WILL HELP US ALL GIVE DEEPER, MORE NUANCED AND LAYERED READINGS.

But we need to be able to read them!

So, in this chapter, we are going to work through a lot of symbols. If you dedicate yourself to the joy of understanding symbols, you will soon be very comfortable with them and, more importantly, at ease when sharing their significance during a reading.

It is helpful to become literate in symbols — to have a wonderful understanding of this language of the soul, a sense of how symbols are constructed, and to explore what that could mean, too. It's important for us to be open-minded and balanced in approaching this subject, as there is a great deal of fearful misinterpretation, appropriation and mistrust of symbols within our cultures. If we buy into this, it will taint the way in which we can 'see' the message shared with us in the context of the cards. Let's come to know the associations and work with the symbols, this universal language, in the context in which they are given.

There is always more to learn, to share and to understand, so when you begin to work with these symbols deliberately, this will greatly enrich not only your readings but also your knowledge and ultimately, your wisdom.

But let's take it further! It would be wonderful for you to draw them in your Book of Shadows and Light while working through their meanings. Doing that will teach you more than simply gazing at them. You will then understand how they are composed, and really begin to feel them. You can meditate with a symbol as your focus. And you can take this further and *embody* a symbol. I'll guide you on how to do this later. I highly recommend it as an unparalleled way to connect with the energy of the symbol.

The Foundations of the Elemental Symbols

Let's begin to work through the symbols together.

FIRE

An upward equilateral triangle: Fire is also represented by literal fire, red tones, and warmth. Sometimes, the triangle is not equilateral. But it points up and is universally recognised.

WATER

An equilateral triangle pointing down: Of course, the element water is also represented by water. Remember in Part I: The Initiate, we spoke a lot about the elements — if that symbol for water is present within a card or a vision you may experience, what could that symbolise? Why is it important? Ask; keep enquiring. Your soul and the Universe will offer you the answers.

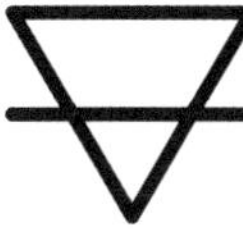

EARTH

A downward-pointing equilateral triangle with a horizontal line running through its top third or sometimes through its base: What else would earth be represented by? Perhaps crystals, Earth itself, roots of trees, stones, soil, seeds … what are earth's qualities? How would you represent these characteristics?

AIR

An upward-facing equilateral triangle with a horizontal line through its top third or through its base: Over to you, dear Adept. Where have you seen this symbol? What else would represent air? What does seeing air in a card mean within a reading?

Begin to look for these simple symbols. Think of how they are often present in very subtle ways — not only within cards but also within nature or the signs and symbols all about us in our everyday lives.

Let's move now to more complex symbols, that, in some ways, could be viewed as being formed by these four elements.

SEPTEMBER 1987, LONDON

•

I breathed, "Oh My God," when I saw the final card — the Star. My favourite! The Most beautiful! Good Omen! Change! To achieve what I have been longing for — a mix of the past and the present that can create hope, faith and optimism.

•

The Star

LET'S EXPERIMENT AND VISUALISE MOVING THESE SYMBOLS AROUND AND INTO relationship with each other. If we begin to merge these symbols, you'll see that we can create symbols you are already very familiar with, like a six-pointed star.

THE SIX-POINTED STAR: Sometimes called the Star of David. But it is also known as an alchemical symbol of the transmutation of elements. Or, a hexagram. Or, the Seal of Solomon.

Clearly, it contains the symbol for air, pointing up, and earth, pointing below. What if we look at this more closely and consider the words, 'As Above, So Below' ... or, air and earth. Spirit and the body.

There are other ways of working with this symbol, seeing the other shapes that appear within it. But just know its (various) names for now and contemplate its meaning.

Let's develop that symbol a little further … let's take the hexagram and imagine it is three-dimensional. Now, we have a new symbol.

THE MERKABA: This is said to be the shape or form the human light body takes on when fully developed. Personally, I do not resonate with this view of a fixed pattern or symbol being the one possible expression of a fully developed light body. Although I have seen this shape, I think interpretation is very subjective and open to question. Our light body shifts and changes, and I do not see the symbols as being hierarchical. (But my view differs from many in the New Age world on this matter.) I simply include this here for your knowledge and for you to contemplate.

THE FIVE-POINTED STAR: Pythagoras demonstrated sacred geometry and the golden mean with the pentagram, which, when surrounded by a circle, is called the pentacle. Many feel that each of the five points represents one of the elements: earth, air, fire, water and spirit, sometimes called ether. It also resembles a human, with arms and legs outstretched. You may wish to practise embodying this symbol: just as we danced the cards, this practice of becoming for a time the physical expression of their geometry can be very insightful and wondrous to work with.

THE PENTACLE MEDITATION

This is a moving meditation. What you will need is a comfortable space, a little privacy, a yoga mat, and these words.

To make this a flowing experience, you could record these words for yourself and play them back as you work with this exercise. Or, you could listen to the recording I've made for you via the QR code here:

Or, you could take turns with a friend, each of you reading and guiding the other through the meditation journey into the pentacle.

Put on some comfortable clothing and be prepared to sink deeply into this experience. Throughout, we will explore symbols by integrating their energies and meanings within our bodies, our auric fields and our energy.

Get comfortable, and take a seat. Let's do the Three Breaths now.

Take a very deep breath in — ahhh, and let it go — ahhh.

Another very deep breath in, and let that go.

And a third, very deep, slow breath in. And let it go. Ahhh.

Now as you continue breathing, I would love you to imagine that your every breath is some kind of delicious elixir that you are breathing in, very gently, with a true sense of gratitude. As you release it, you release out your gift to the world, to the trees, to be transmuted into whatever energies the world most needs right now. Breathing in a gift, releasing out your gift to the world. Keep breathing.

Now, please get to your feet, and place them about hip-width apart. Let your arms become very loose and relaxed. Imagine now that there is a string of light running from above your crown, right down throughout your spine, exiting your body at the base chakra and connecting deep into the earth, very gently. Feel yourself being lifted up by this light at your crown, yet anchored into the earth from the light's connection into the depths of Mother Earth.

Distribute your weight throughout your feet — really feel the heaviness of your physical body moving till it's spread through your heels, the balls of your feet, your toes. You are really planted.

Now, allow your hand to open, and start to feel this energy vibrating throughout you. Begin to sense this line of light, the principle energy, grow and extend into a column of light which you are standing fully within. This energy, this light, this sense of the very particles of the Universe itself are being offered to you, nourishing you. They are all around you, and they are vibrating right through you, right down to your cells, flooding them with this light, till it shimmers out of your physical body.

Keep breathing.

Feel this connection.

Keep breathing.

Now, take your legs out a little wider, heel-toe them out, and float your arms up until they reach shoulder height. Then stretch them back a little, opening your heart right up. Shut your eyes down, and fully enter into this shape. You have now become the standing five-pointed star. Really feel that strength within your legs, the openness of your heart, the extension of your arms, and the lift of the crown of your head.

Then, I want you to see the energy beginning to run from your left foot in a line of light that reaches right up to your crown. Then see it extend as it descends to your right foot.

From there, it shoots through to your left arm, to the very top of your extended right arm, and from there, it will pour back in a line of luminosity to your left foot once again. These living lines of light have also formed the shape of a star, pure energy running through you in that sacred shape.

You have become the star, the five points of which are earth, air, fire, water and spirit. I want you to truly feel that, and feel that energy and the elements move around this shape your body has made. Really deeply feel what it is for you to embody the star.

Soak up this feeling.

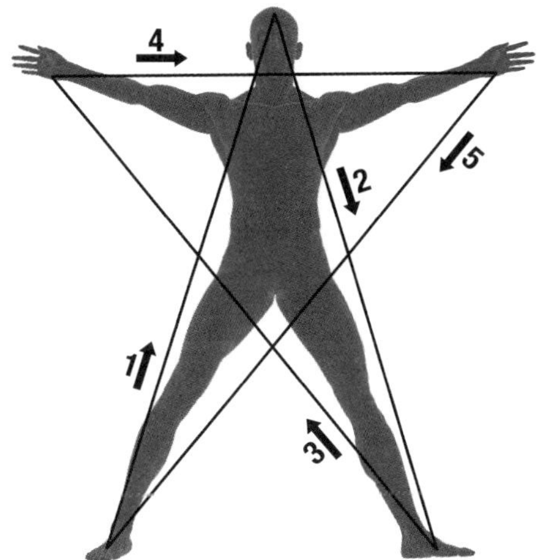

When you are ready, very gently let your arms float back down, and heel-toe your feet back into position beneath your hips.

You will now do the Three Breaths, and as you do, you will return to yourself, but the star will continue to move through you as long as you wish.

Take a deep breath in and let it go.

Take a deep breath in and let it go.

Take a deep breath in and let it go.

Slowly come down to the mat, and lie down. Sink into the mat. Rub your hands together strongly, and place one hand on your heart, and feel that self-love, that lifeforce entering your body.

Breathe deeply in, and out.

And again — in and out.

And again — in and out.

With every breath, come back to the place you began, and become more and more yourself again.

Come up to a sitting position. If you feel light-headed, take your forehead to the mat, or stretch out in child's position, and really feel yourself reconnecting with the earthly, everyday world.

Now though, something has changed. You have found the symbol within you, and experienced its energy. Because of that, you can extend that energy out when you encounter these symbols in your readings. You can share from a deeper place. An embodied, ensouled place birthed from experience.

You are created in a symbolic shape yourself — you are sacred; you are blessed; you are divine.

This meditation is complete. Please make some notes about this experience within your Book of Shadows and Light or your magickal readings journal.

Be blessed. And know you are very, very loved.

Back to the five-pointed star. What do you feel about this star? Where have you seen it used? Have you ever seen it interpreted differently? What do you think fuels these different interpretations? Is there a fixed definition, truths about it (or any symbol) that cannot be denied? Where does this symbol occur in nature?

THE SEVEN-POINTED STAR: Seven-pointed stars form a faery body — two arms, two legs, one head, two wings! And the centre — well, that creates a faery portal through which the energies can move from one realm to another.

THE EIGHT-POINTED STAR: This star is associated with the ancients and with the Goddess Inanna, the Goddess Ishtar and the Goddess Venus. It represents the Galactic and Gaian energies emerging from and returning to the Sun, as they do with the Wheel of the Year and its eight festivals.

The Circle

MAGICKAL WHEN CAST, ALWAYS PROFOUND, THE CIRCLE REPRESENTS THE Infinite, a world between worlds, akin to zero, the place or space of infinite possibility, protection, magick, the womb, the egg and sacred magick.

We could combine two symbols, like the circle and the eight-pointed star, and create the wheel of the year with its Gaian and Galactic energy points. Or, combine the five-pointed star, the pentagram, to create a pentacle.

We cast circles when practising many forms of magick, and in the First Peoples' traditions of the Americas, they developed the Medicine Wheel — a circle showing the four great directions within its boundaries. This great circle was often built into the landscape as a site of respect, ritual and reverence.

OUROBOROS: The age-old symbol of the snake, serpent or dragon devouring itself, looped into a timeless cycle of birth, death and rebirth, represents continuity, the cycle of life and the infinite nature of existence in one form or another. It appears in ancient cultures and philosophies—from the Egyptian to the Greek, to the Norse and the Gnostics—and has inspired paintings, music and architecture.

VESICA PISCIS: The overlapping of the worlds demonstrated. With this symbol, we observe two circles intersecting right in each other's centre. This represents the merging of two worlds: the central position is a place where two worlds meet, where opposites can reconcile, where understanding can be reached, where peace is held, where what is in unison is valued and held precious. I find it a very powerful symbol to work with when conflict is arising, and I find it a valuable ally in partnerships of all kinds.

YINYANG: Is more than simply the eastern symbol of masculine/feminine balance — it is also a complex and mathematically precise diagram of the cycle of the Sun. It is light and dark, the interchangeability of tastes of sweet and sour, hot and cold, the balance of ourselves through opposites — and opposition. Thus, through challenge, we become who we are.

LABYRINTH: Designed to take us deeper into ourselves — profoundly spiritual. For me, the labyrinth can be danced or paced out until one world falls away and the Otherworld rises up before us. As I move into the centre, I let go. When I reach the centre, a gift is given as I spiral or move back out; that gift is integrated into my own self. Labyrinths can be walked with deep solemnity or with chaotic abandon and joy. They have taught me to trust in placing one foot in front of the other until I come to the centre, the very heart of whatever it is I am seeking to understand. Labyrinths can also be worked with to meditate upon a subject, to commune with others, to offer respect as we walk in this sacred pattern.

MAZE: A puzzle, and thus an activity of logic ... a problem to be solved, rather than a knowing, a deepening, an experience, which the labyrinth offers us. Mazes are wonderful at 'trapping' things, so they can often be worked with to restrict or trap ill-intent or malicious energies or misfortune, particularly in folk magick.

SIGIL OF AMETH: Ameth is Hebrew for truth. This highly complex sigil was popularised in magic by the Elizabethan magician, Dr John Dee (who also recognised Glastonbury as a place of healing, and its well as abundant with healing waters). Within this complex symbol of truth are the names of Angels, secret names of God, and codes for the secret language of Angels. If you gaze at the outer corners of the symbol, you'll see those names inscribed. The renowned Kabbalist, Athanasius Kircher, is said to have been the first to channel this esoteric treasure.

One of my favourite places in this world is Cornwall, a land of raw, fierce beauty and energy fresh as sea spray. This shot is from the rock faces of Tintagel, upon which are carved these ancient labyrinths, some say over two thousand years old. Their energy? Wise, pure joy.

The Dance Within, the Dance Without —

Exploring the Spiral

The spiral is an ancient symbol of evolving consciousness and the search for wisdom. It is symbolic for many of the circular (rather than linear) paths of women's knowledge and of the Goddess. Spiral labyrinths are walked across cultures as diverse as the Tibetan and the neo-Celtic …

THE SPIRAL: The spiral is a fundamental shape in all things of this world — and of others! From the nautilus to the Pleiades, the spiral forms the basis of the shape of life. When used ritually, it can also represent the journey inwards, followed by the journey out ... followed again by a journey within an infinite dance. There are spiral galaxies, so when you see this shape, depending on the context, you could contemplate whether it reveals more of your home in the galactic web of life.

INFINITY: Taking the spiral further, we have the symbol of infinity. Adopted by mathematicians to represent the infinite nature of numbers, the symbol itself predates this usage. Magickally, it denotes our lives upon lives, that all is connected, and that energy never dies but is simply recreated. Infinity is two perfectly looped magical circles that are never-ending. It reminds us that we are infinite, as is our energy, and therefore to be mindful of that which we create because it—like us—is eternal.

TRIQUETRA: This symbol is of three in one and has many meanings. It is often used to represent the triad of Maiden, Mother and Crone; birth, death and rebirth; the simultaneous triple world of the Celts; and was popularised by the television show *Charmed*, to symbolise the power of three, the three sister-witches or Charmed Ones of the title.

TRISKELE: The number three is shown in a symbol, but this time, the three lines, curved and in their own spiralling expression, represent movement, the simultaneous existence of the three worlds, and the movement that exists, eternally — all is energy, moving, vibrating. This symbol is also a beautiful symbol to draw and meditate upon when we are initiating, evolving and completing a stage of our lives ... All is interwoven.

Some Linear Symbols

We have already seen the lines within the elemental symbols, but there are other symbols that are created through the use of lines …

AWEN: The three rays represent the breath of inspiration from the Divine — three wizards or witches leaning into each other to share wisdom? Three candles burning brightly? Three drops from the cauldron of Cerridwen. Three rays of light from the Star, the Sun …

THE CROSS: Two lines overlapping create a cross and there are many ways of interpreting this symbol. The four directions are within this symbol, and thus, it has an association in sacred geometry with the circle. From a solar cross and its acknowledgement of the rays of the sun, we have a series of crosses or cross-like symbols that share simple, common elements. For example, we have Thor's hammer, a Northern symbol of protection, which in the Middle Ages was converted to the Wolf's cross — a syncretic symbol interweaving Christian and Viking influences.

THE ANKH: The Egyptian symbol of Eternal Life, a stylised cross topped with a circle. The origin of this potent symbol is the actual hieroglyphic sign for Life, and is also used for magickal protection.

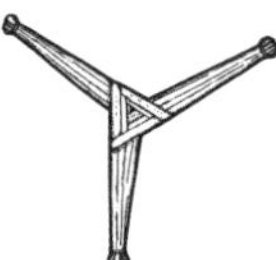

BRIGID'S CROSS: The solar cross of the Irish Goddess of Fire, Sword and Sacred Places, Brigid, is woven from straw or reed, also representing the witches besom, or broom, joined together as we fly to all four corners, yet linked in the centre by Spirit, or Goddess. From her, we all spring; to her, we return.

CADUCEUS: This ancient symbol of the God Hermes represents the marriage of the earthly and the celestial, as the twin serpents twine about a wand that is winged. Hermes, the Greek God of communication and magic, is the father of Hermetic magic and transformation and is involved with both the magickal arts of the earth and of the spheres, or the planets, as we now know them. This symbol is also the spinal column and the double helix of DNA, our angelic self, our earthly self, and overall symbolises a holistic, magical view of who we are as beings.

Into the Natural World:

Organic Symbols

TREES: The Tree of Life is a universal symbol found in practically all cultures and magical traditions. In Druidic lore, it relates to the worship of trees; in the Asatru or Nordic tradition to the World Tree (upon which Odin hung for ten days and nights to become wise); and in the Kabbalistic tradition, it represents the 22 pathways to wisdom via the 10 spheres (or numbers, in the Pythagorean tradition).

THE GREEN MAN: The Green Man, a masculine face emerging from forest foliage, at one with nature, represents humanity's coexistence with the things of this earth. The lifeforce is apparent in the buds and leaves bursting from the green man's visage; his expression varies from ecstatic to astounded, as does ours when we realise that which we share with all other beings that seek the light. The Green Man is represented heavily in Celtic magickal traditions, but is also found in India, and has his counterparts in the Pacific. We are not simply human — we are of the very earth and the things that grow, die and are reborn upon it. The Green Man is often called upon during Beltane. He is found in Christian churches across Britain and, despite mass defacings, lives on in the hearts of pagans worldwide.

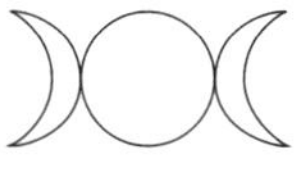

TRIPLE GODDESS: The Maiden aspect, Mother aspect and Crone aspect of the Goddess are most often represented by this symbol, which also embraces the threefold aspect of lunar phases.

OGHAM: The Celtic alphabet of trees, reconstructed by Robert Graves in *The White Goddess*, and found in many Pictish and Celtic stones. Often assumed to be runes, each Ogham or letter consists of a stroke or groups of strokes that represent a tree and its secret magick, healing powers and sacred usage.

RUNES: Nordic symbolic divination wisdom system consisting of strikingly bare, pictorial graphics — some runes continue their life in popular culture today, as in the rune associated with Tyr, used as the basis of the peace sign, and again symbolising Odin's getting of wisdom by hanging upside down on the World Tree. Through gaining wisdom, therefore, peace may come.

OM: Is the beautiful Sanskrit symbol of The Absolute, of the divine principle manifest. It occurs most often in the uttering of the word 'om', the divine sound through which we can come to know our divinity.

AND HOW IT CAN INFLUENCE YOUR ORACLE CARD READINGS

COLOUR HAS POWER — IT IS THE SOURCE. LIGHT CREATES COLOUR, AND ITS different wavelengths stimulate energetic responses within your body and etheric self. Each of your seven energy centres, your chakras, vibrates at a different frequency, and colour therapy can help them maintain balance and health.

You have innate, intuitive abilities to recognise the colours you need, and so do your Querents and Seekers. If they choose their deck, they also choose the tones and the colours within them. Within the reading, the cards that are chosen by the Seeker (in unison with the Universe, on their behalf) will be perfect for their own Oracle card reading. You will become their interpreter.

Simply by gazing at a colour and visualising it, you reconnect with yourself at a very deep level. Each Oracle card is embedded with the intrinsic energy of colour, which you activate simply by working with your cards. Thus, handling them (and reading for yourself and others) is an innately healing, revealing, oracular experience on many levels.

Note the colours within your Oracle card deck and pay attention to the sorts of colours that occur in the spread. Colour is very deliberately there for you to read. Even if it is subliminally informing the reading, the colours will offer their energy and send you their messages. On a personal level, you may find that some of the cards you are most drawn to have hues that have a particular quality.

Please note that the colour and cards you feel the most affection for or attraction to and resonance with will often change over time, reflecting your changing energies and shifting circumstances and, of course, your own personal journey in this lifetime.

Here are some very broad guidelines to colour within your cards:

PINK has the same vibration as divine love, but its many hues have many different subtleties of vibrational energy.

RED empowers you to embrace your power fearlessly, and again, has many different energies depending on its tones, intensity and depth. True red, the red of newly ripened cherries, has a very different vibe to a deep, rich scarlet. Nature will help you feel the energy of the colours.

BLUE enables you to have faith in yourself and speak your truth gently and fearlessly. It is optimistic, uplifting and truthful.

BLACK is the all-colour — it is the colour of change, learning and progression. You are creating your own truth. It is the 'uncolour' or darkness, of depth, of absorption, of the womb, the tomb, the deep earth. It always has nuance and depth and many tones within it.

BROWN grounds you, protects you and helps you trust your own discernment. It helps you identify with all of the earth's creatures and connects you to healing animals. It is a transmuting tone where change can take place. It is grounded and warm, but again, always contemplate the tones.

ORANGE stimulates your own talents, brings joy to relationships and creates an aura of positivity. It radiates cheer and stimulates conversation, gatherings and connection. It is a 'feeling' colour.

YELLOW is a fascinating colour. It can be both energising and uplifting, yet it can also be overstimulating and distracting. If used wisely, sunny yellow can raise your spirits, direct and draw attention, and increase focus. It can be a wonderful colour for those who are studying, who need good cheer, and who wish to enhance their sphere of influence.

TURQUOISE co-creates vitality in your physical and etheric bodies and can support and maintain a strong immune system. It helps us to speak, to share, to maintain loving kindness when we have difficult things to say, and to connect to the sacred within our words.

GREEN is for health, vitality, rapid growth and natural source connections. You may need to get outside more and find a way to bring the love of the woods and the green world into your life, into your everyday moments. It is a healing, loving tone that helps us to emotionally connect.

VIOLET is for your spirituality and for connecting with your higher self. It is a hue that transforms us from a being of the physical world into a being who is of the world of spirit. It is essential when working with this tone to ground, to eat well, and to not 'fly away'. It can make us feel very peaceful, very happy, but it can also lead to disconnect if we do not have the other colours about us.

DECEMBER 25 (CHRISTMAS DAY), 1987, LONDON

•

Every gift I have received, I am grateful for.

But ... the presents in themselves seem like they are for a very little person. Tiny, cute soaps, a stuffed toy, things that are lovely, but they seem for someone much younger, much sweeter, much nicer. They are symbols, perhaps, that others see that I am still so much a child.

It's the child in me who feels unloved. It's the child in me who fears being left. It's the child who feels despised for crying.

•

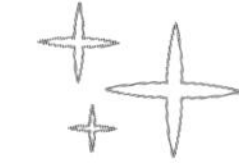

Numbers and How They Can Influence Your Oracle Card Readings

Each number of each card has a meaning.

The symbology of numbers is an ancient art with numerous (haha!) roots, including the Egyptian and Arabic schools of magick, from Pythagoras, continuing through to the Kabbalists, and even to controversial early 20th-century magician Aleister Crowley's numerology, who borrowed heavily from the Kabbalists and Egyptians.

Today, numerology is a fairly mainstream esoteric practice, and there are many best-selling spiritual works which speak of the true meaning within the numbers.

Of course, there are many layers of meaning in your Oracle cards. Please always be aware that the symbols, colours, images, numbers, words and inherent energy of the card are all wonderful cues to activate your own natural oracular talents and enable you to read the cards easily, accurately and with compassion and clarity.

Remember, there are no 'negative' numbers. A number may help to reveal blocks and challenges, and there may be issues for a Querent or Seeker hinted at by the number.

But, we are all here to learn, and we will all have these lessons (and their joyful outcomes) cross our life path — if not in this lifetime, then in one we have already experienced or within the lifetimes we are still to have. In other words, people often feel ashamed of troubles in their lives. We must help ease that burden! Being alive and being human is a wonderful gift and the only way we can bring the soul to fullness and wisdom. Emotions are not bad, they simply are. Sorrow teaches us compassion, if we learn the lesson well. Please see your lessons as gifts for the soul.

PEOPLE OFTEN FEEL ASHAMED OF TROUBLES IN THEIR LIVES. WE MUST HELP EASE THAT BURDEN! BEING ALIVE AND BEING HUMAN IS A WONDERFUL GIFT AND THE ONLY WAY WE CAN BRING THE SOUL TO FULLNESS AND WISDOM. EMOTIONS ARE NOT BAD, THEY SIMPLY ARE. SORROW TEACHES US COMPASSION, IF WE LEARN THE LESSON WELL. PLEASE SEE YOUR LESSONS AS GIFTS FOR THE SOUL.

All cards' numbers will break down to a given series of numbers. So, for example, you could read card 45 as a nine number, as it is 4+5=9. Read it as a nine energy.

You could reduce 14 to 5, as 1+4=5. Read it as a five energy.

This is not to say that in issues of timing—when we are working out a timeframe the card relates to—we reduce the number to its essence. This refers to the energy of the card itself.

ONE: These cards represent a powerful surge of new energy and beginnings of tremendous significance.

TWO: Represents opposing/complementary energies, shadow and light, female and male, partnerships. It also represents the relationship between soul and matter.

THREE: Represents expansion and the end of the first stage of a new project — this is a time to celebrate and acknowledge your journey and achievements so far. It is a magickal number, a very powerful Witches' number, and it is a sacred number.

FOUR: This reflects the outcome of sheer hard work, the use of logic to consolidate your enterprise, and a period of stability to come. It is a very grounded, solid, earthy energy, one which is a foundation of your dreams.

FIVE: Represents an important change, a shift in the energy of a situation. It's a number signifying change, and change—although it is the stuff of life itself—is a quality we resist. When we resist, it hurts. When it hurts, we fear. Five can indicate a level of discomfort with changes and that these changes are not your idea, rather they are being imposed on you. Instead, we could be excited at the wonders of the energies of five, at the opportunity its energy offers us, of the Unknown which is the discovery of the soul.

SIX: Represents the urge to deal with the energies of others. It can signify the sharing of skills and knowledge and the development of talent for the betterment of all. It is a card of connection with family, work partners and community. It is a number of the material world, of creativity and challenges, and of the tests we face in the realisations of our dreams.

SEVEN: Represents the Mysteries, the growth of wisdom and the understanding of the difference between spirit and ego while respecting the role of each.

EIGHT: Relates to bringing together opposing forces — a spiritual balancing act where the dichotomy or the polarised energies are replaced by a holistic understanding. It is a stage of high integrity, of learning respect and courage. This understanding of universal truths is the stage through which we all pass on our journey to knowledge. It is a stage of advanced initiation, after which manifestation and intent work together to create your soul life. It is, on a material level, a card of prosperity and abundance, of a kind of wealth of the spirit, and plenty to go around.

NINE: You're at the edge, the very verge, of completion. Savour achievements, look over them with a grateful eye and see what you have learned from this stage of life. Be grateful for all the lessons, good or bad. Then consider where you would like to create change in your life and make plans for manifesting these wishes and desires. Work on healing any issue you feel may be holding you back, and release what you no longer need in your life. The Universe and the Goddess will be there for you; all you need do is ask for their help.

TEN: This interesting number is at once the sign of reaping rewards, yet also new beginnings. Sometimes, what you have already let go of can return to you refreshed under the influences of this fascinating, mystical number. Joyful moments are to be yours. Simply recognise the blessings you have all around you and celebrate them. Your new cycle will then be activated without fear or pain and with enormous compassion and love.

NUMBERS WITHIN AN ORACLE CARD SPREAD

If a spread is laid out with 10 cards, and within that spread are four two-energy cards, each two simply amplifies the meaning of that number. The meaning of that number—the dual nature of all things—is relevant in the area of your life/the Querent's life covered by the card's position, and you will experience a time where you are working on harmoniously dealing with this natural law. If you experience a reversal of any of the twos, then you'll be more challenged by that area and that position.

DION FORTUNE

Letter no. 47 for October 20th 1940

At 3 Queensborough Terrace we had on Saturday night the experience of being straddled by a stick of four bombs, our head-quarters just fitting neatly into the middle of them, and, though well-shaken, escaping all damage. As the crashes grew nearer and nearer amid a concentration of A. A fire, the conditions were such that the inner and outer planes seemed to merge, and it was possible to see Invisible Helpers at work as innumerable shadowy presences. There were also presences of a much higher and more intellectual grade who seemed to be holding lines of power taut under great tension. Over all was the iridescent dome of protection guarded by great angelic presences. These are among the things we have been visualising and building on the astral and at the moment of testing, it was a wonderful experience to see how potent and tangible they were. The sticks of bombs fell one after the other in roads and gardens and there were no casualties. This is the second time that this has happened in our immediate vicinity. That there are powerful forces at work can hardly be denied.

(From The Magical Battle of Britain, *by Dion Fortune, ed. Gareth Knight.)*

Dion Fortune was one of the Golden Dawn's most influential and prolific members. In time, she went on to found her own group, the Society of the Inner Light. Born Violet Mary Firth, Dion wrote many books on all manner of rituals and aspects of occult lore, including *Psychic Self-Defense*, a book I worked with and which influenced me greatly when I first began exploring the path of the Oracle. She had a battle on her hands to be heard and respected within the Order of the Golden Dawn, and clashed with Aleister Crowley, Samuel Liddell MacGregor-Mathers and A. E. Waite, whose egos were large and difficult to get around. She wrote the standard modern textbook on the Kabbalah, and was deeply involved in a personal exploration of the oracular mysteries, often working as a trance medium or channelling messages from a higher group of angels or 'presences' who were guiding the fate of planet Earth. This peaked during World War Two when she formed a meditative group that would combat the evil forces unleashed by the war through visualisation and the setting up of protective spheres on the astral plane — a great devotion and sacrifice on behalf of all those involved. Every month, a meditation was handwritten and posted to each of the members, outlining a time of day, the meditation and the objective. Much of her interest in the oracular arts and the mysteries was inspired by an instance of psychic vampirism that took place when she was very young. Over time, she developed many ways for individuals to maintain their psychic and energetic health and to avoid being drained by those around them. Dion Fortune certainly had many opportunities to practise this! Some find her hard to read; her books are dense with information, sometimes using allusion to force the initiate to prepare their own mind to receive the mysteries. Her knowledge was real and vast, and she is an example of the oracular life well lived. Fortune was an advocate for disciplined magick and oracular arts; she practised guided visualisation, meditations, ritual and trance channelling. She felt that unless one was well-trained in the mystic traditions, the subconscious may dictate the messages one receives rather than making a connection with pure Source. She was concerned that her students did not indulge their egos but instead work towards enlightenment. She worked with the Tarot in the form of a kind of psychic dictionary, choosing cards with which to meditate. She lived much of her life in London and in Glastonbury, where she was laid to rest. A remarkable woman.

Experientials and Experimentals

- Think of a clean, clear way to describe what you do for people in one sentence.
- Let's work on using symbols as a foundation for a spread. It would be very strengthening for you to find three of the symbols discussed in this chapter within your cards.

- Then, you could take this further … you could find three of these symbols within the world about you. See if there is any relationship between the symbol you saw in your day-to-day life and your daily card, for example.
- What symbols are you drawn to at this time? Why?
- A symbol for a spread: You could begin to contemplate how you can construct a spread with a symbol as its basis. For example, you could find a spread that does this within your deck guidebook or be creative and begin to do this yourself.

  I have created lots of spreads working with symbols as their basis. It's so creative and joyful to experiment with layers of magick when working with the cards. One of the benefits of layouts based on symbols is that the symbols' meaning deepens our knowledge of the messages. I think it helps us grow more intimate with the symbol itself, too. Somehow, through the process of laying out the cards in that sacred shape, the symbol will enter our inner self and our subconscious mind, and we will experience the symbol in a very personal way.

  Here is a quick list for you of some of my symbol-based spreads and the deck they appear in:

  - You'll find the True Love Make My Soul Sing Spread on pages 26–28 of the guidebook for the *Oracle of the Mermaids.*
  - You may wish to try the bewitching Tools of the Solitary Witch Spread — just go to pages 57–60 of the guidebook for *The Solitary Witch Oracle.*
  - The Faery Forest Tree Spread can be found on pages 31–33 of *The Faery Forest* guidebook. It's enchanting to work with this layout.
  - The first edition of the *Wild Wisdom of the Faery Oracle* has a lovely seven-pointed star spread—The Faery Star—on pages 32–34 (or pages 34–37 of the second edition).
  - The Faery Cross Spread can be found on page 34 of the first edition (or 37–38 in the second edition) of the *Wild Wisdom of the Faery Oracle.*
  - Spreads based on circles are amongst my very favourites, and an example of this can be found in a layout called the Seeker's Journey in the *Oracle of the Dragonfae*, on pages 11–12 (both editions).
  - The Circle of Witches is a very wise and helpful spread found in *The Solitary Witch Oracle*, in the guidebook on pages 53–57.
  - Through the Looking-Glass—another circle-based spread—can be found on pages 28–29 of *Alice: The Wonderland Oracle.*

  There are lots more sprinkled throughout all my card decks, but hopefully, this diverse and rich selection will trigger a fascination with combining the energy of the symbols with the divinatory properties of the cards — a potent brew indeed.

- Find a symbol featured on a card within one of your decks, and write about it and what it might mean … why it may be in the card, how it may help within a reading, and how it could be interpreted with a sample question and a sample reading. Write about this in your journal. Feel free to go where the symbol takes you with your words, feelings, thoughts and doodles — all are magickal expressions of your response to the symbol.

The Faery Forest
Card number 14
Name: *Initiate*
Meaning: Curiosity, Warm, Open

I want to draw your attention to the tree within the card. This tree provides a home for others — in this case, a rather wise-looking squirrel peeking out from his or her home, and a place where we know nuts and nesting take place for these lovely creatures.

Let's deconstruct this image a little more, remembering we always do this in conjunction with the question, the spread and the position of the card, and the relationship with the other surrounding cards within a reading. I do not mean that a card's essential meaning changes, but that aspects of its meaning will be accentuated, enhanced or more prevalent depending on context.

We must learn to be sensitive to nuance and to context and all of these variables, else our readings may become stilted, inorganic, irrelevant to the Questioner and one-dimensional.

Flow when you read ... and this flow will be enhanced with practice.

So, to this card.
Let's deconstruct:

TREE: What kind of tree?

LEAVES: What kind of leaves?

COLOURS: What are they? What could they signify?

BRAID: What could this signify?

ANIMALS: What does this animal represent?

TIME OF YEAR/SEASONS PRESENT: How could this be of significance within the reading? Could this relate to timing?

NUMBERS: How could this relate to timing? What do the numbers mean? What energy does it offer the card?

Les Vampires
CARD NUMBER 25
NAME: *THE MONSTER WITHIN*
MEANING: INTERNAL STRUGGLE, PERSONAL CHALLENGES, WANTING TO IMPROVE.

Let's deconstruct this image.

THE CRESCENT MOON: What phase could the moon be in? What influence could this have — consider this, too, in regard to timing.

THE VIOLIN: What could this represent? Stretch beyond the sense of music and into what else it could represent.

THE STAIRS: What could these represent?

NIGHT: What influence could this have on your interpretation?

THE WOLF: How could the presence of this beautiful creature play into your reading? What is the relationship between the Wolf and its Wisdom and the Violinist?

Please look at this image, simple in so many ways; how would the symbology within the card help you interpret the message on the cards? See if you can enter into the world of the card and feel the story before the moment depicted within the card and where it will go — what will happen next with these beings and energies. Will she master the Violin? Will she run with the Wolf? Is there a concert up the stairs where she will play, and will she include the Wolf? Let your intuitive, imaginative genius have some fun, and see where it takes you!

Problem Child:

I've had some feedback in the past saying that the card known as *The Fairy of the Green World* (from the *Oracle of Shadows and Light*) in the centre of this reading below proved a little bit tricky to read. So, I thought I would work with this card for our challenging card.

I've put together three cards, approximating the reading that the student was having some challenges reading this card with.

The card is called *The Fairy of the Green World*, and its primary message is: The Natural World Needs You. Try to see what I am drawing on here for my (freestyle) interpretation below.

So, in the past position, we have *Strangely Lonely: Holding on Way Too Tight*. The student said they had no issues with that card. And in the future position, there was *The Fairy of the Highlands: It's Time to Be Brave*. That seemed to present no problems for the student. But in the centre was the card, *The Fairy of the Green World.* And it seemed to perplex the reader.

Now, I am not privy to the question that was asked, so I am freestyling intuitively here. But if we had a woman come to us and ask us about her marriage, which was troubled, and its future, we could work with something like this, perhaps ...

At the moment, the woman may be involving herself in activities to distract herself, feeling that nature will take its course. She may also be feeling that she needs to get closer to nature, to find some comfort in the situation. She could go to the earth and release some of the energy, the stress that she feels.

She may also find herself drawn to the symbol of the butterfly as a sign of new beginnings. She could pay attention, take walks in nature, and if she sees a butterfly (or winged being), know she is ready to move forward.

She could also work with the lapis lazuli crystal to create a sense of sovereignty for herself. She is intense, gazing into the future and trying hard to see what will happen, but for now, she is afraid of what will come, and she hopes what will happen will be natural, easy and without effort. However, the future card indicates there will be a moment when she must be brave and speak up about her true feelings and desires.

Money may also be on her mind, the sense that she will perhaps not be able to create as much abundance, and yet, the closer she is to nature, the more inspiration she will have, and thus, the more prosperity and fulfilment. She has been searching for wholeness within herself and equality within the relationship but has hesitated to take the steps she needs to create that.

For now, she would do well to recycle more, eat more organically, and do something positive, even in very small, everyday ways, for nature. She has a purpose, she must never doubt that, but the closer she is to nature at this time, the more comfort, strength, independence and freedom she will feel.

In time, she will need to be brave and have the conversation, and stand up for what she feels is right. It's like she is trying to find her truth, to heal from the disappointment, and see what will happen next ... For now, while it is true that nature needs her, she too needs nature — the more connection she has, the less difficult this transition into the new stage of her life will be.

What do you think? Whenever you have a card you find challenging, see if you can avoid being literal. Work with the images, symbols, numbers and colours, and do not forget the primary message of the guidebook. Let it flow ...

With love to you all, dear Adepts.
May your life be rich with symbology,
the language of the Oracles.

Chapter Nine

For us believing physicists, the separation between past, present and future has only the meaning of an illusion, albeit a tenacious one.

— Albert Einstein

Timing and the Cards

In this chapter, we will explore timing and the Oracle Cards. To begin with, I wanted to share with you one of the messengers from the *Oracle of the Dragonfae* — The Time Guardian. Whether you have this deck or not, take a few moments to connect with this energy and feel out the truth of these words before we move to working with time and timing for our readings.

You may wish to read these words (from *The Time Guardian Speaks* section) out loud, as they have power, and almost work as a kind of spell, creating energy that is expansive and calming.

The Time Guardian: You Have Time

> *The Time Guardian speaks:* The feelings you have, of time contracting and expanding, are real ones, not your imagination. Time is a living dimensional being, whose power includes the ability to devote more time to those of us who require it, and for time to speed up when it may be necessary, too. It is in this way that we are able to divine and travel through the threads and weavings of time, and move forward into seeing our future ... in truth, we are already there. And much of who we truly are remains an echo.
>
> The time beings know this, and guard and protect us from confusion. Similarly, they can assist us clearly when we require time to be created. If you feel you are short of time, send a thought message to the Guardian of time, whose domain this is, and his beings will send you all the help you need to meet your goals within the time you feel you have. Know that time is available to work for and with you; you need only tune into it as a dimensional reality, and connect with the time beings.

Call upon the Time Guardian to create the time you need, and call upon them when you wish to speed time up, too. Time will expand to assist you in meeting the deadlines for pressing tasks, and arriving 'on time' will be perfectly simple and easy, no matter the apparent obstacles. Above all, know that you are a timeless being. Know that you are dimensionally vast, that you are protected, cherished and loved by the Time Guardian. From this time forth, you will become the time traveller you were born to be, that is part of all of your inheritance.

About the Time Guardian: This Dragonfae Lord is a keeper of time: he arranges and rearranges its weavings and natural laws, dedicating portions that can expand and contract according to the will, the beliefs and the measure of the heart of the being working with time. He is teaching us all to understand that time is indeed subject to its own special laws, and that if we work with it, rather than trying to compartmentalise and define it—if we return to the lunar and solar and astronomical ways, if we celebrate the time changes apparent in nature all around us with the Wheel of the Year—the timespan we have will be richer, more joyful, our vocations will be discovered and we will no longer struggle to 'cram in' so much to our days.

He is sometimes very tired, as the prevailing human mindset now is of time needing to be constrained and watched ... he encourages us all to experience the natural flow of the energy we call time, and experience its multi-dimensionality. There is one simple way to work with him. Be in the present moment, more often.

Divinatory meanings: Feeling 'pushed for time', that time is moving 'too fast' or 'too slow' for our liking, feeling left behind, or that all is moving forward so fast we are no longer important or relevant. A need to ensure the natural timekeeping is kept. It is likely, when this card comes up, that you may have a theme of running 'late' or of 'never having enough time'. Or feeling that time is not on your side.

Working with the Time Guardian: Nothing would make you happier than to start to greet the sunrise, to enjoy the sunset, to diminish the unnatural lights in your home that give the appearance of a uniformity of time. Time changes, flows and moves as you interact with it. Grow closer to natural time. Give yourself a watch-free day soon, and begin to understand what 'time' it is from the solar position, the moon cycle, and how you feel. It will help maintain an abundance of energy, and it also means that you will be in the flow, making it impossible for you to be 'late' to what it is you are meant to be doing.

MARCH 1990, PARIS

•

I read my own cards this morning. Essentially, they say to take my life step by step. Very gradual shifts. To be careful with change — do not push or hurry myself. To be kind to myself. In this way, I will slowly gain inner strength.

•

Timing and the Beings Within Your Decks

Each of your decks can be used to work with the principles of time and timing within this chapter. The spreads provided for you here later in this chapter will apply to all decks, and the hints and tips regarding the numbers (and working with them for timeframes) hold, no matter which of your decks you may be working with.

First, I would like to share with you a little of the energy that various beings can have regarding time. These can influence your experience with timing and your deck, so it can be wonderful to know a little more about them.

- Mermaids, for example, are very synced into moon phases and tidal ebbs and flows — a more natural, flowing sense of time, a rise and fall, expansion and contraction.
- Faeries are known for being able to shift time — to expand it and to really open time up, almost playing with time. They are very connected to the seasons and to the unfolding of nature's cycles on this beautiful blue and green planet. Within faerie realms, time flows and is woven very differently from that within our human world.
- Dragonfae beings are very powerful and strong, and beings like the Time Guardian can have a direct impact on the time we feel we have. They can help us and time to slow down, be more grounded and strong and still, to let go of the frantic nature of human clock time, and the energy of pressure so many of us live with, which can lead to us feeling disconnected, unwell, stressed and sometimes even unworthy.

- Les Vampires have a very different perspective on time, as they have extended their lifespan and are eternally living in a particular moment, 'frozen' in time and 'ageless'. Nevertheless, there are many cards within this deck that speak about time, as (to a degree) these beings stand outside of time. Yet they have experienced being within it, too, and can observe humans and our relationship to time with very different eyes. There are cards within the deck that can help us to understand some of the unhealthy ways in which humans deal with memory and become locked almost within a moment of time — which prevents them from truly living in the moment and enjoying all the wonders of our fragile, beautiful, precious lives.
- The beings within *The Faery Forest* dwell within places that are most often outside of time — human time. These faery worlds and energetic portals and places have a very different perspective on the linear, driven, urgent way in which so many humans today work with time.

Explore these different takes on time for yourself. Connect with your deck, and see what the beings within it have to say to you about their approach to time.

Timing and Oracle Cards

ALTHOUGH MANY PEOPLE WHO COME TO SEE US FOR READINGS WILL OFTEN wish to know about their soul, others will want to know about very human matters and the timing of the important events in their lives, including significant rites of passage. Over and over, we may be asked, "When will this happen? When will I find love? How long till I have enough money? When will I have a baby? I know I will meet my soulmate — when will I find them? Will I get married? When will that happen?" I know, too, that if I had a reading for a very important matter, I would perhaps find it helpful to have a time frame and would seek clarification on this.

Now, when asked when something will happen, we could simply nod philosophically and say in a sage-like manner, "When the time is right," or "In divine right timing" … but we often wish to do more than that. You'll know from personal experience that you have had moments when time has expanded and contracted. I want you particularly to remember Chapters Two and Three, where we did our work on liminal spaces, and how when we step into that liminal space within a reading—which a true reading both creates and is a part of—we can 'see' into the future possibilities, we can 'see' (or hear, or feel, or know) what took place in the past.

We also read the cards in conjunction with our intuition, bringing them together, weaving them into each other. That way, events can be traced with a kind of timing.

It may not always be to the day or hour, but we can deliver time frames, which can be helpful to the Querent or Seeker. It is a tricky area to work within, as we do not give the Querent the impression that they can simply sit back and events will unfold. We wish to help them also know how to activate the future and bring about the situation they desire.

I feel that if we focus too much on events and timing at the expense of right action and further understanding (which spreads like the Celtic Cross can deliver to us), something of the heart of a reading can be lost. We weave time into our readings, but we offer insight, clarification, understanding and suggestions—given to us by the cards or by our own intuition—to assist the person who comes to us for help. If we are reading for ourselves, this is so very helpful because if we focus too much on the when rather than the how and the why, we can lose sight of the true purpose of a reading.

If we are asked a question with an emphasis on timing alone, I think it's important to wonder whether we are being somewhat squeezed into the position of fortune teller, where we are predicting someone's future. This is a question of fate — is it predetermined? Has what will take place within the Querent's life already been decided? Are we there simply to 'see' this and pass it on to that person?

I do not think so.

Fortune telling, I feel, is not our primary aim. We must be mindful, as we want to do a good job, want to get it right, to receive approval, and may fall into the trap of wanting to please the people we are reading for. We must have a sense of compassion and listening and care, but also detachment. We are not in control of that person or of their future, but we can influence them, and strongly.

There are no easy answers to all the questions this can lead to — simply that we can do our best and deliver the messages as they come with compassion, honesty and accuracy based on our guidance/the guidance of Spirit. We are reading the cards before us, not telling. Fortunes—or futures—are created, not set in stone.

Free will is to be supported and respected, and we assist the person we are reading for by helping them reconnect with their innate sense of divinity and power within any situation. After all, there is always a choice that can be made that can help us to understand and make the most of what has gone before, appreciate the present moment, and take right action. The right choice at the right time—even the decision to remain hopeful—can help us create a future within which we can enjoy our lives, contribute to community, love deeply and learn every single day.

The Story
Will Give You the Time Frame

When we read, as we have been practising throughout this journey together, we connect to what is truer than the truth — the story of the person we are reading for, through the cards they have chosen, and which have chosen to come to them and speak with them. The cards are telling their story, the story of their past (and what created that past), and the present (the influences they are under and the experiences they are having). We then move into the possible future story as it has the potential to unfold, given what is taking place now and what has taken place before.

And yet, it is unwritten. So this part of the story may be considered more fluid, more full of possibilities. Stay with the story, the narrative within the reading, and the timing will organically emerge.

Reading Time

Using a Spread

Many of your decks will have unique spreads within them, some of which can be used to foresee how events and situations will unfold over a coming time period. The spreads I have included below can be worked with, no matter which deck you are using. From the *Oracle of the Dragonfae* to *The Faery Forest*, they will give you positions that will stand in for time frames.

With this structure, you can discover the timing of certain events or the themes months or days may have. This is a strong foundation and platform which grounds the timing in the everyday world of days, months and years.

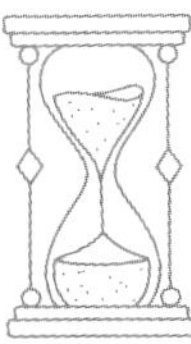

The Cycles of the Moon Spread

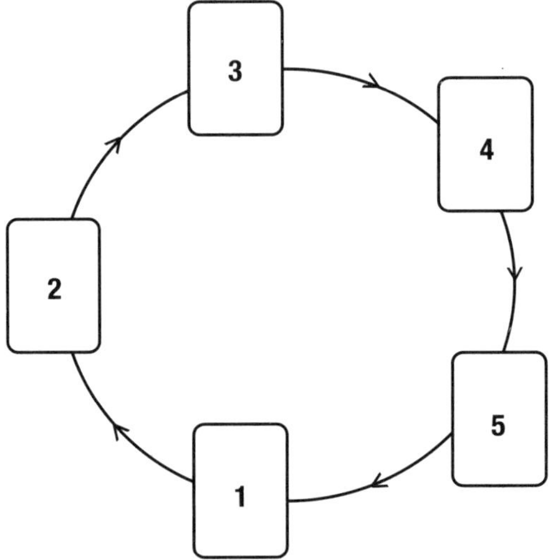

This spread is in the *Oracle of the Mermaids*, and it helps all of us connect with the cycles of the moon and, of course, can be used to see how events and themes will unfold over the coming lunar cycle.

So, as always, first shuffle and cut the deck into three with your non-dominant hand. Then, put the deck back together again.

Now, one by one, lay out the cards in a circle.

You can begin this layout at any stage of the lunar cycle, but for our example, let's imagine we are in the time of the waning moon, and we are wishing to know what will take place over the next cycle of the moon.

To the left, place the first card. This is in the waning moon position, the current time.

Put a card to the right of this, setting up the beginning of a circle ... this is the dark moon card.

Put a card a little beneath this and to the right ... this is the new moon card. To the left of that card, place another card — this is the waxing moon card. And to the left again, place another card. This is the full moon card.

So, when we look at the cards, we see what is happening in the present position under the waning moon, what will take place around the dark moon, what will begin with the new moon, and so on.

Moon phases have an energetic impact, so we can also weave this into the reading. A simple guide to moon phases, their timing and their powers is:

- **WANING MOON:** Withdrawing; a sucking and pulling impact — the card in this position indicates what will be leaving, which influence will be diminishing ... what is fading and on its way out, and what will begin to emerge as the moon moves into her next phase.
- **DARK MOON:** A time to go within and soul-scry — revelations from within. At this time, the card in this position indicates what you can hardly admit to yourself, what lies deep, deep inside that you have kept hidden for a long time, but are now ready to bring out; the heart of the issue.
- **NEW MOON:** A new cycle begins; time to begin your activation of intentions; what will be beginning soon; the initiating energy; the seed of the future; what to watch for and what will grow in power ... make a wish.
- **WAXING MOON:** New growth; continued action and results will come about. How the growth will come about; what to expect as the project grows.
- **FULL MOON:** High tide of power; amplifying and creative. This final card shows you what will come about, what will be empowered.

Of course, you can work with it at any time — you do not need to begin at the waning moon or any phase in particular. It's very flexible. This spread can also be used metaphorically to see what we may need to release, what we will bring in, and so forth, but it also works very well for timing over a coming month.

Say a person came to you and asked, "When will I get a new job?" You could use each of the positions in both their timing aspect and moon phase meaning — saying, "On the dark moon, this or that is likely to take place, and in order for you to create a new job, you may wish to contemplate some issues you have not thought about for a while — these include xyz." Explore those possibilities that have emerged from the card.

Why not work with this spread, once for yourself and perhaps once for another person, just as an exercise? Weave in the timing and the energies of the positions. You may wish to journal this in your Book of Shadows and Light or magickal reading grimoire. I wish I could see how this spread works for you — I love it very much, and I hope you will too. What I do know is that the more you work with it, the more it will offer you.

The Three-Card Spread Extended

You have worked with the three-card spread and are strong with that structure. Now, let's develop this spread so that the timing it covers extends into the future. We do this by placing more cards on the right, cards that represent the coming days, months or even years.

The first thing to do is to establish a time frame to determine the period each card will cover. You could choose for each card to represent a day, for example. Let's see how this would work within a reading.

Shuffle the cards, divide as usual, and then lay them out as you normally would.

Lay your first card to the left — this card is yesterday.

Lay your second card out in the centre — this card is today.

Lay your third card to the right — this card is tomorrow.

But this time, let's go further into the future.

Lay another card to the right for the next day. Another, for the day after that, and then another — and of course, you can cover many days in this way.

Now, depending on the time frame you are working with, you have a spread you can work with to help you see what will be arising over the coming days, or months, or years. All you need to do is set the intent of the time frame each card will represent before you begin your reading.

Bring the numbers that appear on each card into the reading, too — do this intuitively, see what you feel they may represent. You may also wish to use the guide to numbers and their spiritual significance and message that I gave earlier. If you notice the numbers repeating in a pattern, pay particular attention. For example, cards that reduce to five, appearing three times, could mean magickal change is on its way. (Five is one of my favourite numbers, and I see fives so often in my life, usually heralding a significant turning point. They've come to be a major personal sign for me.)

This spread can be adapted to venture into the past, too. Just extend the line of cards from the past-card position. You can also adapt this to include more about today — take the line down from the present-card position. Remember, the cards can represent whatever you decide — hours, days, months or years. They could also represent seasons, moon cycles or sacred festivals. Learn the spread in its essential form first, then venture into the past, present or future using whatever increments of time work for you.

13 Moons

Sometimes, we would really appreciate some guidance as to where we may be over the next year: this layout is excellent for uncovering the themes of your coming year. By identifying areas of opportunity and challenge, we can maximise our chances for a fulfilling year of growth and happiness. It is a wonderful one to offer your clients, loved ones, family—or your own precious self—at the beginning of a new year.

If you would like to add some energetic oomph to this spread, you could conduct it on or around a birthday, at the beginning of the Lunar New Year (around the first new moon of the new calendar year) or on an anniversary of a relationship, for example.

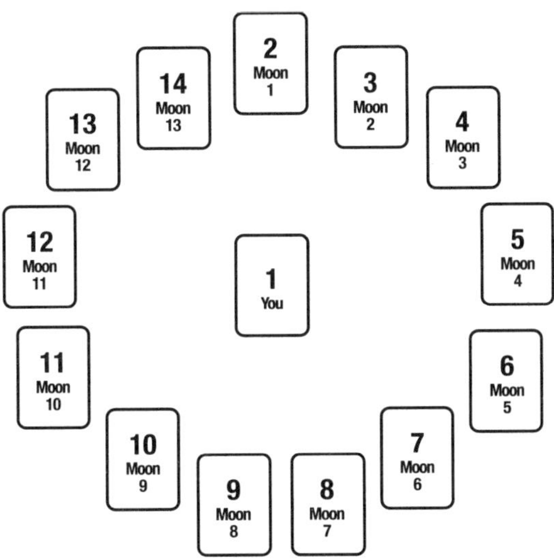

While shuffling, allow yourself to be open to that time ahead — see it opening before you, and ask the beings within the cards to offer you, or the person you are reading for (and with), clear guidance regarding what will unfold over the coming times.

After shuffling, cutting the deck into three with your non-dominant hand (perhaps we could call this the intuitive hand!) and placing the deck back together again, however you wish, turn over the top card.

Put that card in the centre of the spread. This is the theme card, painting a picture of the dominant energies of the time ahead.

Then, lay out 13 cards in a circular formation around the first card you placed down. Each card represents one of the 13 coming moons, starting from the present moon of the reading. The one theme card you pulled, which is placed within the entire spread, represents you—or the person you are reading for—throughout the coming 13 moons.

So, using this structure, you can see that you could create some variations on this, too. You may wish to use this structure to forecast a week ahead, so you would use the same principles, but instead of 13 cards for 13 moons, you could use seven cards for seven days, for example.

Sometimes, when a person comes to see me, they ask me what will happen over the coming year. It doesn't happen often, as many people are not so neat and succinct with their questions — but when it does, I lay out those cards and begin to read. I am a little less used to reading in this structure, so when I do this within a 60-minute reading, I need to be a little more mindful of time (ironically) to be sure I am giving enough attention to each of the cards.

Tarot and Timing

Some of you may have my *Oracle Tarot*, or if you are reading this at some time in the future, you could be working with the very Tarot deck I am working on as I write. If you do, why not try this timing exercise and see how it works for you? I personally do not work with it a great deal, as I prefer to work intuitively regarding timing, using the numbers and the energies of the cards to receive guidance on significant events for people. But this is worth practising as an exercise.

Do not worry if you don't have a Tarot deck — it's worth simply knowing about the technique, and you can save this practice for another time if you ever choose to experiment and extend into the Tarot.

You may wish to take your Tarot, and shuffle, ponder and divide the deck, as you would usually do. Then, lay out your Celtic Cross.

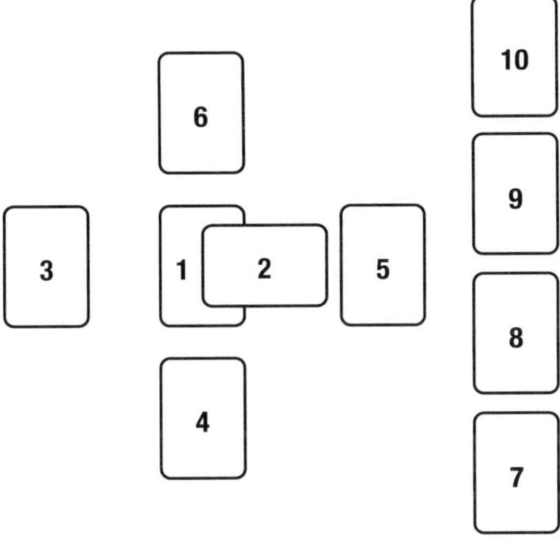

Now, I want you to read, but first, begin to count back from the very last card you laid out until you find your first Minor Arcana card. So, you would not be looking for a Major Arcana card, or a court card, if you are working with a deck that contains court cards. When you find the Minor Arcana card, we are going to use it for timing.

The number of the card will reveal the number of days, months, weeks or years, while the suit will reveal what time frame you are looking at, giving you the key to timing events.

- The suit of coins represents years.
- The suit of swords represents months.
- The suit of wands represents weeks.
- The suit of cups represents days.

For example, if the first Minor Arcana card from the end is the Three of Wands, it will be three weeks until the event. If your first Minor Arcana card from the end is the Six of Swords, it could be six months; if it is the Ace of Cups, it could be tomorrow (one day).

It's important to note that different Tarot teachers suggest different versions of this technique. The Golden Dawn, the secret society whose influence is still so keenly felt, worked with the Minor Arcana to show moon phases and the Aces within the deck to show seasons. I've seen other versions where a teacher recommends wands for days and for summer. So, it is important to find what works for you.

It is a Tarotcentric issue, as the suits are used in this way. Your Oracle cards do not have suits, or court cards, within them.

Non-Linear Time and Our Incarnations

A few thoughts on time. Time is not a line, but more a dimension, or even a series of dimensions which weave into each other and overlap. For example, we may have had an event take place in the past, but its impact may only truly be apparent at a time in the future, when the seeds of a certain action suddenly make their energy known to us.

Similarly, while we tend to think of past lives as having happened in a kind of line in the past, this may not be so. Time is not linear; we may have not only lived before, we may also have already incarnated in the future. So, some people could be from the future, and others could have experienced their last incarnation a great deal of time ago.

We are moving through time, so even the term 'past life' may not be the most accurate. Perhaps we don't incarnate chronologically, from past to present. We may incarnate cyclically. Thus, my next lifetime, or your own next lifetime, could be in what we call the past — we could go 'back', instead of always moving 'forward'. Our soul may need to experience something from 'before', rather than simply having another lifetime in, say 100 years time.

More Expansive Timing — Past Lives Spreads

Would you like to be able to create a past life reading for yourself, your loved ones or your clients? It's entirely possible. Here is a wonderful Past Lives (dimensional lives) Spread for you to work with. This can be fascinating for you to work with personally, or as another way to connect with clients and offer a different kind of reading for people interested in knowing about their soul's journey.

So, centre yourself, Adept. Take three deep breaths and shuffle your cards while focusing on the question of your own incarnations, or ask the person you are reading for to do the same. Shuffle, and then divide the deck into three, put them back together as always, and draw from the top.

We will use 17 cards for this spread.

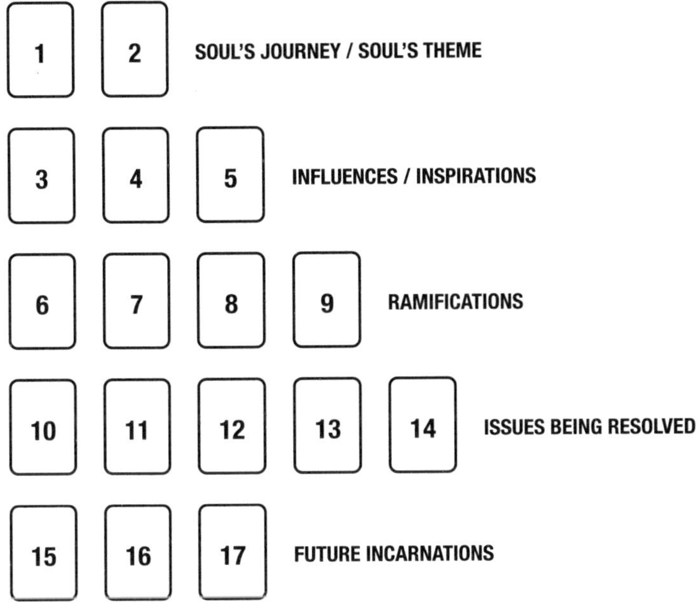

Lay out one card, then another next to it. These are cards one and two.

These two cards represent your soul's journey and your soul's theme … the qualities you are here to experience within your incarnations. Through these experiences, your soul will evolve into these theme's highest expressions.

Lay out three cards on a new line below the first line.

Cards three, four and five show the major influences and inspirations from past lives that you are currently working with in this incarnation.

Layout four more cards, cards six, seven, eight and nine. These cards show the ramifications of choices you made in previous incarnations. Card six will also provide you with valuable guidance regarding who you were; card seven will reveal what kind of life experiences you had; card eight illuminates the kinds of relationships and card nine shares the activities or occupations you engaged in during those other lifetimes.

Lay out five more cards — cards 10, 11, 12, 13 and 14 show you the most important issues that came up for you in your past incarnations. These are well on their way to being healed and resolved.

And finally, lay out three more cards. Cards 15, 16 and 17. These last three cards show you what will come up for you in your next incarnation — remembering though that as we all have free will, we can create and re-create our life experiences from this moment on. The most powerful thing in the entire Universe is the power of now.

Crystals and Timing

I FIND HAVING CERTAIN CRYSTALS OR PRECIOUS ANCIENT TREASURES ABOUT me when I read to be very helpful with matters of timing. Lemurian quartz, petrified wood, fossils and particular amber (my personal favourite at the moment) seem to offer me energy and perspective, influence the reading, and enhance my intuition within the reading. Experiment — see what works for you, and what works with the beings in the deck you are reading with.

THE MARVELLOUS, MAGICKAL MARIE LAVEAU

UPON A GRAVESITE AT NUMBER one, St Louis Cemetary, is a shrine. Money, flowers, gifts and candles lay over the resting place of Marie Laveau, the real-life Voodoo Queen of New Orleans. Marie Laveau is renowned as the first priestess in the United States to charge for psychic services, and is said to have conducted psychic readings for Queen Victoria, desperate to seek out the spirit of her beloved Prince Albert. Born at the turn of the 19th century in New Orleans, Louisiana, Laveau was renowned for her spiritual ceremonies, healing powers, charity work and charms and curses. Many wealthy and politically powerful people consulted regularly with Laveau, who offered protection against personal, physical and psychic attacks, to bend the hand of fate to favour them, or to bring fertility to a mother desperate for an heir to the familial wealth.

The granddaughter of a powerful priestess in Saint-Domingue, Laveau was an intrinsic and necessary part of the culture and high society of New Orleans. In her home on Saint Ann Street, Laveau read for clients using a myriad of oracular tools. She held private rituals in her yard, held Sunday gatherings at Congo Square, and conducted rites of initiation, trance, sacrifice and possession on the shores of Lake Pontchartrain.

Laveau passed in 1881, but her influence over New Orleans has never abated. Her legend as an Oracle only grows stronger and brighter.

Experientials and Experimentals

- Experiment with some of the spreads, and gently find your way into working with the numbers and timing with spreads you may be more familiar with. You may wish to read for another person, and do a practice run on some of the spreads here that are more outside your usual experience.
- Contemplate time, and the passage of time. Wonder about your own experience of time.
- Find a card within the deck that you may not have easily read in the past—your own problem child card—and with the skills you've been practising, look again at this card and see what may be emerging. You may find it speaks to you more openly now.
- Reconnect with liminal spaces, but for your own nourishment.
- On the nourishment of your soul … Take some time for self-care. This is so important, and you have been working hard, and life can have so many demands. It's time to be sure you are being well cared for by the person who most values you, loves you, knows you — your own Divine Self.

And above all, be most blessed
as you enjoy the practice of the Adept.

Chapter Ten

Mythopoetic Realms

The prophet is not diverted by illusions of past, present and future ... The prophet utters fateful words. You glimpse a thing "destined to occur". But the prophetic instant releases something of infinite portent and power ... The best prophets lead you up to the curtain and let you peer through for yourself.

— *Frank Herbert*

Welcome! In this chapter, we are going to explore some wonderful new realms within your Oracle cards, which will bring more depth and a sense of mythic wisdom to your readings. We are going to experiment and play, too, and change our relationship with our cards a little. We will be doing some healing energy work to help us cut unhealthy attachments, refresh our energy and support ourselves emotionally.

A little like bringing a fresh adventure into a relationship, this change gives us a new way of relating, and getting to know our cards better — and it is fun! Joyful learning is so wonderful, and will ease some of the sense of always being at work with your cards. We will go through most of the decks, exploring some of the mythic energies, and some of the deities within the decks. You will find many more when you work with your deck yourself. We'll explore four of the decks, discovering the energies within the *Wild Wisdom of the Faery Oracle*, *The Faery Forest* and many more!

Before we begin, I'd like to draw your attention to the meditational experience of cord cutting and cleansing, which is so helpful when we do this work. If you are very sensitive, we can sometimes become depleted. At those times, we can be easily influenced by other people's energies, develop areas of stuck energy, or just feel stressed or drained, so you will find cutting the cords very healing and rejuvenating.

Help restore your vitality, and give yourself the thirty minutes to immerse yourself in this healing work. Use the meditation whenever you wish to cleanse and clear — every day, or once a week, would be an extremely nurturing and uplifting practice for all Oracles — particularly those who walk the path of the Adept.

Cord Cutting – Psychic Surgery for Oracular Freedom

One of the most powerful moments in my spiritual learning was being introduced to (and practising) cord cutting in a group workshop. I hadn't done this before, although I had heard of it, and the teacher guided us through the process. What became clear as the teacher's voice calmly continued is that the process took on a life of its own. At first, I followed along and found some cords, which—with the help of Archangel Michael's sword—were cut with a little resistance. After a palpable tug, like a stitch being pulled, the cord kind of popped free and was cut and cleared. If there was any damage at the root of the cord, I asked another angel, Raphael, to bathe this in green light. This all went smoothly — until I came to a part of my body where I could see an immense tangle of strong, deep roots twisted in and out of each other, deeply embedded in my belly and extending right through my body to the spine. The roots were wrapped around all of me, it seemed, and had worked their way into my own spinal column and nervous system. I wasn't alarmed, but I felt a wave of deep, profoundly painful emotion, and I could feel some of who these ties belonged to. It seemed to me that as I worked through them, some did not even come from this lifetime. They were hurts and harms, betrayals of myself (by me!), and cruelties from others that may have happened lifetimes long ago. Since this first time, and through years of practice and cutting others' cords, I have found that many of us have such deep-rooted cords of attachment to people, places or patterns from other lives. Some of these may even have been lived as Oracles, in which lifetime we were punished for our gifts and our service to the community was repaid by suffering and rejection — or even death.

I CAME TO A PART OF MY BODY WHERE I COULD SEE AN IMMENSE TANGLE OF STRONG, DEEP ROOTS TWISTED IN AND OUT OF EACH OTHER, DEEPLY EMBEDDED IN MY BELLY AND EXTENDING RIGHT THROUGH MY BODY TO THE SPINE. THE ROOTS WERE WRAPPED AROUND ALL OF ME, IT SEEMED, AND HAD WORKED THEIR WAY INTO MY OWN SPINAL COLUMN AND NERVOUS SYSTEM. I WASN'T ALARMED, BUT I FELT A WAVE OF DEEP, PROFOUNDLY PAINFUL EMOTION, AND I COULD FEEL SOME OF WHO THESE TIES BELONGED TO. IT SEEMED TO ME THAT AS I WORKED THROUGH THEM, SOME DID NOT EVEN COME FROM THIS LIFETIME.

This process took a long time within that first workshop, and in the end, there was a bloody, malformed 'being' on my lap who had dwelled within me. It was enraged at being ousted from inside of me and was howling like a baby in protest. It was not evil in any way, but it was filled with negativity and toxicity and resentment. It was out of me — I could feel the weight on my lap, and I felt immense compassion for myself and this creature for this suffering. With a lot of work and persistence, I have cleared this being from my energy field and returned the energy to the Universe. It is a process that takes work, and which I repeat on occasion, as we are all inclined to create cords. While some dissolve simply, others are ages old, or very powerful, or deeply rooted within our sense of self. It is very simple spiritual hygiene to do this work and to continue to do this as needed. It will never harm you, and it will always leave you feeling fresher, brighter, lighter, freer — and fear will dissolve along with the cord.

Cords of attachment can be cut with an athame, a witch's knife, and I have often done so. These cut on the energetic planes and are very helpful, but you can also use your hand as the blade. Another option is to cut the cords through visualisation and intent, and by working in alliance with divine beings who are happy to help you clear.

I tend to work with Archangel Michael and his sword of blue fire to cut through cords. Remember, these can emanate out from your chakras in any direction, so be sure to visualise the angel or divine helper cutting the cord from the direction it extends. Be sure to check for cords from your sides, your back, even sometimes along limbs. Many of mine seem to extend from my solar plexus or heart chakras, but cords can attach or grow from your entire energetic body, so be sure to scan your entire body, not just your front.

You need not be angry or upset at the cords or the people who may be continually renewing the energy. That won't help — in fact, it will strengthen the cord.

I like to see the angel, or often the Goddess Brigid (whom I work with most, and nearly always for illness) with their healing sword, passing the blade through the cords. As they are struck by the light—the light that slices through the living energetic cord—the energy of the cord begins to dissolve and be transmuted and ultimately returned to the Universe.

If you have many cords—or a tangle, as I described—it's important to 'cauterise' the endings or roots so they do not regrow and can then drop away. I have experienced Archangel Raphael's healing green balm applied to these cord ends, but Brigid has also cleared the ending, almost pulling it forth from my body like a holy gardener weeding her garden. Then, she heals the place it was attached to, ceasing any leakage of energy.

You can go chakra by chakra or focus on whichever cord seems thickest and stickiest and most in need of detachment. If you feel daunted, just scan through your body, choose one that seems simple to work with to begin, and allow your divine surgeon to help you. Sometimes, I have worked with faery surgeons, and their work is so precise and delicate — almost like spiritual microsurgery.

After doing a reading, I often scan my body by closing my physical eyes and passing a hand down about half a metre in front of my body, from my head to the base chakra, and behind. This can be helpful if you have readings one after the other, or just have a connection to a person that you feel would best be peacefully dissolved.

The same can apply to situations that occur again and again. Find the cord by scanning with your third eye, and ask the cords between you and the pattern to dissolve.

You may need to do some sea-salt bathing, or swim in the ocean, or carry a protective smokey quartz or piece of obsidian for a while after cord cutting — because sometimes our patterns long to be re-established, and this will ward off those energies that we no longer wish to have in our lives.

Cord cutting can also be very helpful for disturbing dreams, poor sleep, illness and psychic attacks. It's a simple, under-used, very powerful tool you can work with to cleanse and protect yourself in your path as an Oracle.

Deities, Myths and Legends

Within Your Oracle Cards

Many of you will be familiar with deities: Gods and Goddesses, divine energies who many cultures have revered and honoured throughout the ages.

Within your decks, there are lots of interwoven energies. We could be drawn to working with certain decks when we need their energy. For instance, I have returned to the *Oracle of Shadows and Light*, really thriving on the healthy encouragement of the beings within the deck to maintain my personal boundaries—to avoid those who would drain and use us, without really caring for us—and to be honest and authentic, to live from my truest self. They help me reclaim myself, redraw my boundaries, and steer away from drama and addictive behaviours (both those of others and those that I possess and can be triggered in my day-to-day life).

The Mermaids have a very watery, emotional energy, very nurturing and understanding, and so compassionate. I can feel my heart lighten and feel almost held when I work with them. Even if the message itself is not positive, such as in the card 24, *Soul Cage*, I can really feel myself being taken care of by them, and there is a deep emotional connection I experience with them. They help me to love, and to love myself.

Why are they so powerful? One reason is that, within each of the decks, there are deities whose energy was gracefully offered to enter into the decks and gratefully received. There are also cards that contain echoes, or shades, of myths and legends. I'll weave some of these into this chapter, too, so you can explore these more deeply if you wish.

JANUARY 5, 1988, BRIGHTON

•

Dreams last night – marriage figuring in them. Being in the country and wearing a diamond ring – the one Gran gave me. I think I was pregnant. Driving off in the family car, stuffed into a white dress. I was also enrolling to study, talking with other feminists. Thoughts, anxious, of whether I could handle all the activities. The sequence of my dreams is confusing.

There was a tall woman made of light walking towards me, but I could not see her face. Too much light. I do not know who she was. But she knew my name.

I awoke with her voice saying my name echoing in my ears.

•

DEITIES AND MYTHIC ENERGIES WITHIN THE ORACLE OF THE DRAGONFAE

BRIGID: Brigid is a triple Goddess of three aspects, and her Maiden form and season is that of spring. Traditionally in Ireland, young women walked ceremonially from house to house to deliver blessings at this time. Brigid is warm and creative, being a Goddess of the forge and flame, and she is solar in association due to that life-giving brightness and as she shares that vital force that she has in such vast quantities.

THE PENDRAGON: To me, this card contains the Arthurian energies in Dragonfae form. So, there is Arthur and Uther Pendragon (Pendragon means 'Chief Dragon'), which connects deeply with the masculine side of the Avalonian energies.

TIAMET: The story of Tiamet is deep, wild and cosmic in its scale. Her complexity scares some folk away — but know when we work with this ancient one, we work with our own ability to rebuild ourselves, taking the parts of ourselves that have been scattered and seemingly destroyed and rebuilding, recreating and rebirthing ourselves. If you wish, explore her a little more. There is a great deal of bias about her, so read carefully.

MORGAN LE FEY: King Arthur's older half-sister is a Faery — part Dragon, part Crow, and perhaps a Goddess. Morgan was a wise woman, a Lady of the Lake, and a priestess of the Triple Goddess. She is described as a necromancer and is said to be able to transform into a Raven at will. She ultimately took her brother Arthur from the battlefield of Camlann (where he was fatally wounded by their own son) and returned the dying King to Avalon, or Glastonbury Tor, where he sleeps to this day, awaiting his land's great need — or perhaps still undergoing great healing.

GRIAN: The Solar Goddess of Ireland. She brings light, hope and growth and is the Sun, sunbeams and summer's bliss after darkness and cold. A Dragonfae deity who brings life to the world, Grian breathes loving power and productivity to all. She is associated with making manifest your dreams, firing up your enthusiasm, igniting your own internal sun, and being bright, strong, warm, loving and powerful. She is the Dragonfae goddess for whom the ancient temple of Newgrange in Ireland is named — New-Grian, or Grian's place. It is at the winter solstice each year that Grian's rebirth as the solar Goddess returns life to the land, and her first great act is to bring her sword of light into the centre of the womb of the earth that is this 4,000-year-old temple at Newgrange in Ireland. In visions, Grian can appear to be part Fire Dragon, part Faery, part Goddess, and is often seen with bright flames and small Dragons all about her. She is heat and life and the ignition of dreams.

AINE: Aine is an Irish Faery Queen, and at times, she is also referred to as a Goddess, a Mermaid and a Dragon. Her domain is the moon and all that falls under moonlight. The rays of the moon are a kind of crystal cleansing, and her domain is specifically that of healing and regenerating the sacral or sexual regions for both men and women. It is said that when Saint Patrick first arrived in Ireland to bring Christianity to the people of the Old Ways, he claimed he exorcised Aine from Ireland in or around about 432 CE; at the same time, he was asking his God to protect him from "the spells of women and druids". Aine's very name means 'radiance, glow, bright', and while Patrick may have claimed to have banished her, how can one banish the light of the moon? She can bring happiness in love and prosperity to families and lovers, and can eradicate the guilt people so often feel in sexual relationships about enjoying their sensuality fully! She is described in folktales as "the best-hearted faery woman who ever lived — lucky in money and love". Wherever there is moonlight, there is Aine, and she can gift you with her ability to see clearly when all seems dark about you.

She works with us to heal sexual issues, guilt around femininity, dissolving any residual or conditioned thinking regarding women being 'sinful', and reclaiming your worth and right to love fully, prosper and be happy. Her speciality is cleansing these energetic woundings from the light body under moonlight.

AINE'S VERY NAME MEANS 'RADIANCE, GLOW, BRIGHT', AND WHILE PATRICK MAY HAVE CLAIMED TO HAVE BANISHED HER, HOW CAN ONE BANISH THE LIGHT OF THE MOON? SHE CAN BRING HAPPINESS IN LOVE AND PROSPERITY TO FAMILIES AND LOVERS, AND CAN ERADICATE THE GUILT PEOPLE SO OFTEN FEEL IN SEXUAL RELATIONSHIPS ABOUT ENJOYING THEIR SENSUALITY FULLY! SHE IS DESCRIBED IN FOLKTALES AS "THE BEST-HEARTED FAERY WOMAN WHO EVER LIVED — LUCKY IN MONEY AND LOVE". WHEREVER THERE IS MOONLIGHT, THERE IS AINE, AND SHE CAN GIFT YOU WITH HER ABILITY TO SEE CLEARLY WHEN ALL SEEMS DARK ABOUT YOU.

DRAGONFAE PLAYTIME

For those of you working with the *Oracle of the Dragonfae* deck, why not find out more about one of these powerful deities? Work with them and explore their energy for yourself. Learn their stories, and your deck will speak with you even more clearly.

- Make a Brigid's Cross.

  There are so many online tutorials, and I really like the ones that are traditional, from Irish folklore. You can make one from rushes or reeds, but paper can work just as well. I had a friend make me a Brigid's Cross and gift it to me at Imbolg, and this loving, sisterly gesture touched me to my core.
- Light a flame.
- Plant snowdrops if the season is right.
- Build or do something solid, constructive, in honour of Tiamet.
- Look through your cards and find the energies within them that feel very strongly those of a God or Goddess.
- Why not take your Grian card for a walk in the sun? She is so wonderful to work with when you require empowerment or when you are self-sabotaging action on dreams. Enlist her help for activating dreams into reality, for grounding and completing concepts, for staying motivated and excited about your life and self, or for believing in your power, asserting yourself, protecting your own boundaries and expanding your energetic influence in peaceful ways.
- Have a sunbath with Grian … call her name, and allow her golden energy to warm, fill and nourish your own internal chakra of power and autonomy. See how this makes you feel.
- Or, work with Aine beneath the moonlight, and ask for her healing, her love and her laughter.

A MANIFESTATION RITUAL WITH THE DRAGONFAE

Let's spend some time experimenting with introducing magick directly into our work as Oracles. I'm going to offer you some spells, rituals and alternative ways of working with your cards. I find many readers enjoy branching out and refreshing themselves through taking a different approach to working with the cards, both for personal use and within healing work. I have worked with them in many ways over the years and I can't wait to share these inventive and creative techniques with you! We'll begin with the *Oracle of the Dragonfae*.

Dragonfae are very helpful when it comes to manifesting … which is a skill that can be drawn upon for crafting and casting and developing your skills as an Oracle.

The Dragonfae have told me time and again that we can create so much if we are willing to do what needs to be done if we work with timing, and if we create magickally. Instead of manifesting something to ourselves, the Dragonfae, the fae and the various beings I have connections with insist that we manifest from within ourselves — that we create and add to the world and work with the abundance of natural energy all about us to bring forth our dreams. In doing so, the world itself changes, and we begin to experience life as purposeful, peaceful, loving and exciting, too.

So, how do we work with these beings to create from within ourselves the physical manifestation of our dreams?

There are simple steps we all can follow. I'll share them with you.

Firstly, you need to clear prior to the dark moon. By clearing, I mean several things.

Begin with a space clearing. Declutter and give away belongings that you no longer have a personal connection with. Without becoming laborious over this, contemplate — what does this item bring to my life? What does it say to me, and about me, to others? Contemplate giving it away. Now, this will take time, but please complete this while the moon is dark ... not new (you will know when it is new by the smallish silver sliver in the sky).

Then, rearrange items in your home to refresh and rebalance the space. Where is the heart of the home, what keeps that heart beating? Shift and rearrange, ever so slightly, or with great vigour, till you can feel the beat of your home's heart again.

Then, conduct a smudging or smoking ceremony. Using herbs that are in tune with your energy, smudge your space. Ask a friend to smudge you, too, before you do this.

Once you have cleared the house, energetically sweep it using a Witch's broom or a broom you use, which you can also smudge for this purpose.

Then, bring in something new to the home, something that represents the energy of the new life you are creating. It may be a plant, a statue, a painting or an ornament. But this is a symbol of the new coming in and being welcomed right into the heart of your home.

When this has been done, at the next new moon, I would like you to take out your *Oracle of the Dragonfae*. While shuffling, I wish you to undertake something of an examination of yourself — and be very, very honest here with yourself. Say to yourself:

"Dragonfae beings, please reveal to me now what is holding me back ..."

And write down, "What is holding me back is ..." and then let your pen write ... let it flow ... let it pour out ... let the truth come.

Now, when you have written down your answer using this simple method of automatic writing, I want you to choose a Dragonfae being who you will work with for the next moon period. Yes, that's right — choose. You can always allow the divination process to come forward and allow a being to come to you, but for this practice of manifesting, and because you are drawing forth from within yourself a creation that will have a great impact over the following year, I want you to choose.

WHICH DRAGONFAE GUARDIAN TO WORK WITH?

HERE'S HOW.

Let's look at what the issue holding you back is likely to be.

For each card, there will be a matching energetic resonance.

So, for example.

CONCERN	CARD NUMBER	CARD NAME
For deep and abiding, unshakeable self-love.	1	*Melusine*
To open your heart, feel warm, beautiful and alive.	2	*The Lady Grian*
For protection in a relationship.	3	*The Lovers*
To release anger/resentment/rid your life of conflict.	4	*Apalala*
To create friendships and happiness.	5	*Lady Titania*
To feel physically more fit and comfortable, happy with growing older and wiser.	6	*Grandmother Magicks*
To have more time to relax and complete projects.	7	*The Time Guardian*
To find the right teacher.	8	*Nimue*
To find a peaceful, healing home.	9	*Morgan le Fey*
To find creative solutions to problems.	10	*Queen Oonagh*
To find out about old magicks and ancestral lines.	11	*Queen Mab*
To feel sensual and free to love who you wish.	12	*Aine and the Guardian*
To seek a just outcome.	13	*The Lady Alfreda*
To feel worthy and deserving.	14	*The Green Lady of Y Ddraig Goch*
To rebuild your strength.	15	*The Dragonfae Goddess Tiamet*
To connect with understanding allies and people who will help you.	16	*Gwynne and Elluish*
To reclaim the missing parts of your soul.	17	*New Moon Fae*
To overcome fear-based thinking and behaviour patterns.	18	*Tatsuya*
To be responsible and clear karmic debts.	19	*The Wild Huntress*
To clear issues with your own Father, Father–God figures, or issues to do with unhealthy expressions of masculinity.	20	*The Pendragon*
To become more perceptive.	21	*The Listener*
To know right action.	22	*The Morrighan*

CONCERN	CARD NUMBER	CARD NAME
To shift body shape/excess weight/food issues.	23	*The Lovers at the Feast*
For emotional freshness and flow.	24	*Andelle*
To grow your business.	25	*Lady of the New Buds*
To heal from a breakup.	26	*Pellinor and the Lady*
To have more joy and laughter.	27	*Chenguang*
To overcome betrayal and deception.	28	*Drystan**
For unity and healing in volatile relationships, and healing within the body.	29	*Brigid*
To manifest a wise advisor/mentor/ethical and clever professionals in your life.	30	*The Elder*
To heighten and make keen your intuition.	31	*The Dawn Watcher*
To ease through a stage of life (e.g., menarche, motherhood, menopause).	32	*Lady Luna's Magick*
To see opportunities at the right time.	33	*Hideki's Door*
To grow your wealth in responsible, life-affirming ways.	34	*Oroki*
To farewell the egoic mind.	35	*Chumara*
To release guilt.	36	*Wu-Wang*
To create a beautiful relationship or marriage.	37	*Gaia's Dragon*
To grow your power in loving ways.	38	*The Sovereign*
To watch your dreams come true.	39	*The Blue Lady*
For success and victories.	40	*The Guardians*
For knowledge and truth amidst a fresh start.	41	*Dragonfae of Rebirth*
For dreams of guidance.	42	*Dreamcatcher*
To get clear on what you want and where you need to be.	43	*Fernia*

* A word on Drystan — he is a trickster, but in this context, he will teach you how to identify those who are not worthy of trust.

So, now you have chosen, or have been chosen by, a card that will help you either clear or create with the alliance of the mighty Dragonfae. Remember, there is a Law of Creation, and you are the Source, so to be abundant, you must connect to yourself as Creator. The Dragonfae being will assist you with this in many ways.

Clear your space, have with you something to offer the being. A small crystal, flower or herb will suffice.

Call in the being and make this simple. They do not need an elaborate invocation. So, for example, you may say: "I ask the Dragonfae Goddess Tiamet to join me now. I ask for her assistance in rebuilding my life, my workplace and my home." (Whichever area it is you seek to rebuild — as she rules architecture, home structures and renovations, Tiamet is a wonderful Dragonfae energy to work with for these issues. She can repair so much, resolve conflicts and help you traverse challenges as you build your life's home!).

Ask her to speak with you.

Write down what you get.

Thank her, and place your offering on your altar.

Farewell your Dragonfae guide, for now.

Now, act on the guidance.

WHAT TO EXPECT

Repeat each day: Incredible results
Repeat once a week: Tangible progress
Once or twice in the moon cycle: Positive change
Once: Good advice will be given

The guidance may seem interesting or a little strange from time to time, but the Dragonfae are also immensely practical beings. They are not fluffy. They will offer clear guidance based on what you need to do and create. Then you must act.

For in the acting, you become the creator. Do not hesitate to follow the guidance.

The Dragonfae will never tell you to do something that feels wrong to you. It may feel odd, but it will never feel wrong. They will give you practical advice, too — and if you follow it step by step, you will be amazed at what you begin to create. And what you can attract. But mostly, what you create.

Remember, they are wise and powerful, magickal beings who are your kin. They are a part of you. When you reconnect with them, you reconnect with lost parts of yourself, and by doing that, you become whole. That is true healing, and from that place, abundance and manifestation flow like water downhill!

DEITIES AND MYTHIC ENERGIES WITHIN THE ORACLE OF SHADOWS AND LIGHT

THE *SHADOWS AND LIGHT* DECK HAS MANY STRONG ENERGIES WITHIN IT, BUT let's explore the energy of the Goddess Kali first. This fierce, primal, instinctive Goddess is the great Hindu deity of death and rebirth. She is often depicted as dancing on skulls, a bloodied knife in her hand and a necklace of skulls about her neck. This symbolises her ferocity. She will kill off the old in your life — just know, when you invoke her, that there will be some destruction. Her energy is NOT malicious, but it is very 'no-turning-back'. She will also help protect you from any abusers — so definitely invoke her if you are being bothered or harassed or bullied, and you want it to stop.

There are many other energies woven into the deck, some in quite subtle ways. I'll include some here for you to explore.

AMARA THE MENEHUNE: The Menehune are ancient Hawaiian nature spirits who reside primarily within waterfalls — an almost perfect liminal space that so many of us have experienced. They are said to be very small, and beautiful, and wise. They can help us clear our energy fields and connect more deeply with the primal side of nature, uplifting us while teaching us and offering wisdom that is to be experienced. How could you connect with them?

FAIRY OF THE HIGHLANDS: There is Goddess energy woven into this card — who could She be?

FACELESS GHOSTS AND THE HAUNTED GIRL: This card has a strong Japanese cultural tradition woven into it — what do you think that might be? To learn more, you could explore Japanese culture; you could also have some fun with this and watch *Spirited Away*, a wonderful, legendary film by Hayao Miyazaki/Studio Ghibli.

You could also spend some time with the card *Dress of Alchemy* and explore the history of alchemy and transmutation, or *The Winged Seer* and deities with sacred eyes. Look within the imagery of the *Violet Angel* and her wings, the kinds of feathers she has, and the meaning this could bring to the card. Or explore *Voodoo in Blue* and deities who clear and banish, and the *Pink Lotus Fairy* with her Kuan Yin-like energy … so many cards to explore on this mythic level.

SHADOWS AND LIGHT PLAYTIME

- Set a boundary, and keep to it with *Voodoo in Blue*.
- Think of the *Grumpy Red Fairy* — be more like her (like your authentic self), especially in regard to someone who is taking advantage of you.

- Watch your thoughts, and when you begin to go into destructive thoughts, which can be repetitive and extreme, work with Kali.
- Spend some time in meditation or do some gentle, restorative yoga with the *Pink Lotus Fairy*.
- Get up early and celebrate the dawn; set intentions and wishes with the *Violet Angel*.
- Try working with your Spirit eye, or third eye, with *The Winged Seer*.
- Be brave and take assertive action with a situation or person you've been afraid of.

DEITIES AND MYTHIC ENERGIES WITHIN THE ORACLE OF THE MERMAIDS

Let's do some work with a few of the many legends and magickal energies woven into this powerful deck. Knowing more about their myths and stories will help deepen the experiences you have when reading for yourself and others. No knowledge is wasted, if it is applied with wisdom.

You may wish to explore the card *The Selkie and Her Skin*. Read about the Selkies in my book *Mermaid Magic*, or watch a film like *The Secret of Roan Inish*, one of my personal favourites, which captures Selkie legend and energy so beautifully.

To understand the card, *The Crane Bag*, you may wish to create a Crane Bag for yourself and discover more about the deities within this card … (to find out how, there is a whole section in my book, *Witchy Magic*, devoted to this process). To explore card 44, *Homeland*, explore the section in *Mermaid Magic* about the amazing qualities turtles have. To understand *Imramma*, the card and the soul journey over water, think deeply about your own journeys, and perhaps read some of *The Lost Lands*, or explore some of the Celtic myths concerning Imrammas.

The more you understand about Atlantis, Lemuria and the Celtic sea lands, the more you will have to offer when you speak with this deck. It's a wonderful journey, delicious and deep and neverending. So do not treat it like homework but like an adventure!

I like to immerse myself — explore in the physical realm through travel, watch movies that creatively explore the sacred energies, or listen to music that inspires me. Mermaids work very well, as do faeries, with a creative approach.

Here is a beautiful story I wrote some time ago, *The Merrows of Tír fo Thuinn*, which has rarely been seen. If you read it, you will understand so much more about your deck and the magickal mermaids within it. You'll find some playtime suggestions after this story.

The Merrows of Tír fo Thuinn

The Mermaid

A mermaid found a swimming lad,
Picked him for her own,
Pressed her body to his body,
Laughed: and plunging down
Forgot in cruel happiness
That even lovers drown.

— W.B. Yeats

If you stand at the ragged cliffs of Land's End, Cornwall, and turn to face the west, you will gaze out over the grey-green seas that cloak the lost land of Lyonesse. Fly through the damp veil of the heavy mist on your coracle of dreams, and you will arrive at the land of the ever-young. In that land, with its green cliffs and faery song, you will find secret coves, pebbled beaches and pearlescent tidal pools, reflecting dreams, bringing you home to this land's windswept shores. And all of these liminal places of mer-magicks overflow with the song and the compassionate energies of mermaids whose purpose is to rescue souls, awaken us to love, and walk between the worlds. Those mermaids are known as the Merrows, and they are Ireland's own shapeshifting maidens of the sea.

While writers like the visionary 19th-century poet W.B. Yeats explored the world of the Merrow with mistrust, the Merrow in the folktales of southwest Ireland are more often enchanting lovers of human men and shepherdesses of the sea creatures. Instead of cruel beings who drag human men down, they are the ones who rescue them, raising them up and breaking them free from the harrowing torments of the underwater Soul Cages of legend.

Soul Cages and Merrow-Men

You see, the male Merrow is a jealous being, and when he sees the love between the Merrow-maids and the men of the land, he grows ugly with his rage. Many Merrow-men were once handsome and splendid, but because they have grown habitually jealous and suspicious, they have lost their beauty and offend innocent eyes.

They stalk the lithe, lusty seamen the Merrow-maids love. They rock their *curroughs*, stir evil winds, and raise waves so high they fling the beautiful young men from their vessels. The Merrow-men then gather them from the sea, dragging them to the deep beneath the waves. There, the Merrow men entrap the princes of the earth in cages of kelp and coral — the Soul Cages of legend, in which the prince lies suspended between life and death.

But for every man kidnapped and thrown into the Soul Cage, there is a Merrow-maid who will free him from this antediluvian dungeon, swim him to the surface, and start his heart once more with kisses that are part song, part spell. When the breath of Merrow and Man unites, the prince returns, alive once again, forever changed. This defiance, of course, further enrages the Merrow-men, who then grow uglier, and the Merrow-maids love them even less for their wrath.

Merrow-maids not only free captives from Soul Cages and revere all that is beautiful and powerful in the masculine, they also sing the wind, raise or quiet the waves, and some can even draw the clouds out from behind a raincloud. They are the treasured protectors and kin to the seals, the cetaceans and the beautiful shy leatherback turtle, too — and while they are wary of the shark (who is not?) they are respectful of their energy and purpose, knowing they too have their part to play in oceanic magicks.

Shapeshifting Merrow Magick

The word Merrow comes from the Gaelic *muir*—the sea—and *oigh*, meaning maiden. As feminine creatures of the waters, they are changeable, mutable, translucent, flowing, ever-moving, reflective, emotional, and life-bringing. This mutability extends to their form, as Merrows, like many magickal beings, have the ability to move between forms.

The Merrows form when within the saltwater world is a young woman from the waist up — a maiden of translucent, luminous pearl-like skin; large, ovoid pale grey, green or blue eyes; and hair painted every shade of red, from glowing vivid scarlets, saffrons and the soft blush of peach — or green. Like the changeable colour of water in a shallow pool, their hair's kelp-like strands flow back from their pearly brow. From below, they have the form of an aquatic creature, most often a dolphin.

They are renowned for their exquisite, lilting voices, their tone conveying infinite gentleness and love, everything raising in inflexion at the end of each phrase, sounding like a question, whether or not it is. The Merrow flows; they change, they reflect, and they help us to enter the realm of wonderment and contemplate life in a far more fluid way, dissolving boundaries that are no longer serving us in an instinctive, feminine, watery way.

The Magick of the Cohellen Druith

It is well-known amongst those who have loved or lived amongst the sea maids that Merrows have two magickal objects that allow them to move between the land and the sea. These are known as *cohellen druith*: a red cloak and a red cap, said by some to be made of feathers. Other Merrow-folk whisper there is no cloak nor cap at all, but the cloak the long scarlet waterfall of some Merrows' red hair, and the red cap, hair bundled up on the head of the merrow. Whatever its origin, the red cloak and the red cap of feathers are part of their legend.

This wearing of the cap and cloak allows the Merrow to shift seamlessly from sea to land creature — so keeping their *cohellen druith* safe is paramount for the ability of the Merrow to return to the sea.

Merrows in Human Form

When a Merrow is in human form, you may see, if you look carefully, that she walks a little strangely — her legs are often strong and powerful, but her feet are unnaturally long and slightly out of balance. Webbed toes, but her gait suggests she has yet to learn to cope with the heaviness of life on earth. The lack of gravity in the water makes her movements fluid and dreamy, but on land, she moves slowly, heavily and carefully, as though she has only just learned to propel her body through the air.

Merrows in human form never leave the ocean for long ... they sing to the waves, and ones who have been stolen often cry at the shore, wondering why they feel they are never home, trapped by the loss of the *cohellen druith* and their memory of Tír fo Thuinn.

If a Merrow chooses to wed a human for love, she will sometimes cut her long green or red hair and dye it, and secret her *cohellen druith* in a safe sea cave where no one can find it. If her man breaks her heart or betrays her by taking her cloak and cap, she will find them, and she will return to the depths to heal and allow her salty tears to merge with the sea.

Sometimes, greedy men cut the Merrow's hair, or steal their *cohellen druith* late at night while they rest on a beach under starlight after rescuing some from the Soul Cages, or sleep deep on a rock after shepherding the precious leatherback turtles into warmer waters.

This happens more often than it should, as a Merrow bride is much sought after, not only for her beauty, voice and compassionate nature, but also because she is said to bring great treasure — gold, pearls, corals … great catches in nets will come to the one who gains her for their own. But those who seek her and take her without loving her, against her free will, will never truly benefit. And those who steal her *cohellen druith* can never keep them for long. Some who have stolen the maid of the sea mysteriously become captives of the Soul Cages ... and no Merrow can, or will, hear their cries for help.

Merrows and the Sea Creatures of Tír fo Thuinn

The Merrows not only help the men of the waves and the currents, but they are the friends of the sea creatures — including perhaps the most famous of their friends, Fungi the dolphin, of Dingle. Fungi made Dingle famous, and while he is likely to have passed due to a long and wonderful lifespan, his legend lives on.

Merrows may be sensitive, but they are very courageous, and they fearlessly interact with sharks, the 'police' of the seas. Merrows send their healing, mellow energy to the sharks, gentling them and encouraging them to take time out and bask in the warm gulf-stream shoals. Sharks love the rich offerings of the Irish waters, and it is up to Merrows to ensure that sharks use their authority and patrolling capacity in ways that are just. Even so, Merrows know just when to avoid a shark!

While it is mostly the Selkie, sisters of the Merrow, who care for the seals in the colder northern waters off Scotland and the Isle of Man, the Merrows interact with the seals too in Ireland's waters. In Clew Bay and Tralee Bay, many Merrows play with the grey seals, playing with the pups and teaching them how to fish and fend for themselves — and which fishermen to avoid.

Many Merrows are found in the Shannon Estuary in Ireland, playing and working with the pod of bottlenose dolphins that have made that waterway famous. The Merrows, through their work with the sea-loving humans, have encouraged the lawmakers to establish Ireland as a sanctuary for cetaceans — the 24 species of whales, dolphins and sweet, shy porpoises that call the Irish waters home.

PLAYTIME WITH THE MERMAIDS

- Enjoy a sea-salt bath. Splash and play, feel joyful as you let go of what no longer serves you. Feel the freedom and joy of the mermaids, and know how strong and loving they are — and you are, too!
- Consider visiting Ireland, Scotland, Cornwall, Hawai'i, Polynesia, the coast nearest to you, or a river that runs to the sea — even the bathtub can provide the most marvellous of mermaid adventures!
- Learn more about Atlantis, Lemuria, or some of the Celtic coastal lands.
- Read W.B. Yeats or a book about Mermaids.
- Swim in a red swimsuit to evoke the red caps or red cloaks of the Merrows.
- Grow your hair, or play with dying your hair red — that Merrow energy again!
- Take up a watery exercise, one that is playful and delightful.
- Connect with the bottlenose dolphins.
- Make a donation to a sea conservation society.
- Free the masculine divine that is strong, beautiful and supportive of female power.
- Free yourself from the Soul Cages life can construct around all of us.
- Use your voice in uplifting, enchanting ways. Tone carries magick and deep meaning. Speak softly, deeply, and with 'song' in the sound. Sing out loud and have fun doing so!

DEITIES AND MYTHIC ENERGIES WITHIN THE ORACLE OF THE SHAPESHIFTERS

Many deities take on the form of animals, and most are associated with at least one animal — and some have many animal associations. Viewing the deck with this in mind, we begin to open up to the presence of deities within the cards.

The Raven, for example, is a form taken by various deities, such as the Morrighan, Odin and Morgan le Fey. In folklore, there are many qualities that we humans can learn from. This deck offers us a way to understand the world of animals, of which we are a part, and yet, not a part, as we have separated ourselves so much from nature and, thus, from ourselves.

Working with the beings who came to me in this deck gave me a great opportunity to research and connect with so many of these mystic familiars, as I called them, and commune very deeply with nature. This deck also ties in animism, the philosophy that all is alive and sacred and is a part of Shinto. Shinto and Buddhism are the two dominant religious/spiritual influences on Japanese secular culture. The Shinto belief of animism teaches that everything can have a spirit or soul. That everything is alive and ensouled — from trees to birds, to stones, to flowers, to inanimate creations, like dolls or cars, and cups and jars. It's a beautiful experience to be in a culture that treats everything respectfully because everything is living, everything has a spirit. It conveys a respect, a gentleness, and a grace that stunned me when I first experienced Japanese culture and made me feel clumsy and inconsiderate by comparison.

THE SHINTO BELIEF OF ANIMISM TEACHES THAT EVERYTHING CAN HAVE A SPIRIT OR SOUL. THAT EVERYTHING IS ALIVE AND ENSOULED — FROM TREES TO BIRDS, TO STONES, TO FLOWERS, TO INANIMATE CREATIONS, LIKE DOLLS OR CARS, AND CUPS AND JARS. IT'S A BEAUTIFUL EXPERIENCE TO BE IN A CULTURE THAT TREATS EVERYTHING RESPECTFULLY BECAUSE EVERYTHING IS LIVING, EVERYTHING HAS A SPIRIT. IT CONVEYS A RESPECT, A GENTLENESS, AND A GRACE THAT STUNNED ME WHEN I FIRST EXPERIENCED JAPANESE CULTURE AND MADE ME FEEL CLUMSY AND INCONSIDERATE BY COMPARISON.

I love the way the Celts depicted deity — never in humanoid form, always as animals, shapes, and perhaps, at best, part-human. To me, this is very much a part of the energy of the *Oracle of the Shapeshifters*. It is not a Celtic deck, but that feeling of metamorphosis and a deity having many forms is a part of the deck's energy and message for you.

Let's look a little more deeply at some of the cards and see where this connection between animals and deities can take us. To begin with, let's explore the card *The Faery Bee*. If you have the deck, have a look now. What mythic energies does this card connect with, apart from the Bees and their energies? I'd like to offer to you the Melissae …

I spoke about this in *The Lost Lands*, and I'll recap it here: bees gift us with the tasty nutrition and geometric beauty of honeycomb, whose antibacterial qualities boost our immune system and heal wounds. In Avalon, bees that were encouraged and communicated with ate from sacred healing herb gardens; their honey had special, powerful properties, much like Manuka honey does today.

Beekeeping was a sacred task, and the modern-day attendants of the Glastonbury Goddess Temple are called Melissas. So, within this card is this energy of the Priestesses, and they serve a Queen, the Goddess. It is not servitude; it is service. Thus, a way to read this card could be that the person has ample support and help in their lives, and when they seek to fulfil their own purpose, they will inspire others, who will be of assistance. They must work with this power wisely.

Why not explore the idea of the Melissae for yourself?

Let's look now at the card known as *Kitsune*, which is accompanied by the message, "I will show you who to trust."

Many of you will have experienced the energy of this being, Kitsune. But how much do you know about him and the Kami he serves? Kami are Shinto, not equivalent to a God or Goddess, but more a Great Spirit, and Inari is one such spirit. Her/His shrines are found throughout Japan, and the red gates made in her honour are instantly recognisable.

Inari brings grain (specifically, rice grain), which, in rice-dependent Japan, is a symbol of abundance, prosperity and good fortune. Kitsune carries the grain for her — just one of his many tasks. Sometimes Kitsune are depicted as white, at other times red-eared, and other times just an 'ordinary' fox, golden. Perhaps consider learning a little more about Inari and Kitsune to deepen your connection with this card and the deck.

You could also explore the card *Mermaid in a Koi Pond* and look into the legends of the Koi.

What do they turn into? How do they do this? What happens when they are forced into a smaller space? Have a play with this idea, and see how it makes you feel to think that if you, too, become like the Koi who breaks free of the smaller pond, what could happen to your readings? To your skills? What could you do? This is not about ambition but about being able to fully become your true oracular self.

PLAYTIME WITH THE SHAPESHIFTERS

- Spend some time with animals, and go through your deck and find cards with animals you find very appealing. Learn more about which deity they are associated with. There may be several.
- Decide to learn more about magickal familiars, and if you do have an animal companion in your life, invite them to share in your readings. Find a card where there is a magickal familiar whose energies you would like to explore more and spend some time in conversation with them.
- Consider where you can grow and expand — where are you playing small, like the *Mermaid in a Koi Pond*?

- Work on protecting yourself magickally with the *Albino Alligator*, and wonder which Goddess' energy could be within this card.
- Find a source of ancient knowledge, or think of connecting with Elders in some way. Ways I love to connect to those ancient sources of knowledge include watching documentaries about ancient sacred sites. If I can go to them, even better, I will do that and connect deeply when I am there. There are many old trees and places all around us that hold these stories of timeless wisdom, including stones, crystals, air and the earth. I've included some of the stories of the historic oracles within this book just for this purpose — they can be the wise elders you seek, if you wish. I make a point of chatting with older people, as I become an old person myself. I also explore different cultures and am especially interested in their stories and legends, their rites and lore. Ancient knowledge also lies within us, in the DNA we share with some of our ancestors. So your own ancestors could be more easily connected with at times like Samhain, when the past ancestors are so very present, as are our future ancestors, too. Samhain is on October 31/November 1 in the Northern Hemisphere and April 30/May 1 in the Southern Hemsiphere. Dark moons are also very helpful when connecting with older energy forms because their energy helps us see right into the past, as if scrying in a dark mirror of the Universe. From journeys to sacred sites to a simple walk on the earth, the ancients are everywhere — in the earth, air, fire and water of the elements, and the small moments and precious memories of our lives.
- Work with *The Black Cat*—bring back some magick—and think about which Goddess could be working within this card.

I hope you've enjoyed our time with these mythic energies and deities within your cards. In the next chapter, we will look at *The Faery Forest*, *Wild Wisdom of the Faery Oracle* and *Les Vampires*.

ELIPHAS LEVI — THE ALCHEMICAL ORACLE

Eliphas Levi was the magickal name of French occultist and oracle Alphonse Louis Constant. Levi was an Oracle whose work focused on alchemy. He worked on reviving many alchemical aspects within the Tarot and began the work of linking (or discovering?) the way the Kabbalah and the Tarot interacted. His was a true source of wisdom — his fame was a by-product of his intellectual stature and his ability in other, more literary areas. Some say Levi coined the word 'Tarot' from the Latin word rota, for wheel or circle. He saw within the use of the cards the symbolic quest for meaning that we all must take throughout this lifetime. Also an avid Egyptologist, he was interested in numerology, and he captured the imagination of all who were embraced by his charisma, presence and generosity. Eliphas Levi died in 1875; his master work is the *Dogme et Rituel de la Haute Magie* (*Dogma and Ritual of High Magic*), published in 1854–6.

Experientials and Experimentals

- Give yourself time to work on one or two of the playtime suggestions within this chapter.
- Play with a spread, but this time with a focus on the deities, the colours and the numbers in the forms of energies and dates. It could feel a little clunky at first, but you'll soon begin to feel it all getting smoother and the information falling into place.
- Take you and your cards out on a little trip into nature, even if it's just out into the garden for a little while to feel the sunlight and breathe the fresh air.
- Make sure you have fun this week — take a break from tension, drama, negative self-talk and burdens. Create a stress-free time out for yourself where you have fun, laugh and let go.
- Be sure to work on boundaries and self-care — be kind to yourself, be authentic and respectful, and do your best without strain and guilt. In this way, when we read, we will be more able to deliver quality messages without our egos attaching to worry about what others may think of us.
- Write a list of the ways in which becoming an Oracle card reader can benefit you and be of service to others. Consider avenues to do this work in loving, creative, supportive ways.

Chapter Eleven

Revelations

Recollection of the outward events of my life has largely faded or disappeared. But my encounters with the 'other' reality, my bouts with the unconscious are indelibly engraved upon my memory.

— Carl Jung

WITHIN THIS CHAPTER, WE WILL DELVE INTO SOME OF THE LEGENDARY BEINGS TO BE DISCOVERED IN THE *WILD WISDOM OF THE FAERY Oracle*, *The Faery Forest* and *Les Vampires*.

You also have two layouts to work with at the end of the chapter, layouts that can help us understand the purpose, beauty and challenges within our important life relationships. But first, to the beings!

FROM MY BOOK OF SHADOWS AND LIGHT, DECEMBER 2006, QUEENSLAND.

•

I can sense and sometimes see the spirits of place all about me. There are soft blurs that may be beings in the bush, and I can see the details of the plants and the flowers about me spiralling into faces and gestures. The Green Man looks out from tree after tree ... It was hard to drive without being distracted – perhaps the two days of ritual and power and song and companionship have changed my sight for a time? I seem to be able to see both with my physical eyes and my Spirit eye. I can see into the world, to the realms beyond. If this continues, I will have to pull over throughout the drive, as I have done now, for surely seeing all this, while beautiful and a gift, is not meant for when I need to drive on the highway!

•

DEITIES AND MYTHIC ENERGIES WITHIN THE WILD WISDOM OF THE FAERY ORACLE

THE GREEN MAN: The Green Man is a primordial, ancient God of the Green World, and he is fertility, promise, new life and the ecstatic rush of spring in the world. He is so powerful that even when his ancient places were destroyed and churches built over the forests where he was the Lord, the people of the Church were sure to create depictions of him within their stone walls. Thus, when you visit amazing places like Westminster Cathedral in London, you can find the Green Man — even amidst the takeover of the wild green world, there he is. He is most often depicted as simply a face made of living leaves and trees.

When working with him, see what he is made from in the depiction — often, he is oak; at other times, vines. This changes the energy somewhat each time and will help you read the image. To really know him, learn more about the Sacred Trees and their language and meaning. If you have *The Lost Lands*, there is valuable information within the Avalonian Imramma section on these magickal ancient trees and their distinctive energies. By knowing them, too, you can use them for timing. He appears many times in the *Wild Wisdom of the Faery Oracle* and within *The Faery Forest*, too.

ELEN OF THE WAYS: This Paleolithic British Goddess is the keeper of the pathways and directions our soul can take in a lifetime. She helps us move through transitions and find our way when we are lost, and provides us with all we need to survive in harsh times of change and challenge. She is associated with labyrinths, reindeer, winter and ice, gateways and paths, and is considered by many to be The Horned (or Antlered) Goddess. She—or her energy—appears within several of the cards: *Golden Gift*, *Gatekeeper* and *The Secret Path*.

MERLIN: Merlin is the great sage of pre-Christian Britain from the time of the Druids. The wise Druids read the stars, the trees, the animals and the stones. They protected these natural things, as they saw them as they truly were: sacred. To the Druids, everything on this planet—everything—was a repository of consciousness. We also have the facility to be so connected with the natural world through our own innate psychic abilities, as expressed through the 'clairs'.

Merlin is able to help you turn your power up or down: if you feel bombarded with messages, respectfully ask him to make them simpler and clearer and turn them down a notch. It is hard for those on the etheric plane to work with us unless we are absolutely clear. (Be ready for communications with the plant kingdom after connecting with Merlin!)

GNOMES: These wise beings are the keepers of the treasures of the earth — minerals of all kinds, including crystals, are under their protection. The gnomes encourage us to bring our dreams into reality by digging deep … committing to hard work, and activating our tenacity. Gnomes are patient, hard-working elemental beings who find great satisfaction in their labours. Thus, they can assist us humans in finding work that will satisfy us, challenge us, and reward us greatly.

Gnomes can also show us ways to become more organised, patient, thorough and careful. When we connect with them, we create structure and become very earnest about our work and the creation of prosperity. They are slow in their approach, and this very grounded, solid approach can see us safely into old age, assisting us in saving and making wise investments that will support us for years to come, as gnomes also teach us to revere the blessings of our later years.

They intuitively guide us to create lasting wealth, the kind that endures, and can help us to find homes, inheritance and value in the land. Gnomes, more than any other elemental, reveal to us the practical processes that need to take place in order for us to bring our visions into the material plane in an enduring fashion. They are about legacy.

PLAYTIME WITH THE WILD WISDOM OF THE FAERY ORACLE

- Take a walk with your faeries this week. Walk softly on the earth, and look for faery doors, sweet little mushrooms, butterflies and dragonflies, and most of all, ladybirds.
- Tune in to a being within a card and ask for your faery name.
- Eat wonderful organic food; plant-based is most friendly to the fae.
- Plant some thyme — it is a faery flag, letting the fae know that they are safe and welcome and will be protected.
- Draw the seven-pointed star, then place a card in the centre and speak with that card or the beings within it.
- Choose a card you'd like to explore more and work with the following meditative journey into the cards.

JOURNEYING INTO A CARD

WITH THIS EXERCISE, WE ARE GOING TO HAVE QUITE THE ADVENTURE. I HOPE you are ready to come along with me and enjoy this deep exploration into your cards.

First of all, what I'd love you to do is take some time and choose at least one card from one of your decks, one which you'd like to journey within. To literally go within the dimension of the card. There is a strong tradition in cartomancy of venturing into the cards and exploring their worlds in a visionary way. This can be quite intense, so initially I'd suggest you choose a card you're already comfortable with, one that you've previously had good experiences with. Further down the track, you can work with cards you feel less positive about, but for now, choose one you will feel happy to explore more. That way, your first experience will be a great one.

Before going ahead, read through this exercise a couple of times, and make yourself familiar with the process. After you do this exercise several times, it will come easily to you. Find a space where you're not going to be disturbed. Switch off your phone. Create a very comfortable, cocoon-like atmosphere. Maybe burn some beautiful essential oils. Really create a very nurturing, sacred atmosphere. What you should have near you is your Book of Shadows and Light (or your magickal reading grimoire) so that you can record what happened during the journey once you come out of this deep, deep place.

So, now you've got your card, sit or lie down. Be comfortable and warm enough in a private and quiet space.

Take in those three magickal breaths.

Deep breath in, *ahhh*, and let it go, *ahhh*.

Deep breath in, *ahhh*, and let it go, *ahhh*.

One more deep breath in, *ahhh*, and let it go, *ahhh*.

I want you to take your card and, very softly, in the way we have spoken about within this book, gaze at your card. I want you to let your eyes soften. Just allow your gaze to drift over all the different parts of the card … I want you to see it almost as if it were for the first time.

See the colours, the number, the scenery within the card, the kind of land it appears to be in, the symbols and the season. Notice if there are any animals or beings, and observe the way the sky is, the way the earth is. Tune in to the kinds of energies that seem to be within the card — let your eyes move over all the elements and commit this card to memory. Don't force it or strain; don't worry about a perfect image. Just take your time and allow the parts of the card you've been aware of to enter into your memory.

When you feel ready, close your eyes. Now, I want you to reimagine your card, but this time, it materialises within your Spirit eye, an emerging picture on the screen in your mind. Just let all the elements emerge; some elements will come forward, others may step back — be aware that this is significant.

Notice the image of the card getting bigger and bigger on the screen of your mind until it's as large as the doorway to your home; it's a gateway you're visualising. I want you now, if it feels right for you, to step through the gateway into the image itself, stepping right through into the world of the card.

So now you are within, across the threshold, on the other side of the gateway. Look around you. Start to use your senses on the other side. Be curious and become aware of any changes. What is the temperature like? What are your senses telling you? How does the air feel on your skin? What can you see? What sounds are present? Take a deep breath in and really smell all about you. Notice what you can sense and feel within this world of your card. Now, you may wish to begin moving — moving, walking, swimming, flying towards a being or a place in the card. It could be a Goddess, one of the faeries, a mermaid, a shapeshifter or an animal. It could be a castle, a tree, a stone circle, a star … just move towards that being or place, and when you reach them, introduce yourself. Let them know who you are. And now, I would like you to thank them for allowing you to visit within their world.

If it feels right for you, you may wish to ask the being (or the object or the space) within the card three questions. For example, about them, the world of the card, the energies of this card or the energies within the deck. Bring your questions to this being; ask them about their world, show your interest and desire to understand. Really allow yourself to open up to them so they can feel your energy. Pay attention to the answers that come, in whatever form they come. They may use language, gestures, colours, symbols or sounds.

Once you have received those answers and messages, thank them. Then, seek their consent to explore this world again, and next time, more deeply. But for now, thank them, ask for their permission to return, and then—respectfully—just turn around and very gently return to the boundary of the card. Look out from within the card, and you'll notice you can see yourself in the room you began this adventure. You may be lying on a yoga mat or the couch or sitting very comfortably on a chair … just see yourself and see where you started this journey. I want you now to take hold of the borders of the card, and without any difficulty at all, you are going to step back through the gateway to your own world. Notice the sensations shifting and changing, the temperature, the smells. Gently, you rejoin your body. Really reimmerse in your body, lying down or sitting, in your time and place … in your world, in your home, in your body.

Look now from your body to the doorway, and see the card—the gateway—and see it grow smaller and smaller, until it is again the same size as the card when you originally began.

We will return to your world taking the same magickal deep breaths with which we opened the gateways; only this time, the in-breath fully restores us to our body, place and time.

Deep breath in, *ahhh*, and let it go, *ahhh*.

Deep breath in, *ahhh*, and let it go, *ahhh*.

One more deep breath in, *ahhh*, and let it go, *ahhh*.

When you are ready, begin to wiggle your fingers and toes, and know you are returned to this world.

Gently open your eyes.

Take a moment, then stretch, sit up and give yourself a gentle little shake.

But before memory can fade, take your Book of Shadows and Light and write about the messages you received. Note anything down you wish — it's all significant, it's all sacred.

You've connected with a very deep energy with the card, and this is now a part of you, part of your personal experience. You are now woven into the energy of this card, not in a way that traps you or imprisons you, but in a way that helps your energy speak from a place of deep authenticity because you have truly connected.

You will now have even greater confidence when providing readings for others.

You may wish afterwards to go through the deck and make a note of some cards you may wish to journey with in the future. You could decide to experiment with cards that include gateways or doorways or pathways. *Secret Doorway* and *Follow Me* are wonderful cards to journey with.

You might find cards that relate to this moment in your life appealing. You might choose a card that speaks to you of future desires, and with that card, you can investigate your own future. This is a very ethical and principled way of working with the boundaries of time and your potential future.

I'd love you to do this journeying into the cards as a regular part of your practice.

In time, you'll find yourself moving through some of the cards you find more challenging. You'll learn so much, you'll have wonderful adventures, and I know the cards will welcome you into their various otherworlds and homes. You are safe doing this work. There is nothing to fear, and you are very, very loved by the beings and places within the deck — some of the places may even feel like home.

Be sure to ground yourself after doing this exercise: drink some herbal tea and eat fresh fruit, and really enjoy the experiences that opening up to your cards and entering into them can offer you.

I offer you my love, and especially so many blessings as you embark on these oracular adventures.

Blessed Be.

Owls have been a part of many an Oracle — spending time with these birds of prey, allowing me to be this close, even snuggling into them, filled me with respect and awe. I love Goddess Blodeuwedd, so meeting these owls in Avalon (Glastonbury) will be an ever-treasured occasion.

DEITIES AND MYTHIC ENERGIES WITHIN THE FAERY FOREST

This deck has a very interesting blend of deities and energies who came through to me in very ancient sacred sites, primarily throughout Britain. This isle was successively settled by different peoples throughout history, who brought their Gods and Goddesses, their energies and beliefs with them — so the deck contains deities of the Vikings, of the Norse, and of the Old Ones of the lands we now call Britain. They all live with each other in a very eclectic, yet … well, harmonious isn't quite the word, but they all manage to live alongside each other without conflict. It works.

There is an immense amount of old faery energy within this deck, and it all comes together quite beautifully — just as the beings do themselves in the old sites, the ancient places, the Wild Green Worlds where they dwell to this day.

Avebury, an ancient stone circle, has defied many attempts to defile her serpentine energies, vortexes and personality-filled stones. I read between these stones (known as The Cove) within the northern inner circle on my handfasting anniversary. My partner and I later repledged our love between these two sacred beings.

FRIGGA: This complex Norse Goddess (also known as Frigg) has many aspects to her, but one that came through strongly while she spoke with me was just how very much she had to offer, how clever she was in terms of being sure we had enough, and she showed me an immense treasure chest which was hers. She shared the treasure, but she ensured she and her people had plenty — metaphorically, it was a very powerful symbol, as the treasure was not simply about money, which is so often our modern default mode. It was about the treasure within our lives and the appreciation that helps that grow.

SALU: Salu is very bright, shining and full of love — she came to me whilst in a forest, near an old burial site of the ancient people, which has been occupied by successive peoples, including the Anglo Saxons … but she felt very old, although her energy was so youthful. She spoke to me of the necessity of the Light and of the Sun and of how, when we are healthy and vital and well, we are kissed by the Sun (which is what she shared with me her name truly meant). She encouraged me to share with you all the necessity for natural light and for sunlight in particular.

Energetically, I feel she speaks to us of coming out of the darkness of our thoughts and into the light, so we can be well and have balance. She also speaks of a moment when we come 'back to life' after being in a kind of near-death state for a time. This need not be literal, but it could also mean when the soul is sick … when we are suffering spiritual or emotional ennui, Salu and her light make the soul well again.

ENERGETICALLY, I FEEL SHE SPEAKS TO US OF COMING OUT OF THE DARKNESS OF OUR THOUGHTS AND INTO THE LIGHT, SO WE CAN BE WELL AND HAVE BALANCE. SHE ALSO SPEAKS OF A MOMENT WHEN WE COME 'BACK TO LIFE' AFTER BEING IN A KIND OF NEAR-DEATH STATE FOR A TIME. THIS NEED NOT BE LITERAL, BUT IT COULD ALSO MEAN WHEN THE SOUL IS SICK … WHEN WE ARE SUFFERING SPIRITUAL OR EMOTIONAL ENNUI, SALU AND HER LIGHT MAKE THE SOUL WELL AGAIN.

AWEN: This beautiful word refers to pure Inspiration, the breath that blows to flame the sparks of fire in the head ... The muse and the divine poetic gift, given to bards, druids, priestesses, artists, singers — all of us! To be with or to experience Awen is to be full of inspiration that has at its heart a deity, an element, the fae or a magical beast ... it is beyond classification in the ordinary sense. The priestesses would breathe with Awen to bring life to their inspirations and purpose as individual priestesses and as a community.

Awen is represented by different sigils. However, it is the source itself, and chanting Awen brings you not only inspiration but also the name of creation, inspiration, source, beginnings, endings, birth, death and rebirth. It is also worked with to invoke the truth. Within this card (also titled *Awen*), you see the personification of Awen, perhaps in the form of the faery being who gifted the Goddess Cerridwen the 'recipe' for Awen, which then was brought through into the world of the humans, too.

RAGNAROK: Such a deep card, and within it are Universe-cracking revelations and legends. Ragnarok is the end of days in Norse mythology, and when we see this card, we know that the life of the person we are reading for is changing deeply, and there may even seem to be destruction taking place. The image within the card is fascinating, as there are many aspects of Ragnarok, but one part of the legend came to me in the forest.

It was about the Goddess known as Saga, who turns to see the flames of Ragnarok. In this image, I feel we are seeing Her turning from the flames and readying herself to warn others. For Saga, as her name suggests, is the Goddess of Story, cyclic time and narrative — she is so very present within this card. So, with the narrative of the cards, we can forewarn others of their own Ragnaroks, helping them avoid harm.

FREYR: He is so very strongly associated with the Elves and came through to me at an old burial chamber known in our time as Wayland's Smithy. To me, he is the greater form of Wayland the Smith, who is an Elven King. He is about the bounty within your blood and bones — your DNA has so much wisdom. He is fertile, powerful, able to move and change, yet extremely bound to that place (he said, as he watched over those who came to the site, to be sure they were well if we asked for this blessing).

When we make offerings to him, he can turn them into greater blessings within our lives. He gives us all the gift of movement—agility and exploration, travel and discovery—and with his help, we can harness energy and be propelled forward into the next stage of our lives with abundance and plenty.

GNOMES: (They are present within the *Wild Wisdom of the Faery Oracle*, and they have a significant presence, too, in *The Faery Forest*.) Gnomes dwell deep within the earth and are very strong beings. They offer inspiration that is so grounded and achievable that they can almost seem like very solid counsellors, rather than an elemental.

They are particularly helpful for people who tend to be unable to choose or find it difficult to settle and focus. They offer a kind of calming influence, strong and solid and slow. For some of us, being so attuned to the mercurial pace of modern life can feel very strange. But it is so beneficial to have this solidity and this density. By connecting deeply with the gnomes, we also undergo transformation and integration; just as the earth takes whatever falls upon it and transforms it, when we connect with that deep, earthy, root energy, we transform and transmute, too. They are very helpful when we are exploring expressing ourselves in ways that can become very real, very strong, very solid parts of ourselves. Gnomes also help with confidence around our physicality.

So many of us are surrounded by messages of not being quite good enough, physically: that ageing is somehow wrong; that to even have a body is somehow unspiritual. Gnomes help us to connect with the tangible, sensual sacred in the form of our body. They show us how to enjoy physicality, to exercise, move, and eat well — and with great enjoyment, with the companionship of others. They can help us release weight or gain muscle mass and bone density to reconfigure our bodies in a form more suited to our souls. These help us to be stronger and have an unwavering sense of self, of core values, and of being well and healthy.

Gnomes are of the green world — the great old forests and the ancient trees that are so much a part of this deck. Thus, they help the earth breathe, and the healthy roots of trees help her hold on to her deep magick. If we wish to connect with Mother Earth, working with the gnomes is a deep and rewarding way to feel her from the inside out. By respecting her, loving her crystals and minerals, and choosing simple, ethical ways to spend our money, we help support her through this great shift in Mother Earth's story.

The gnomes can encourage us to recycle, eat organically, and grow food, too — particularly anything that grows beneath the earth, such as root vegetables and pulses.

Gnomes are the antithesis of the disposable culture that is now all around us — they teach us to find the value in what we have, or to create new ways of working with what we have. They also show us to respect what is useful, what is practical, what can be worked with. They adore gardeners and can help you to grow the most wonderful foods and keep the soil fertile and healthy. They help us to take care of the health of the trees, the animals and the earth herself.

THE NORNS: The Three Norns are central figures in Norse mythology, and while the card *The Faery Norn* does not depict them directly, their echoes are found within the card. They are the carvers (through runes) of destiny and the weavers (through threads) of fate. The Norse concept of fate is not that we have a soul contract, nor are we unable to rework our destiny — it is a weaving between our own choices, our own soul's path, and the influences about us.

It is well worth looking into *wyrd*, and its influence on destiny and time. The Norns are three 'sisters' who dwell beneath Yggdrasil, the world tree, and they either carve their runes of destiny into the tree or weave the threads of beings' lives together. Their energies can be said to correspond to the past (the Norn Urdr), the present (the Norn Verdandi), and the future (the Norn Skuld). It is not quite so neat as that, as the Norse concept of time is cyclic, and we know from exploring time in Chapter Nine that all can exist together. So when that Norn energy appears within this particular card, ask yourself, what is she stitching? Who is it for? Why is she alone? Which Norn is within this card? Does the being within the card wish to change her destiny? Or is she musing about the past? Or immersed in the present? And, as always, learn through enriching, wonderful examinations of the world's great mythologies, which have so much to teach us all.

PLAYTIME WITH THE FAERY FOREST

• Work with Awen ... sing, chant or simply say the word over and over. Its power becomes clear when you sing and chant the sound. Look for rays of light, and if you feel the moment of divine breath flowing inspiration upon you, take a moment, step into the energy, and absolutely absorb it all.

• Read some of the great Viking sagas or watch a television show like Vikings to get a feel for their energy. (This can be quite violent, so check in with your intuition as to whether it will affect you adversely.)

• Experiment with runes this week — see which shapes appeal to you, and practise drawing those that seem to call to you.

• You may wish to visit a green world near you — just an hour or two of walking will help connect you to the energies of these deep green spaces.

• Work deep old faery magicks — ask the Old Ones for their assistance.

• Garden, recycle and practise loving action on behalf of Mother Earth. Plant something green and good, and watch it grow. You are contributing to the lasting energy of the green world when you do this simple, magickal thing.

• You may wish to work with the Past Life Spread in Chapter Nine, to see where you may have dwelled once upon a lifetime.

• Read *The Book of Faery Magic* (by Lucy Cavendish and Serene Conneeley) to discover more about the old, wise energies of faery, or *Witches and Wizards* by Lucy Cavendish. Its pages contain a great deal of information about Anglo-Saxon magick, which, in turn, worked its way into this wonderful, rich deck.

DEITIES AND MYTHIC ENERGIES WITHIN LES VAMPIRES

Les Vampires has a very interesting energy, and some of the energies came through to me within cathedrals and places of great established religions — which was fascinating, as I have, shall we say, 'issues' with lots of organised religions, and particularly Catholicism. Yet through they came.

The energies of Rome and the great ancient families of the Italian city-states—the Medici and the Borgias—are included within the deck as a very baroque gathering of beings. Yet, the deck contains some of the purest energies, too, including those of Christ within the card *Compassion*, which clearly references Michelangelo's *Madonna della Pietà*. Magdalene's and Mother Mary's energies can be found intertwined throughout this deck's symbolism and guidance.

I was concerned that people would be offended by some of the inclusions, particularly *Compassion*, but to date, there seems to have been none. I did not set out to offend, not at all, but it is a subversive deck, iconoclastic and challenging in its way. I find the imagery and messages to be exceptionally beautiful and comforting — strange it may be, but as the vampires say, to go through darkness, you must travel with those who know the territory.

THE LAMIA: In the *Jealousy* card swirl the conflicting energies of Mount Olympus and the vengeful ways of the God Zeus, who cursed the Lamia to a vampiric existence. Within this card is the wisdom of this ancient story, which, to me, gives us so much more to draw from when we work with this card.

CHRIST AND MOTHER MARY: The *Compassion* card directly references the Pietà and thus holds within it the energies of Christ, sacrifice and Mother Mary. The compassion within this card called so strongly to me. The idea of carrying and helping someone when they are 'beyond' help is present and tangible within this card, which can offer understanding and compassionate support when reading. So that supremely loving energy of the Mother is within the deck, as is the compassionate love of Mary as Mother, who looks over us all when we find ourselves within moments that have broken and betrayed us. As she did for her son, she will come to help soothe and heal us.

I had a personal epiphany many years ago when I first went to Glastonbury that helped me reconcile my childhood love of Mother Mary and my path as a Witch, which seemed so at odds. When I went to Glastonbury in 2005, I found my way back to her, and to peace. I think it had a great deal to do with where I was staying, not only in such a special town, with such sacred energy, but the cosy bed-and-breakfast I'd chosen was well-loved for its Goddess-themed rooms. I was so excited to see which room I would receive — would it be Rhiannon? The Lady of the Lake? Imagine my bewilderment when I was ushered to the Mother Mary room. It turned out to be a great blessing to me, and I felt Her in that room, and Her healing worked its magick on my wounded child's heart, reawaking a lost, tender part of myself. She is like that within this deck; she is a loving energy, so present and generous — perhaps she is especially so amidst the most 'fallen' of all the beings.

PERSEPHONE: The energies of Persephone are within the card *That Death Will Come …* the myth of her descent into the Underworld at Mabon each year, of the frightening grief and torment of her Mother, the Goddess Demeter, which brought endless winter to the world, and of the pomegranate which keeps her relationship with the Underworld alive are all within this card. There are many versions of the myth, and while some versions speak of Persephone being abducted by Hades, there are earlier versions in which she falls in love with Hades and runs away with him, choosing to leave her mother.

Working with this card and this energy will help you understand and move through grief, separation and sacrifice, and the return to joy that comes to all of us who grieve. It is a reminder to laugh (as Demeter returns with the Sun and warmth through laughter and the humour of the Goddess Baubo) and to know that to love is like going underground — the promise Hades and Persephone make to each other is fulfilled through the pomegranate seeds she eats whilst within the Underworld. Thus, she has her life as Lover and her life as Daughter. The Wheel of the Year turns, and we ourselves find our way through grief, separation and change.

UNICORN: We have explored Unicorn energies throughout this book in regard to other cards in other decks, and it is as present within this card as any other, but in a very different form. (Such is the energy of *Les Vampires*.) The card *Transgression* speaks of the breaking of natural laws and of 'sin'.

Within this card, the allegory of the Maiden and the Unicorn is referenced, with the Maiden outliving the Unicorn. Perhaps this Unicorn has been killed, in which case, a great sin has been committed for nothing is more sacred, pure and rare than the energy of the Unicorn. The Unicorn's magnificent and distinguishing spiral horn—the alicorn—is a sacred shape that recurs across nature and contains the code upon which life itself is based.

THE UNICORN'S HORN EMANATES FROM THE CENTRE OF THEIR BROW, THE REGION IN WHICH OUR THIRD EYE AND THIRD EYE CHAKRA ARE LOCATED. THE THIRD EYE CONTAINS OUR CAPACITY FOR INTUITION, PSYCHIC ABILITIES, CLAIRVOYANCE, COMMUNION AND COMMUNICATION BETWEEN WORLDS. SO WE CAN WORK WITH THIS INFORMATION, TOO, WHEN WE SEE THE UNICORN WITHIN THIS DECK AND THE OTHER DECKS WHERE THEY APPEAR.

The spiral is a perfect manifestation of the divine sequence, a numeric code discovered by ancient sages where each successive number equals the addition of those preceding it. This symbolises the continuing growth of everything: that everything in this world exists as a result of everything that goes before. As it is above, so it is below. When this Unicorn was killed, that sacred balance was disturbed.

The Unicorn's horn emanates from the centre of their brow, the region in which our third eye and third eye chakra are located. The third eye contains our capacity for intuition, psychic abilities, clairvoyance, communion and communication between worlds. So we can work with this information, too, when we see the Unicorn within this deck and the other decks where they appear.

MARY MAGDALENE: A beautiful card from *Les Vampires*, *Redemption* resonates with the energy of Mary Magdalene and the sacred bloodline — Mary Magdalene and Christ's children. Gnostic Christians believed that Mary Magdalene had been the loving partner of Christ, and within her was held the sacred blood of the Holy Grail. The Grail also corresponds to the womb and alludes to the amniotic fluid of the sea. Thus, the *Redemption* card holds oceanic energies and points to our relationship with water, emotions and empathy.

Mary Magdalene is a sensual, loving Goddess, and she leads the way to true repentance: for the lack of respect shown to sexual women, the degradation of the sacred feminine, and the rising again of the Holy Bloodline within us all.

THE MAENADS AND DIONYSUS: Within this deck are entwined the vine-like energies of Dionysus, an ecstatic, frenzied energy that needs liberation, else we can erupt with chaotic emotions and behaviours. In Dionysian lore, we learn of the Priestesses of Dionysus, the Maenads, who tore their victims to pieces with hands and teeth — so consumed by the trance and bloodlust of the worship of Dionysus.

Their name means 'raving ones', so consumed are they by a kind of madness that is both divine and very dangerous. This card speaks to us of the need for safe spaces in which to unleash our primal energies. When we repress them within our cultures, we can often fuel a great hunger, which—when denied and ignored—can override our conscious minds and rise up as an insatiable thirst, a tide of madness.

We see this all the time. It is no feature of an ancient world but of humanity and our hunger, thirst and desperation to connect with the Divine, which can quite often see us succumb to dangerous behaviours. Like the Maenads, we can lose our minds and become raving ones unless we safely work with these energies and ground ourselves. No human being is immune to this madness. We need safe spaces and ritual environments to unleash our primal energies, that ecstatic dance of the Maenads, where we can worship the Gods. Please know when I say we must work with these energies in healthy ways, I am not suggesting at all that we harm others in an ecstatic fever — harm none. But our souls desire to enter into wild spaces, and we must do so or risk becoming repressed and arousing the Maenad within us, whose primal energies can arise and behave in ways that are beyond our power to constrain.

Because this card has Dionysian energy, you may find that there could be addiction or mental health issues with people when working with this card, depending on how it appears within the spread.

PLAYTIME WITH LES VAMPIRES

- Explore the story of Persephone. How does knowing her story—in its various versions—help you within readings and bring depth to your understanding of this card? In the story of Persephone, laughter in the form of a Goddess named Baubo works a kind of miracle, lifting negativity and dissolving despair, transforming all with the utter magick of laughter. It's an essential component of the myth, so find a way to make laughter a part of your journey with this card (*That Death Will Come*) and bring the sunshine back into your life.
- You may wish to read several times this week in the darkness of night. Work with some of the spreads from this deck, and contemplate areas where you have been helped through the darkness in your own life.
- Wonder about life beyond death and even about death within life. We often let ourselves 'die' long before our physical bodies have left.
- Imagine you are no longer able to live within the daylight and enjoy the energy of the Sun — really allow yourself to feel the life force of the Sun feeding you, and be sure to give thanks for the great miracle that this truly is.
- You may wish to watch a television series in which some of the energies within are depicted. If you are after something very 90s and pop culture, try *Buffy the Vampire Slayer* for her ambivalent relationship with the Vampire called Angel. Or you could watch *The Borgias*, whose energies are within a particular card in this deck, one which speaks of family sins and domination.
- Eat and drink wonderful food, wines or juices this week — feast the senses that the Vampires can no longer engage with.
- Find a way to connect with your own soul's wild, ecstatic energy — perhaps dance a card that inspires you this week!

- For a complex, fascinating literary take on Vampires, I recommend Anne Rice's *Interview with the Vampire*. Inspired by the death of her daughter, it is an ode to immortality, love, passion and mourning.

To Understand the Relationships in Our Lives

THE SIGNIFICANT OTHER SPREAD:

In Part One of our journey together, The Initiate, we spoke of honouring the sovereignty of other souls when it comes to readings. However, as you are now deepening your relationships with the cards and have proven your dedication and commitment, you could now work with the cards to understand your—or your Seeker's—interactions with others. We can do this in compassionate, non-invasive ways.

Let's say we wish to uncover some of the challenges within a relationship we may be experiencing. We'll work with our reversals, as we did in Part One.

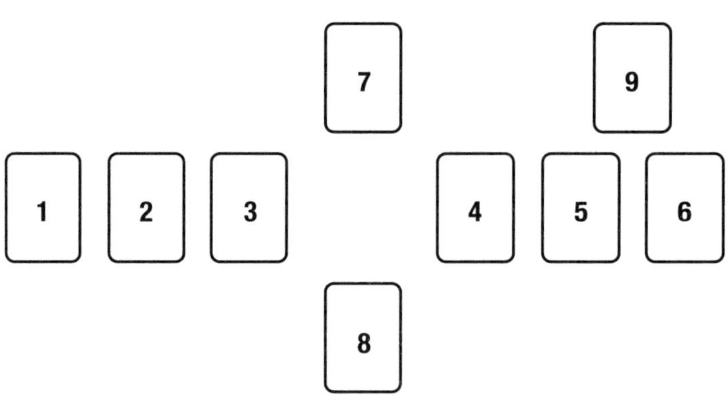

Shuffle while mulling over the question. When you feel it is the right time to cease shuffling, do so. Then, split the deck and put it back together in the usual manner. Now, split the deck into three piles, turn the top card on each pile around and put them back together again. Shuffle thoroughly and split once again.

When you have put your deck together again, take three cards from the top of the deck and lay them out on the left in a line. Then, take three cards and lay them out to the right, again in a line. Then, take three more cards and lay the first above the lines, the second below the lines and the third to the right.

The set of three cards on the left represents your partner or the person you feel a connection with. The first card you put down indicates their true feelings, the second is their public face and how they behave towards you, and the third is the direction in which their feelings will develop.

The set on the right represents you. The first card here, card four, indicates your true feelings; the second, card five, your public face and how you come across to this person; and the third, card six, the direction in which your own feelings will develop.

The card above these two groups, card seven, indicates the destination of this relationship. The card below, card eight, indicates the potential problems, blocks and challenges and the lessons from this union. The card to the right, card nine, will give you guidance regarding the right action in this relationship.

Always respect another person's sovereignty, and know you are reading their feelings in the context of understanding your relationship and their impact on you. You are seeking to understand more about them so that you can have a more healthy relationship.

SHARED INCARNATIONS SPREAD:

I DON'T OFTEN WORK WITH THIS SPREAD, BUT WHEN I DO, IT GIVES ME VERY trustworthy insights regarding my soul's relationship with another person's soul. To me, it is an ethical way of working with the cards to more deeply understand the reasons I am having certain challenges or blessings with another human being. We work with the cards in a way that is respectful and not intrusive, and we seek the highest good of all concerned.

This spread builds on our spread from Chapter Nine, where we worked with past lives. It's an amazing spread to clarify past lives and the soul purpose of a kindred spirit, and it is wonderful, powerful, insightful and healing — especially for those of us in what feels to be a fated relationship, or where one partner feels this way, and the other does not!

First, I want you to choose a card that represents the person you're involved with. This card is going to help give you very important information about your relationship with the other person. Put this 'signifying' card to one side, as you will soon be using it.

Now, take the rest of your deck and begin to shuffle. While shuffling, think about the relationship you are in and a part of, and ask, "What past lives have I shared with this person?"

When you have completed shuffling, split your deck into three, put it back together, and then fan the cards out before you, with their backs to you, so you don't know at this stage which card is which.

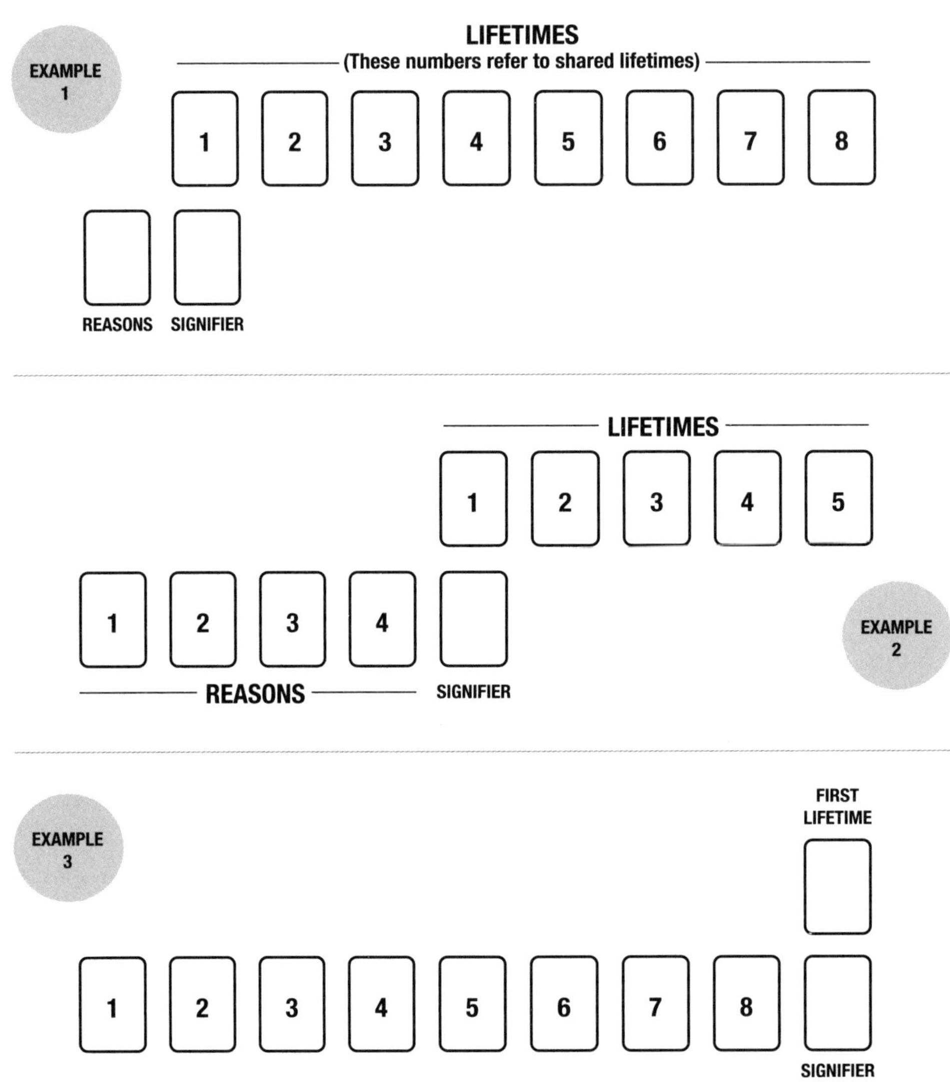

Hover your left hand over the cards and choose nine cards from the deck. Take these nine cards and add the original 'signifier' card you chose to represent your friend or partner. Now you have 10 cards. Shuffle once again. When it feels right, just stop shuffling.

Now, we begin to lay out the cards. Start to lay them out from left to right, right side up. Now, when the 'signifier' appears, place the next card above it. This card, with the 'signifier' underneath it, indicates the very first lifetime you have shared with this person. The cards following that indicate consecutive lifetimes. The very last card indicates your current lifetime together. The cards prior to the 'signifier' indicate the themes of your journey together and the reasons you chose to incarnate together and be with each other again in this lifetime. I know this can be a little confusing, but when you have the cards in your hands and laid out before you, it will become clear.

So, if the 'signifier' is card two, then you have had eight lifetimes with this person, and the final card is the one you're working on together now. The third card—the one that is now on top of the 'signifier' card—reveals your first lifetime together, and the next seven show other lives you've shared and the issues you dealt with then. Card one, to the left of the 'signifier', reveals the reasons for you incarnating together now.

If the 'signifier' is card five, then this current lifetime is your fifth life together, and there are four cards (cards one to four) to represent the issues you are dealing with now.

If the 'signifier' is card nine, then this may be your first lifetime together, in which case card 10 shows you what this lifetime is about, and every card preceding it reveals the issues, lessons and gifts you are bringing to each other's lives now.

If the 'signifier' is the first card you put down (card one), then this lifetime—represented by the last card—is your ninth incarnation together. To clarify your theme, the reason you have shared so much, pull a further card randomly from the deck. This card will give you a message regarding the deeper meaning of your soul journey together.

Finally, if the 'signifier' is the very last card put down, card 10, then you may be nearing the completion of your incarnations. Of course, you may have shared many more incarnations with some souls; however, for the purpose of this spread, I tend not to go beyond this number, as otherwise, the reading could become infinite! You can always explore more another time. The cards prior to card number ten represent what you are going through in the present lifetime in regards to the person you have sought more information about, with whom you are potentially sharing your final incarnation.

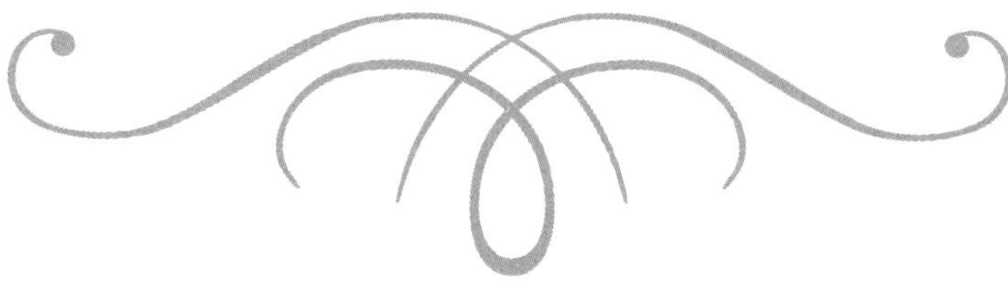

THE ROYAL WIZARD WHO SPOKE WITH ANGELS: DR JOHN DEE

"A MARVELLOUS NEUTRALITY HAVE THESE THINGS Mathematical, and also a strange participation between things supernatural … and things natural ..." Dr John Dee is truly one of the world's most influential and fascinating real-life Oracles. A bona fide mathematical genius, a political and occult advisor to Elizabeth I, and a dedicated, visionary occultist, Dee bridged the worlds of mystery and politics during a very dangerous age. To this day, Dee remains an astonishing character, one who has never lost his hold on the public imagination and who has never quite garnered the respect he is due. Along with his genius, his passion for the occult and his determination to pierce the veil and connect with the unseen world, Dee created an occult language and system that is more popular today than ever before — Enochian Magic.

During his colourful eighty-one years of life, Dee was arrested at least twice for sorcery and more than twice for treason. Banished from Britain and then later called home from exile, Dee's obsessions gathered him into the whole gamut of human experience — the glittering favour of the royal court, great poverty, intense relationships, sex scandals, a beloved family, buried treasure, public condemnation and physical attacks. He was the darling of the powerful and brilliant Elizabeth I and became her watchful eyes and her spy — some say Dee began what was to become, in time, the British Secret Service. He was an outcast, who nevertheless managed to keep his head, follow a scandalous Magickal path and even inspire William Shakespeare to write *The Tempest*, a play featuring a powerful magician, Prospero, modelled on Dee.

That he managed to live as long as he did is testament to his wit, daring and courage — and his lifelong value to Elizabeth I.

Experientials and Experimentals

- Simply work through some of the Playtime Activities for this chapter and enjoy.
- Work with a spread, and delve into some legends and myths, and see how they weave together. Feed your beautiful mind and fill it with the wonder of these ancient myths, legends and stories — which are all, as the saying goes, "truer than the truth".
- Be sure to undertake your 'card journey' exercise, and most of all, take very good care of yourself afterwards by grounding with nourishing, wholesome foods.
- This is a wonderful time to pause and go back to the beginning of Part Three: The Adept, and revisit some of what we worked with. How do you describe yourself? Journal a little until you feel you've reached a good description of yourself, and perhaps contemplate the Trial by Fire (Chapter Seven) once again. I know it can seem daunting, but when you put it into practice, it can be very empowering.
- Commit to self-love this week, and do something wonderful for yourself.
  With brightest blessings for your explorations of oracular Magick and Wonder.

Chapter Twelve

We can predict the future when we know how the present moment evolved from the past.

— Carl Jung

Dear Adepts,

As you have been working through this third part of this book, you have developed your skills at working with the Oracle cards. You've strengthened your abilities in so many ways and have deepened your appreciation and understanding of the beings within the cards, too. Your meditations have helped you to clear and cleanse, refresh and reinvigorate yourself, and you have stepped through the borders of this world and into the Otherlands of the cards.

There have been new spreads to work with and new ideas to ponder, and we've uncovered a final realisation — that there will always be more to discover and learn and experience.

Right back at the beginning of Part Three: The Adept, I gave you all a challenge, and that was to pass through a test. All tests are opportunities or gateways. They provide for us a borderland, which offers us the chance to change by stepping through the gates. One part of our life ends, another begins, and we walk on. You did not step back. You kept walking onwards.

Your own trials will come again and again — as a reader, as an Oracle, simply as a human being. There is no avoiding that which tests us. What you have developed, and what you now have a great deal of support in accomplishing, is the moving through the gates — moving through the fires of change. Always be good to yourself, but know that the fears and the clever persuasion of the egoic mind, which will arise when a little shocked or confronted, will take place within our lives.

APRIL 6, 1990, PARIS
TAROT READING

•

Eight of Discs – problems at hand in the past, the lovers of the past, or the ways of loving have ended. Learning new ways was absolutely necessary, as was new directions.

Two of Discs – a separation, a breakup of a present partnership, probably by agreement. Indicates heavy demands on my nature, inability to cope.

Hidden, unconscious factors – new beginnings with problems attached. Plans, new things still worth doing, but maybe not immediately. Choosing when, and allowing when, is vital. How will I recognise the moment when it comes?

Perhaps more importantly, how will I meet the moment?

I hope I choose courage, and do not shrink away from destiny, for she may not come so willingly if I turn my face from her too often.

•

The Trial by Fire is not, and never will be, compulsory. But I encourage you once again to consider taking on this task (detailed in Chapter Seven) in order to break through some of the barriers you may have placed about yourself. This is of particular relevance if you wish to read for others and read professionally. This sacred practice will reward you, challenge you, trouble you, inspire you, delight you, puzzle you. What I hope you have seen, from your work thus far and the way your energy is changing, is that your courage is growing, your sense of adventure is sparking, and deep within you, a candle of knowledge and wisdom has been lit. It was always there, but now its light shines more brightly than ever before.

You are unique and amazing. Within this book, I have shared trusted methods, ethics, techniques and practices that are here for you to return to, again and again, in your own particular and personal way. Each of you will take your own road, and one day, perhaps our roads will cross and we will meet to discuss and share our experiences. Please know you have my support, both here and in the Otherworlds.

Please keep yourself fresh. Laugh often and loud. Read and explore the sacred world in ways that are vital and fun — with trips and journeys. Make it tactile and sensual. Stay well, and move. There is no better time than now to take up a spiritually satisfying and physically healing practice of movement. I more than encourage you; I urge you to be sure to take care of your wellness and to find your joy in the wonderful, simple things of your everyday life.

During my time creating decks and reading for people, people have often asked me for suggestions for blending your decks. It sounds complicated, but truly, it is a lot of fun! Some of you may wish to shuffle two decks into each other and work that way, with one large 'superdeck' for a time. This can be a wonderful practice. Personally, my cards live in their own homes much of the time, and I rarely work with this technique. When I do, it is nearly always rewarding, but I take care afterwards to move my cards back into their homes. That is simply my practice. It is practical for me as I move around so much, and so that sense of order is very important for me to stay grounded and 'together' in my head, as well as literally organised.

The other method I use is taking my cards and asking two or more decks the same question. I find this works best with the three-card layout or the day-to-day variation of

YOU SEE, OUR OWN PERSONAL ENERGY ALWAYS COMES INTO PLAY HERE, AND THUS, WHAT WORKS FOR ME—WHILE IT IS LIKELY TO WORK FOR YOU—MAY NOT FOLLOW SUIT. SO, IT IS BEST TO TAKE THE SUGGESTIONS AND THEN EXPERIMENT FOR YOURSELF. WHAT YOU WILL FIND WHEN DOING THIS WORK IS THAT YOU WILL GET TO KNOW YOUR CARDS AGAIN, IN A DIFFERENT WAY, BECAUSE YOU ARE GIVING THEM A DIFFERENT CONTEXT TO WORK WITHIN.

this layout we worked with in Chapter Nine on timing. Every deck can work with another deck. They all know each other, but there are natural affinities I've found when working with certain decks together. Please do not take my word for it — experiment for yourself.

You see, our own personal energy always comes into play here, and thus, what works for me—while it is likely to work for you—may not follow suit. So, it is best to take the suggestions and then experiment for yourself. What you will find when doing this work is that you will get to know your cards again, in a different way, because you are giving them a different context to work within.

The conversation is lit up from a new angle, and you will notice different nuances and shades of meaning within your cards. Changing things up keeps us fresh and shakes us out of habitual thinking and routine. There is a wonderful aspect to ritual and routine, our practices, which ground us, keep us safe and set us up for our readings. But if we do not refresh these from time to time, they can become rigid and stale.

This is as much a matter of personal energy and personality as it is of practice. Some people who are more flighty and scattered do well not to change up too much initially — they need the grounded, solid approach to balance their mercurial natures. Others, who love their rituals and get very comfortable within their practice, need the shake-up to stay fresh and aware; otherwise we can become a little heavy and dulled in our approach.

Remember what we learned back in Chapter One with the Oracle of Delphi? Know thyself — your own foibles, eccentricities and strengths, and yes, acknowledge your weaknesses. This does not make us 'negative' — it means when we acknowledge what we are not so good at, we can find ways to receive support or develop skills that will help us.

None of us are perfect. But you are a perfect child of the Universe and of the Divine. You are here on a spiralling journey towards the fulfilment of the soul, and your life is beautiful and full of meaning. You are sacred. Your existence is sacred, and you matter to the Universe. You are its own manifestation, a precious fragment of the Divine. Be good to yourself. Be kind. Be real. Take the time to do whatever it takes to become more like that shining part of your soul that is most good, most wondrous, most divine.

Getting Out There

You may never read for others, and that is okay. But if you do wish to read for others and take this work out into the world, you may be wondering how to do that. Please work on the way you show who you are to the world. Remember in Chapter Seven when I asked you to contemplate how you would describe yourself in a sentence? Of how you would write about yourself? Of what you may place on a business card or a website? Of how to capture your own unique essence ... It may be time for you now to consider how to get the word out in both a practical manner and a spiritual manner.

By practical, I am referring to the pragmatic and common-sense, 'real-world' strategies. These can include the following:

- Decide what you would like to do next and try some of these ideas out.
- Register a business name — feeling official can make a difference!
- Create business cards to share.
- Begin to create connections with people who run festivals and consider having a stand or sharing a stand with another person to share costs.
- Creatively share who you are with the world. This could include sharing information about what you do, and how, via social media. You could set up your own Facebook or Instagram page, and Youtube or TikTok.
- The way in which you share your messages will be most valuable when they are very true to you — your passion and intent must shine through. Tone and the way you express yourself is essential to people understanding your energy and who you are.
- Develop a website that stands alone because it is YOU!
- Put some of your income aside for further education — be it in the form of travels, research and wonderful books, experiences you wish to have, or courses you would like to take.
- Consider your tone in your posts and communications — work with your own voice to be sure you are lovingly expressing your own authenticity in the world.
- Have some beautiful photographs taken for you to use on your site, your posts and cards. The more these emerge from the truth of who you are, the more creative and energetically filled these are, the more people will feel them and respond.
- Look within other fields of creative, soulful work and see who has authentically created a business that shines from the heart. You'll notice that people usually share their story, and how that story has led them to their work, which they are profoundly

passionate about. You need to find YOUR story and discover why you are passionate about that. It's got to be real — it must feel true and shine out from all the 'me-me-me' stuff that is out there. Why is it important for others to know your story? Or know about your work? Find a way of creating connection, relating, empathising … work on the way you tell the story.

- Speak from the heart, but find ways to speak that are engaging, real, and perhaps a little different!
- The very thing that makes you odd, weird, crazy, insane, different, quirky and not at all able to fit in is often the very thing that the world needs and this is the thing that will give us our voice. You must find that way to sing your oracular song out into the world.

  There are many aspects to getting your work out there, and it can seem overwhelming at times. It's also an art. Just as I was writing this, I was 'told' to look at Facebook for a moment, and while there, I noticed so many people marketing themselves, but in very heavy-handed, literal ways. That's not how to do it … we need to be true, build relationships and connections, and speak from our hearts in words, pictures, and then, of course, in our readings, too. Everything must be true to you.
- Because it's so vital to your success at being seen, it's essential to find a way to speak about who you are and what you do that connects with other people. Because they will feel something from your words and your pictures and your energy. It needs to be real, authentic, sustainable, human. It needs to be about a relationship between you and the people who will come to you. Your energy is what will draw people to you, or otherwise, and how you communicate this energy and your skills is essential.
- Daunting? It certainly can be … When you feel that sense of, "It's too much, I don't know how to market myself/set up a website/fill out a form/do the paperwork/describe myself," I would always recommend that just take those three deep breaths and listen to Spirit for a moment. None of us know how to do everything.

Open up to Spirit, and find help. Learn a little about design, and wonder about what pleases the eye and how to take elements you love and incorporate them into your own marketing — the creative sharing of who you are with the world.

Then, break it down into little steps and do several of those each day. Some days, we won't get very much done. Other days, we will achieve so much!

Breathe, keep going, and find ways to shine your light out into the world.

Because the world needs you, Oracle.

Energy Exchange

There are many of us who remain in a place of doubt about whether we are worthy of receiving in exchange for a reading. Please know this: you are worthy. You deserve to be paid for your time, your skill and your energy. It is up to you now to place a value on your work and honour yourself sufficiently to receive.

The form this takes place in is up to you, of course. But please make a commitment to yourself to receive for your readings from this time forth.

It is a rare thing in this world of instant food, give-it-to-me-now satisfaction, immediate downloading and fast, fast living to be asked to take the time to do the work. But you have done so, and I want you to be very proud of that. All the work you have done matters because of the commitment to the path it has shown. And that work is now a part of you — you are richer, deeper, more grounded and much more solid on your feet. You are like an athlete who has trained and is ready. You have developed, and you are stronger for the work you have done. Well done.

Please make a firm commitment to ethical oracular practice. There are many grey areas, so I would recommend you check in with yourself from time to time. Be sure to remember the sacred nature of the privacy of your clients, consent, and of establishing and being worthy of the trust we share with those we work with. This is important not only for the people we work with and read for but also for our very souls. I don't mean that you need to be secretive or grandiose about this, but simply safeguard your boundaries and respect the people who have placed their trust in you.

Please be sure to give yourself a great deal of outdoor time, fun, laughter and delight, too. Amidst all the intensity and seriousness of this world and of the work we do, we must allow our spirit that soaring freedom of lightness. It will make us all better Oracles.

Spellworking with Your Cards

Over the years, many people who have come to love my cards have asked me for some suggestions on how to work with the cards in combination with spellwork. I am including these spells here. Spells are not to be cast frivolously, but they can be done with joy and delight, so read through the material here, follow the guidelines, and deepen your relationship with your cards!

If you wish for more pointers on casting circles and other suggestions here, you could consider working with one of my books, like *White Magic: An Inspiring Guide to an Enchanted Life*, *Witchy Magic*, or *Spellbound: The Secret Grimoire of Lucy Cavendish*.

THE SEVEN-POINTED STAR SPELL

This is a beautiful spell that connects you deeply with your own magick, the faery (elemental) and Dragonfae realms, and with your own instincts and wild self. Lots of that instinct becomes layered over in our lives, so we lose some of our natural intelligence and power — our Wild Self. And if you've ever wanted to work with the beautiful, clever fae and the strong, wise Dragonfae, well, this spell will swing the safe door wide open!

You can work with most of my decks with this spell.

Note: You'll need to cast a large circle for this spell to have enough room to work within. Be generous. This spell is best cast outside. Please use large jars to place the candles within, and have a large jug of water nearby, just to be sure all is safe and well when working with fire outside.

Find a place you can return to, where there is a tree growing. From that tree, there must be a branch that overhangs the space. It doesn't need to be a large tree! What's more important is that the tree is healthy.

TIMING

Full moon — greatest potential.
Time: 3.33 (pm or am) or 9 (pm or am).

YOU WILL NEED:

- Sea salt for casting circle (as a protective barrier).
- Incense suitable for the fae! Some incense is made from cow dung, which the faeries don't mind, but it's not their favourite. You could make your own flower blend to burn from thyme, lavender, eucalyptus and rose. Or, choose an incense that is made with other natural ingredients — the faeries will adore that!
- Ritual bath blend — I make my own, and I tend to tailor the blend to the requirements of the working, so they can vary. Generally speaking, I am inclined to work with a blend of nine drops lavender, nine drops frankincense and three drops sweet orange. I tend to always have those three notes — one soothing and relaxing, one protective and strong, one cheerful and uplifting. Sandalwood substitutes beautifully for frankincense, and any citrus-based oil or orange neroli will add a note of encouragement and optimism. I may pour these directly into the bath, or I may make up a separate bottle with plenty of the blend to use regularly. I nearly always work with the nine or three drops, and sometimes I add some energy to the blend by chanting words (usually three times, or three times three) over it to infuse the blend with intentions.

- Four candles — two for the spell, one for the fire quarter, and one for the bath.
- Some crystals — rose quartz, and one for a dragon (they love most any crystal, but one will find its way to you!).
- A key — any kind, decorative or just an old key! This is a symbol for the faerie.
- One bottle of blessed water.
- An image of a faery or a Dragonfae from one of your Oracle card decks. I would suggest working with a being who you trust and who you can make direct eye contact with, if at all possible.

PREPARATION

Prepare first with the ritual bath. It is powerful and will cleanse you prior to spellcasting, readying you by clearing any debris of the day and gently introducing the energies you are bringing in. It is truly the beginning of the spell.

Light a candle during the bath. Inscribe on this candle the seven-pointed star as a sign to the fae. Have your card nearby, and gaze at the Being within the card.

After the bath, pat yourself dry gently, and dress in clean, comfortable clothing. You may wish to paint the seven-pointed star upon your forehead.

CAST THE CIRCLE

Consecrate the area first. Do this in a deosil direction — anti-clockwise in the Southern Hemisphere and clockwise if you are in the Northern Hemisphere. Then, mark out four quarters — the north, south, east and west.

Choose the elemental locations either geocentrically—according to where they are most present in your actual location—or choose to work traditionally, which many people do, regardless of which hemisphere of this blue-and-green planet they live within. Traditionally, east is air, north is earth, west is water and south is fire. I prefer to work geocentrically but feel absolutely free to explore for yourself. We always, regardless of hemisphere, begin in the east, no matter what element you decide to place there. That is because it is the direction of the rising sun. So, as an example, the direction you place water could be east if you live on the east coast or west if you have a great body of water to the west).

Water: Place a small bowl with a few drops of the sacred waters here.

Fire: Place one candle here. Again, inscribed with a seven-pointed star.

Earth: Place the crystals here.

Air: Light the incense here. Please do this with charcoal and a fireproof container. Disperse it with a feather or your breath or hand.

In the centre, place your card. Prop it up with a natural object, like a crystal.

Cast the circle by sprinkling the area outside of the four quarters with a touch of the blessed water in a circle.

Follow this with the salt.

Remember to go in a deosil direction (anti-clockwise direction in the Southern Hemisphere or clockwise in the Northern Hemisphere). We are following the natural path of the Sun, whichever hemisphere we are in.

Chant three times, or 3 x 3:

*Hear me now, my *faery kin*
I ask for you to step within
The borders of this sacred space
Outside the laws of time and space
I ask for you to hear my song
And come to me, where I belong
Into this place, none may come
Who wish me ill, who'd harm loved one
This Circle's bound by sacred rite
Holds love and power, green world delight

*You may wish to change faery to Dragonfae, for example.

Then say three times:

My intent is firm and strong
No thing enters that does not belong

Awaken in turn each of the elements: pour the water into the bowl, knowing as you do so that you ease your thirst and allow yourself to flow.

Light the candles and know you ignite your spirit and motivation.

Light the incense and stir the smoke with your breath, feeling your thoughts grow clear and your breath deep and strong. Feel the space purify.

Hold the crystals to your heart for a moment and breathe into them. Then put them back on the ground/surface. Feel their strength pour through you, and pour yourself into them. Allow the earth to love you, and love her in return.

Within this sacred space, say as you walk:

Cast a circle round about
Magick stay in, doubt stay out
Cast a circle round about
Magick stay in, doubt stay out
Cast a circle round about
Guardians stay in, doubt stay out

(Do this three times, or a multiple of three — nine is best!)

Standing in this space, take a deep breath in and pick up your card. Feel the presence and energy within and of the circle.

Now, draw upon the ground with a stick a seven-pointed star within the circle, large enough to stand within its centre.

When you have completed that, place the card in the centre, along with the crystal, the thyme, and the faery key.

Hold the crystal up to the sky, then to the ground, then to your heart. Extend your hand and show it to them. Say:

Ignite my soul and set me free
Unbind from me all locks and chains
I am Wild and Free again
Allow my Soul its truth and Spark
Whether brightest light or deepest dark
**Dragonfae — my Ancestors of Strength and Wild Pure Power*
Come to me this Sacred Hour
I ask for your flame to light within
Midst nature's heart I call to thee
I'm honoured by your trust in me

*You may wish to change this to faery, if you are working with them …

Place the stone again on the ground. Breathe. Allow any messages to come through that may. Write them down on one side of the paper.

Next, take the rose quartz, hold it to your lips, to your heart, and then to the sky. Extend your hand, offering it to them. Say:

My kin, my friends, I ask you here
To guide me, show me, always clear
I honour you with this good stone
I vow to keep clear your home
And honour you with thyme and herb
The clarity you so deserve
Please do share with your human kin
The secrets of the faith within
Bright heart I bring and offer you
Faith and care and action too
Gwyn Ap Neath and Mab the Queen
Show me the lands of sight unseen

Place the stone on the ground.

Sit and feel the sun, the weather, its shifts ... feel the fae come to you now ...

If there are any messages, write them down.

Now, take your faery key and tie it to the tree branch.

This is the symbol of our meeting place. Together, we declare the boundaries. We choose the time and place.

Make any statements of INTENT you may wish to make or feel inspired by.

THANK THEM ALL!

When this is done, say:

By Faery Place, I cast this spell
Into me, your power swells
I thank you now and welcome all
This new life brings, I hear your call

Take your pouch.

Place within it the crystals (except for the dragonstone and rose quartz) and thank earth.

Place within it the waters (just a sprinkle will do!) and thank water.

Place within it a little of the incense, and thank the air.

Place within it a little wax from the candle, and thank the fire.

Place within a little of the thyme, the faery's green flag.

As you tie the pouch off, say:

The power of this spell now within me
As I do will, so mote it be
As I do will, so mote it be
As I do will, so mote it be

It is time to thank and farewell this circle for now.

Trace the circle round in the opposite direction to that which you cast it, saying:

My circle is open, but never is it broken. My circle is open, but never is it broken ...

Take a moment to breathe and feel the energy shifting. Then say:

I close the door to this sacred space.
This is for us, our holy place.
None can follow me from here
Our way is safe, and calm, and clear

Clear the area of all tools and items, and bury the salt. Anything that seems like it does not belong, clear it away. Leave the stone, the quartz and the thyme there overnight. If they are there in the morning, you may collect them and bring them in, all except for the thyme, which must remain behind.

Eat some salads with some flowers, like nasturtiums or honey cakes.

Carry your pouch on you for a moon cycle or for longer. Pop it under your pillow.

Return to this place often for healing, magick, divination and connection. And, of course, for your oracular work — because this place is now very sacred, and very connected to your readings and to the beings within the cards.

Meeting the Goddess Brigid's Flame at Sister Rita's home in Kildare, Ireland. Now enshrined within the Solas Bhride Centre, the flame has burned for thousands of years, tended by Priestesses and Nuns, and shared with those seeking peace and healing. I often write my Oracle card decks by its light.

BRIGID'S FLAME SPELL

I sometimes work with the cards in my spellwork. You could cast this spell, working with the *Brigid* card from *Oracle of the Dragonfae*, placing it upon your altar. This spell is from my book *Spellbound: The Secret Grimoire of Lucy Cavendish*, but I've changed it up a little, just for us.

Use the forge of your mind to create today. This day is a crucible … what you bring to this day will ripple out into time and space, creating tomorrow after tomorrow. Think well and hard on dreams and what it is you wish to create with your life. This does not have to look like anyone else's life.

YOU WILL NEED:

- One candle, beeswax.
- Orange sweet essential oil.
- Gold dust.
- A blue cloth.
- Your *Brigid* card from the *Oracle of the Dragonfae.*

TIMING

Sunday is a day of beauty and initiation. Brigid is a Mother Goddess who has three forms. This day, we ask her to re-light your fire within.

IMBAS IS A WORD OF IRISH ORIGIN AND IS THE IRISH VERSION OF THE WORD AWEN, WHICH IS WELSH. BOTH AWEN AND IMBAS REFER TO THE DIVINE BREATH OF INSPIRATION, TO A SOURCE OF CONNECTION THAT IS OTHERWORLDY. IT IS THE FORCE THAT DRIVES ART, CREATIVITY, VISIONS AND WONDER. WE ARE WORKING WITH THE IRISH WORD FOR THIS ENERGY, AS BRIGID, LIKE IMBAS, IS IRISH. I THINK USING THE OLD WORDS HELPS TO CONNECT WITH DEITY ON A DEEPER LEVEL.

CAST THE CIRCLE

Set up your altar with blue cloth, and anoint the beeswax candle with orange sweet. To do this, take the bottle of orange sweet and place three drops or nine (multiples of the magickal number three) on one palm. Gently rub the oil between your hands, then take your candle and roll it between your hands until most of the oil has been transferred to the candle. Wipe or wash your hands if you wish. Place your Brigid card in the centre so she is upright. You may wish to have her in a frame or even leaning against your cauldron.

In the invocation, I mention the word 'Imbas'. Imbas is a word of Irish origin and is the Irish version of the word Awen, which is Welsh. Both Awen and Imbas refer to the divine breath of inspiration, to a source of connection that is otherworldy. It is the force that drives art, creativity, visions and wonder. We are working with the Irish word for this energy, as Brigid, like Imbas, is Irish. I think using the old words helps to connect with deity on a deeper level.

Connect with her image, and as you do, say these words:

Sweet Brigid, my Mother, light from the ashes of my spirit
An undying flame
Light within my deepest parts
Your fire, your spark
Reignite my heart
Until the brightness that's mine
Flows from me and shines
Out into the world
In word and in deed
Of your flame, of your fire
I shall always have need

Sprinkle the gold dust around the candle and rays of light will spread from this.

Nine rays, three rays of Imbas, the three drops of knowledge and of Holy Light.

Then, light your candle, saying:

As I light this candle
So my fire is rekindled
A flame eternal
To inspire, heal, comfort and warm

Do this, and place the healing flame of Brigid where you feel it is needed.

Hold your hands just above the flame and feel the heat.

Scoop it up in your hands and hold it over your heart.

Feel Brigid's love warming you.

Hold your hands over the flame again and scoop up that heat.

Hold it over your lips so your words be warm and true.

Again and again.

Finally, look deep into the flame of Brigid and know this is a healing flame, one which will bring peace, harmony, compassion, courage and wit to any time and place.

Brigid is your Mother and will care for you.

You are within her forge when you light this candle.

You are creative, caring, independent and reborn each time this candle is lit.

Thank her, and write down in your Book of Shadows and Light any messages, feelings or thoughts you may have had.

Think for a moment and resolve to have courage, and to burn bright and steady, like her flame, and forge a great life, as her forge creates over and over again.

Blow out the flame, sending wishes into the week as you do so.

Wait till the wax is cooler, then roll the candle in the gold dust. Carve a Brigid's cross upon the candle.

Use this candle to light other candles and each time you cast this spell.

Close your circle, and enjoy a deep, peaceful sleep.

When you work with your cards like this—which, admittedly, is quite a complex spell—you will enter into a different relationship with them. It becomes really interactive. It is something to experience rather than to describe. All I can do is encourage you to make some time and try this for yourself.

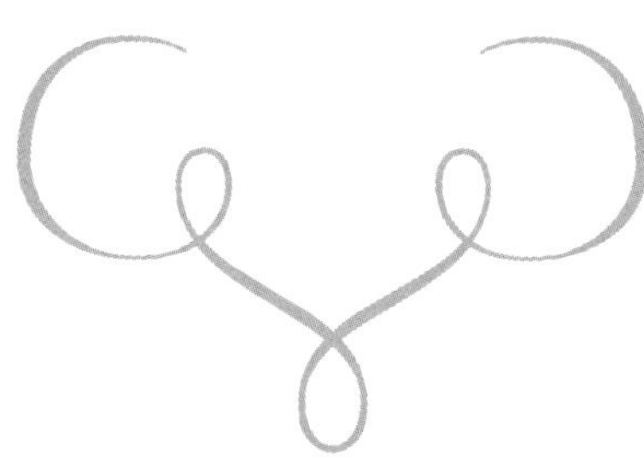

TOO BRIGHT A STAR — ROSALEEN NORTON

In Australia in the 1960s, the avant-garde gathered in Kings Cross, the city of Sydney's bohemian hub. At its very core was the mysterious, talented and infamous Witch and oracular visionary, Rosaleen Norton.

Rosaleen was an extraordinarily talented artist whose work was labelled depraved and corrupt her entire life. Not that this daunted her!

In 1949, she met the poet Gavin Greenlees, and they became lovers. Greenlees was inspired by Roie, as those close to her called this Witch, and her work found a growing audience hungry for her courageous depictions of taboo beings. Her erotic and prophetic 1949 exhibition in Melbourne was raided by police, who confiscated her art and charged her with obscenity.

The court case was notorious. Known as the Witch of Kings Cross, Rosaleen shared the oracular symbolism within the works, and the case was dismissed. But her fame had taken root and began to grow. Her whole life was punctuated by court cases, police arrests, book burnings — but she continued on her path, driven by visions of Pan, Gods of the Old Worlds and their sensual adventures.

Harassed on a habitual basis by the authorities, Rosaleen still drank fearlessly from the cauldron of life. When she met Sir Eugene Goossens, a Knight of the Realm and famous conductor, they became partners in experimental sex magick, led skyclad (naked) rites to the Pan, practised trance channelling and altered states of consciousness. With Goossens' patronage, Rosaleen played host to international artists, and more and more devotees began to gather in Rosaleen's tiny Kings Cross apartment for the Rites to Pan.

Rosaleen Norton's *The Art of Rosaleen Norton* was republished—without censorship and scandal—in 1982 and has never gone out of print. Sadly, Rosaleen did not live to see this respect — she died in 1979, staying true to her oracular visions of otherworlds and a purely pagan path. Today, she is revered as a wild, witty, courageous oracular visionary who painted dreams, and wandered the spirit realms few dare to experience.

Experientials and Experimentals

- Please go back and think more, and work again on the suggestions for describing yourself and your own particular oracular gifts and interests.
- Ponder how to go about getting the word out and act on one of the suggestions in this chapter.
- Reflect on your own journey so far. What are your strengths as an Oracle? What came naturally? What are the areas where you need some more development? What are the opportunities before you? And what holds you back? You could even do a spread on this — ask the cards!
- Do some work with blending the decks — experiment, have fun and see what happens.
- Perhaps gather with some of your friends and practise.
- Plan your next steps work with a journal or Book of Shadows and Light to organise your time and keep you on track with your commitments. This is especially essential for those of you who will be reading professionally.
- Fall in love with the cards all over again — head out for a day trip into nature, and enjoy!
- Make a commitment to learn more about the beings within your deck through study and reflection.
- Most of all, care for yourself — make a special time this week to have a massage, go to a dance class, see a film at a cinema, organise a gathering with like-minded souls or attend a meet-up group. Nourish yourself.

Sometimes, a different perspective can work wonders. I might gaze at a layout from above or upside down to see if the shift reveals unexpected relationships between the cards. Here, I've stepped back to see if I can spot any cards 'speaking' to each other. A tree-like perspective, perhaps!

A Farewell for Now ...

Brief were my days among you, and briefer still the words I have spoken.
But should my voice fade in your ears, and my love vanish in your memory,
then I will come again ... And if this day is not a fulfilment of your needs
and my love, then let it be a promise till another day ... Know therefore,
that from the greater silence I shall return.

— *Kahlil Gibran*

So here we are. At an ending, and a new beginning. Another threshold. But this time, instead of entering the shadowlands, you could be said to be entering the light of the Illumined path. The path of the trained, wise, compassionate Oracle.

You've travelled through your cards, and you've had the bravery to go deep and see the journey through. I want you to know that all the exercises and experiences, all the stories shared, the people you've been inspired by, the fears you've faced, and the secrets and dreams you've shared in your magickal journals have joined together to create a solid foundation of skill within you. It's all a part of you now. Being an Oracle is a living part of your soul and your identity in this lifetime.

Just like the Oracles of old, you've worked and trained your intuition, and you've reached into spaces and places that may have once seemed out of reach. You've devoted yourself to a special path that isn't for everyone — because you have gifts inside you that will always need to be expressed and a light within you that longs to shine out in the world. You have developed your ability to sense what is happening, to feel with more sensitivity, to express the messages with kindness and clarity, and to bring someone else into the experience that oracular readings can be.

You are to be congratulated not only for your grit and commitment to yourself but because you have learned so many new skills. You have made space in your precious life to nurture and grow the innate gifts you always had. You may have discovered talents that slept until now, awaiting you to realise the cosmos of possibility that whirls within you, longing to be expressed into the world. You are a creative force.

I know just how much effort it takes to give yourself the time and space to do this. It isn't easy.

All these gifts you have, all the skills you've developed, have made you a fine Oracle card reader. You can take this anywhere you wish from this time forth. Be imaginative, daring, and always follow your dreams.

And when you falter (and we all do), return to the cards, to the lessons, and keep those Books of Shadows and Light, your magickal journals going. They'll sustain you.

I hope that, as a side effect of doing this work and sharing the adventure with me, some healing has taken place and a sense of worth is solidly, unshakeably within you. I would love for any fears you had about reading for yourself (or for others) to become less powerful than the strengths you've developed; the belief that's come from doing the work. I want the voices that once said you couldn't do it to have been proven wrong forever. May your inner choir sing a beautiful new song in praise of your efforts and hard work.

I hope you have danced a card and fallen asleep with cards on your pillow and tangled in your hair. Or awoken from a dream with a message so strong you've needed to write it down, because it related perfectly to a card that you just couldn't get clear on. I dream that you're reading for others with so much kindness and compassion that your light is shining brighter than ever before out into the world.

Give yourself permission to be imperfect, to have days when you're better than others, to feel ebbs and flows in your energy. Know there is a time to withdraw, recede a little and nurture yourself, and a time to explode forth into view and share your beautiful energy and your oracular work with others.

Some call it light work, yet it contains shadows, and you have walked in both the sun and the moonlight on your path as an Oracle card reader. Just as my tears and heartbreaks led me to my first readings, I hope any pain you ever experienced in your life becomes fuel for the most wonderful journey of discovery, self-love and self-respect.

You are a powerful, wonderful light of an Oracle card reader!

Know you are very, very loved.

With so much love for you, and may all that is good and wise bless you.

For you are now an Oracle.

Lucy

)O(

LUCY CAVENDISH is a true free spirit: a Witch and writer whose works are cherished and trusted around the world. An exciting voice in the field of inspiration, she is loved for her vision, compassion, wisdom and humour. She has that rare ability — to connect deeply with her readers.

Her work is notable for its breadth and depth of knowledge on sacred rites and sites, magickal history, witchcraft, folklore, alternative spiritual practices and intuitive traditions. Lucy's original creations have struck a chord with contemporary seekers ready to create lives of courage, spiritual adventure and magick.

Lucy's books and oracle decks are available in many languages, and she's a popular guest on television programs such as *Studio Ten*, *The Project* and *The Morning Show*. When she's not writing or recording her popular podcast, *The Witchcast*, you'll find Lucy drinking tea, surfing in the ocean or wandering deep within a faery forest.

You can discover more about Lucy by finding her on social media, listening to *The Witchcast*, wherever you get your podcasts, or by visiting **www.lucycavendish.com.au**

IMAGE CREDITS

P29 Image of Kassandra: Evelyn De Morgan, Public domain, via Wikimedia Commons, sourced from https://commons.wikimedia.org/w/index.php?title=File:Cassandra1.jpeg&oldid=982753328

P85 Image of Inanna: Detail of Burney Relief (Inanna), cropped and converted to black and white. Gennadii Saus i Segura, CC BY-SA 4.0 <https://creativecommons.org/licenses/by-sa/4.0>, via Wikimedia Commons, sourced from https://commons.wikimedia.org/w/index.php?title=File:Relieve_Reina_de_la_Noche_(ca._1800_a.C).jpg&oldid=750507441

P183 Image of merkaba with crystal: יאחוקיו, CC BY-SA 4.0 <https://creativecommons.org/licenses/by-sa/4.0>, via Wikimedia Commons, sourced from https://commons.wikimedia.org/w/index.php?title=File:Kristal_ball_in_Merkaba_(cropped).jpg&oldid=459466177

P185 Graphic of human figure: © Blue Angel Publishing

P187 Symbols:
Labyrinth: File:Hemet Maze 49x49 grid.png: Watchinderivative work: Jeff G., CC BY-SA 4.0 <https://creativecommons.org/licenses/by-sa/4.0>, via Wikimedia Commons, sourced from https://commons.wikimedia.org/w/index.php?title=File:Hemet_Maze_49x49_grid.jpg&oldid=768129810

Maze: Original: User:IceySVG: User:MichaelFrey, CC BY-SA 4.0 <https://creativecommons.org/licenses/by-sa/4.0>, via Wikimedia Commons, sourced from https://commons.wikimedia.org/w/index.php?title=File:Picture_maze.svg&oldid=904188110

P190 Symbols:
Ankh: Alexi Helligar, CC BY-SA 3.0 <https://creativecommons.org/licenses/by-sa/3.0>, via Wikimedia Commons, sourced from https://commons.wikimedia.org/w/index.php?title=File:Ankh_(SVG)_01.svg&oldid=795843715

Brigid's Cross: RootOfAllLight, CC BY-SA 4.0 <https://creativecommons.org/licenses/by-sa/4.0>, via Wikimedia Commons, sourced from https://commons.wikimedia.org/w/index.php?title=File:St_Brigid%27s_Cross_(three_arms).svg&oldid=1007178787

P191 Image of Green Man: Carving in Sutton Benger Church, Wiltshire. Somerset Greenman, CC BY-SA 4.0 <https://creativecommons.org/licenses/by-sa/4.0>, via Wikimedia Commons, sourced from https://commons.wikimedia.org/w/index.php?title=File:Green_Man_carving_in_Sutton_Benger_Church,_Wiltshire.jpg&oldid=732087121

P197 Image of Dion Fortune (Violet Mary Firth): Unknown author, sourced from https://lafelguera.net/autores/dion-fortune/

P220 Image of Marie Laveau: Painting *Woman in Tignon* by Adolph Rinck, Public domain, via Wikimedia Commons, sourced from https://commons.wikimedia.org/w/index.php?title=File:Woman_In_Tignon.jpg&oldid=1083389583
NB: Historically, a great number of portraits of Creole women have been widely attributed as portraits of Marie Laveau. However, it is now believed that she was never photographed nor sat for a painter, so there is very little chance that the portrait above is a true depiction of Marie Laveau.

P245 Image of Eliphas Levi: Public domain, via Wikimedia Commons, sourced from https://commons.wikimedia.org/w/index.php?title=File:Eliphas_Levi.png&oldid=946142353

Photos of/by the author on pages 43, 57, 65, 79, 103, 113, 129, 139, 149, 154, 188, 253, 254, 281, 285: © Lucy Cavendish

P85 Photo of Lucy: © Mel Chamberlain

P177 Photo of Lucy: © Leonie Dawson

Notes

Notes